W9-DAS-682

# BASIC NEEDS AND DEVELOPMENT

# Basic Needs
# and
# Development

Edited by
**Danny M. Leipziger**

Foreword by
**Paul P. Streeten**

 **Oelgeschlager, Gunn & Hain, Publishers, Inc.**
Cambridge, Massachusetts

International Standard Book Number:   0-89946-021-6

Library of Congress Catalog Card Number:   80-19938

Printed in the United States of America


**Library of Congress Cataloging in Publication Data**
Main entry under title:

Basic needs approach to development.

   Includes bibliographical references and index.
   1. Economic development—Addresses, essays,
lectures. I. Leipziger, Danny M.
HD75.B37      338.9′001      80-19938
ISBN 0-89946-021-6

# Contents

# List of Figures

# List of Tables

# Foreword

*Paul P. Streeten*

In responding to Danny Leipziger's request to write this foreword, I thought the most useful contribution would be to highlight the distinct features of the basic human needs approach as they emerge from this book and other sources and to concentrate on the practical policy issues. For this purpose I have drawn on the work done in three areas—first, concepts and measurement; second, country studies; and third, sector studies. From these I try to draw briefly some general lessons that, I hope, will be found useful by policymakers.

## BASIC NEEDS

The objective of a basic human needs approach to development is to ensure that all human beings should have the opportunity to live full lives. To this end, the approach focuses on securing access to minimum levels of consumption of certain basic goods and services. The basic needs approach, like other poverty-oriented approaches, attaches fundamental importance to poverty eradication within a short period as one of the main objectives of development. It defines poverty not in terms of income, poverty lines, and deciles of the income distribution, but as the inability to meet certain basic human needs on the part of identifiable groups of human beings. Poverty is characterized by hunger and malnutrition, by ill health, by lack of education, of safe water, of sanitation, of decent shelter. A vital aspect of the elimination of poverty, then, consists in securing access to these goods and services by the poor so that people have the opportunity of leading lives free from hunger, disease, and deprivation.

If we accept the objective of the basic needs approach, how do we translate it into action? For operational purposes, we must distinguish between three different aspects of the basic needs approach—supply, demand, and institutions. There must be adequate production or imports of the goods and services in question; there must be adequate purchasing power by the poor to buy them; and the organizational arrangements must facilitate access and delivery.

The institutional framework has tended to be ignored in many conventional approaches to poverty elimination. In the basic needs approach, however, it is of crucial importance. Three types of institutions are important: basic needs are met by the market, by public services and transfers, and in households. The activities of the household are particularly relevant to the basic needs approach. The household allocates among its members incomes earned by members who are employed for wages, and it produces goods and services for its own use. While its own production may account for as much as 40 percent of income in developing countries, it forms a much more substantial proportion of basic needs sector activity. Moreover, household activities play a crucial role in converting education, health, and nutrition into improvements in the quality of life of individuals.

The public sector is also important in a basic needs approach, as a producer, as a maker of rules, and as a source of finance. Health, education, sanitation, and family planning are commonly concentrated in the public sector. Transfer payments and subsidies are paid out of public revenues, and the government makes and enforces the laws to which private transactions are subject. One reason why the basic needs approach is necessary to supplement the previous development emphasis on minimum incomes and poverty lines is that the income approach has tended to neglect the household and the public sector, which in turn has led to the neglect of basic needs where these sectors figure prominently. Analysis of the public sector must cover administrative and political arrangements, such as the combination of participation and central support, the forms of democratic participation, and the social structure.

The bulk of previous work has been concerned with policies that enable people to earn enough income to buy in the market the goods and services required to meet basic needs. The generation of remunerative and satisfying jobs and the exercise of free choice to buy what is wanted remain central to a basic needs approach, broadly interpreted. If little is said about these aspects here, it is because the novelty of the basic needs approach consists in emphasizing the relatively neglected institutions of the household and the public sector.

A basic needs approach requires combined emphasis on the supply of basic needs goods, the demand for basic needs goods, and the appropriate institutional arrangements for access and delivery. Failure of any of these can lead to failure of basic needs performance.

## COUNTRY TYPOLOGY

It has been customary to construct alternative scenarios and to derive from them projections on the number of poor in the year 2000. The base case scenario of the World Bank yields 600 million poor, and the pessimistic scenario, 710 million. On more optimistic assumptions about aggregate growth, aid, and trade, it arrives at an estimate of 470 million poor.[1] Additional assumptions about redistribution of income and reductions in fertility rates can bring down the number of poor to 300 million.

A basic needs approach to eliminating the worst aspects of poverty seeks to look deeper than the aggregate income figures and, by more precisely directed measures, to achieve fulfillment of basic needs at levels of income per head below those indicated by a poverty line—that is, in a shorter period. For this purpose, it is helpful to distinguish between different types of country, and different sectoral approaches.

The basic needs success stories are illustrated by three types of economies, from an institutional and political point of view—the socialist planned economies, such as Cuba and the People's Republic of China; some market-oriented economies with special initial conditions with respect to land distribution and special policies, such as Taiwan and South Korea; and the "mixed" economies, of which Sri Lanka is the outstanding success story. It is interesting to note that such different political regimes as North and South Korea, China and Taiwan, and Cuba and Costa Rica show excellent basic needs performance.

For those interested in eradicating the worst aspects of poverty by the year 2000 in nonsocialist, low income societies, Sri Lanka has some important lessons to teach. Its remarkable performance was initiated in the colonial era. But Sri Lanka has made very substantial progress in the rapid improvement of many social indicators since the last war, at levels of income per head below $200. A major factor has been high levels of public expenditure on primary education, health, and food subsidies. Social programs and food subsidies account for about one-half of current government expenditure and 10 percent of GDP. These services have, until recently, been available to a large segment of the population. The food ration accounted for about 20 percent of calorific intake among families with very low incomes. A cutback in the availability of food rations in 1974 was accompanied by a sharp rise in the death rate, indicating the importance of the food ration for health.

It is commonly believed that Sri Lanka's economy is not viable in the long run because the high levels of expenditure cannot be sustained and because these expenditures reduce economic growth. However, the programs were in fact sustained, with a respectable growth rate, for over twenty years following the last war. Poor economic management, adverse movement in the terms of trade, and poor monsoons led to severe problems in the 1970s. But with economic reforms and more selective programs for the lower income groups, it appears that Sri Lanka is again able to combine successful performance on basic needs with economic growth. The Sri Lankan case shows the importance, for a mixed economy, of consistent and reinforcing efforts on the side of supply (through public sector and production planning), the side of demand (i.e., adequate incomes), and by institutions (especially public services) for success in basic needs to be achieved.[2]

## ADMINISTRATION AND MANAGEMENT OF BASIC NEEDS

Institutional, organizational, and administrative problems are encountered in countries that have failed to meet basic needs at all stages of the policy process. Formulation of policies is heavily affected by political considerations, with insufficient understanding of the relations among the administrative and bureaucratic structure, the economy, and the society. Policy implementation suffers from inefficient bureaucratic procedures, lack of qualified managerial staff, lack of coordination among ministries and between national and local units, and poorly trained or motivated civil servants. Policy evaluation is virtually nonexistent, because the information base is inadequate, and research and experimentation capabilities are absent. Basic needs programs impose special administrative requirements, because they are often somewhat experimental, extending to new areas and involving different procedures.

There is no panacea for the host of institutional problems faced by the developing countries, especially the poorest. Most of these issues cannot be disentangled from their social, political, and economic context. In addition to management training, two changes may contribute to the efficiency of basic needs programs. One is to restructure organizations so as to make them fit the functional requirements of the programs. In many cases, this is likely to involve decentralization, but with appropriate links with higher levels and national organization (as in the organization of health services, for example). If administrative procedures are developed to increase staff participation in decisionmaking, this may increase staff commitment and also the responsiveness of the program to local needs.

Second, participation by the poor for whom the projects are organized in decisionmaking and service delivery may increase the efficiency of basic needs programs. The major beneficiaries are often willing to supply labor, materials, and finance to establish the services. Most basic needs programs require participation for their success—for example, in education or health and sanitation, the cooperation of the public or patient is essential to the effectiveness of the programs. Hence, achieving a high degree of participation is far more important in these programs than in more conventional types of economic activity. In many cases, the participation of women is especially important, and this may lead to some conflict with traditional organizational forms, which are generally male oriented. Experimenting with organizational structures and decisionmaking is an important element in developing an effective basic needs approach.

## FINANCE FOR BASIC NEEDS PROJECTS

The question of finance with regard to basic-needs-oriented projects is particularly important for three reasons. First, because on the whole, recurrent costs are quite heavy in relation to capital costs. This means that any system must allow for continuing financial support, rather than a once for all commitment for capital costs. Second, the obvious solution to the recurrent cost problem—levying charges to cover these operating costs—may be both difficult to administer and undesirable because the social benefits of the projects very often far exceed the private benefits to the individual consumer. This is clearly true, for example, of vaccination programs or programs of health education where the beneficiaries are the community at large as well as the individuals participating in the program. In other cases it may be difficult to charge for the services because they are provided communally and the benefits are not appropriable. Third, since a major objective of basic needs programs is to provide universal access—especially to provide access for the very poor—any system of charges is likely to debar the very people for whom the programs are most essential. Yet despite these problems, unless some system of generating finance on a continuous basis forms an intrinsic part of the programs, they are liable to be limited in coverage and in duration, as the central government becomes overburdened with fiscal liability.

Experience on the individual sectors' financial problems suggests the following conclusions:

1. In some areas, charges to cover recurrent costs are reasonable from the point of view of social and economic efficiency. In these cases, which include shelter, water, sanitation, and some recurrent medical costs, charges probably offer the best solution. But charges should not be levied—or should be levied at much reduced rates—on the poorest consumers. The poorest consumers may be financed by cross-subsidization from richer consumers or from general government revenues.

2. For programs where user charges are not desirable or feasible as a system of finance—much of education and health—planning the financing of recurrent costs should form an intrinsic part of initiating projects. If the local community takes on (as it often does) responsibility for some proportion of the capital costs, it may also be able and prepared to undertake a similar commitment for overall recurrent costs. Similarly for aid donors, it should not be assumed that the central government automatically will be able to undertake full funding of the recurrent costs of these types of projects indefinitely.

3. Central government financing is likely to be required for subsidy programs—for example, for nutrition and for other services for poorer consumers. To limit the government's financial responsibility while enabling the poorer consumers to partake in the programs requires selective policies, so as to confine the subsidies to those most in need. Such selective policies are very difficult to implement for administrative and political reasons. It may be easier to plan effectively for some types of programs than for others—for example, providing subsidies on foods primarily consumed by the very poor. Where this is so, larger subsidies on this type of output might be used in preference to smaller subsidies on a number of types of output, each requiring complex administrative procedures.

## SECTORAL LINKAGES

There are strong linkages and complementarities between the supply of various basic needs goods and services. The efficacy of the output of one sector—in terms of its impact on the quality of life—depends largely on the availability of other basic needs goods or services, and costs can often be reduced by joint supply. It can be shown, for example, that the impact of investment in sanitation facilities on health depends on education in personal hygiene and that the effectiveness of expenditure on health depends critically on the nature of the output of other basic needs goods. Thus curative medical services are likely to be rather ineffective if people are chronically malnourished, use germ-infested water, have no sanitation facilities, and follow poor health practices in their lives. In some cases, action on one front without simultaneous action on others can be actually counterproductive. To provide water without drainage can lead to pools of stagnant water that attract insects and spread disease. A few examples illustrate these linkages with respect to impact and costs.[3]

Malnutrition leads to a high predisposition to disease and to fatalities from disease. In Mali, the high death rate among children who have contracted measles is more accurately attributable to a fatal combination of malnutrition, diarrhea, and often malaria and measles. A study covering Recife and parts of São Paulo State in Brazil showed that 50 to 70 percent of all deaths of children under five were nutrition related and that there was an even higher proportion for those under one year. The study also showed a strong interaction between malnutrition and infection: 50 to 70 percent of all deaths from infectious and parasitic diseases had nutrition deficiency as a related cause. Specific nutritional diseases are responsible for some major diseases, and malnutrition, in turn, is seen to be partly the result of chronic ill health. Malnutrition among women leads to fatigue (and less attention to household health and nutrition practices), high maternal death rates, low birth weights, and malnourishment among breast-fed infants.

Further evidence of intersectoral linkages includes the following: poor sanitation conditions are widely observed to be a major contributory factor to many infectious diseases. However, in Sri Lanka education (boiling water) appears to substitute for clean water. In Mali, Somalia, and Gambia, evidence has shown that weaning practices affect health as well as nutrition; health practices (particularly providing food and liquid during measles and liquid during diarrhea) affect the recovery rates from these diseases; education affects health through its impact on conditions of food preparation and personal hygiene; the health (including the nutritional status) of people affects their willingness and capacity to learn; and malnutrition in infants can affect their mental capacity permanently.

In analyzing the complementarities on the cost side, consider that to dig trenches for water supply simultaneously with those for drainage can lower unit costs; water, sanitation, and shelter, particularly, are more economically constructed together. While it is controversial whether agricultural extension workers should teach people several skills or whether they should concentrate on a single skill, there is less controversy over the fact that nutrition, family planning, and hygiene are most efficiently taught by the same people.

The manifold linkages between sectors with respect to both impact and costs have led some to conclude that a basic needs approach is essentially multisectoral and requires integrated projects covering a number of sectors. But in most countries (and at the international level) organizational structures tend to be along sectoral lines. In some cases, the required sectoral collaboration may be achieved by establishing links between different projects; in others integrated projects may be preferable.

## SECTORAL PRIORITIES

The interdependence between the sectors raises the question of sectoral priorities: must all the basic needs outputs be provided simultaneously—which would impose impossible administrative and financial costs in many countries—or can a set of sensible sectoral priorities be established for meeting basic needs? Whatever the resource situation, a rational basic needs program should take into account the interactions between sectors. At this stage we know too little about the relationships to come to a definite conclusion about priorities and linkages, but there is enough evidence for some suggestions.

The linkages described above provide some pointers to priorities. For example, education, and especially female education, appears to be a likely priority area: even without additional output from other sectors, female education may improve nutrition and health practices and reduce fertility. But without education, provision of sanitation and clean water are likely to be ineffective in improving health status. Education can (as it appears to do in Sri Lanka) substitute for such improvements. Sri Lanka's high life expectancy was achieved while only 20 percent of the people had access to clean water. In contrast, in Egypt over two-thirds of the population have access to clean water, yet child mortality rates remain high.

Improvements in nutrition are critical to improved health. But increases in food supply alone will not be sufficient to improve nutrition. Much depends on the distribution of food among and within families, in turn depending on the distribution of purchasing power, the relative price of the various foods, and spending patterns among families. Aggregate food supply is in excess of requirements in Cuba, Brazil, Indonesia, and Egypt; yet there is very considerable malnutrition. In Brazil 37 percent of Brazilian children were estimated to be suffering from first degree malnutrition, 20 percent from second degree malnutrition; in Indonesia 20 to 30 percent of children were shown to be malnourished according to a survey of heights and weights; in Egypt chronic malnutrition is widespread in rural areas, where one-quarter of the children are stunted. In contrast, in Sri Lanka, with a significantly lower supply of calories per head, a survey in 1969–1970 showed that only 25 percent of the population earning less than 400 Rupees per month consumed less than 2200 calories per day, and only 5 percent, less than 1900.

While health is a major objective according to a basic needs approach, the evidence here suggests that health services, as conventionally defined, may not be an important input, just as formal schooling may not be necessary for education. Curative health services of a Western type are rendered more or less useless in the absence of the other conditions for improving health. For example, in a village in Gambia, the British Medical Research Council provided specific curative treatment to each child in need. There was only a small difference in child mortality between this village and a "control" untreated village.

Much depends on the content as well as the area of particular basic needs sectors' output. For example, the content and method (learning by rote or learning to think) of education is clearly important in determining its effects. The health sector may be largely confined to curative medicine, or it may be extended to include a good deal of health education and nutrition.

Several country studies provide some insights into sectoral linkages and priorities and the causal processes at work, but it is difficult to know whether the results can be generalized from one country to others. Taking data from a large number of countries, an attempt has been made to see whether there are any systematic relationships, across countries, between achievements on basic needs—defined in terms of life expectancy—and performance on various basic needs input indicators.[4] The inputs examined include (in addition to income per head) primary school enrollment, the ratio of female to total enrollment, access to clean water, availability of doctors and nurses, level of nutrition, public consumption as a proportion of gross domestic product, the degree of urbanization, and the income share of the lowest 40 percent of the population.

The data were analyzed in a variety of ways, which in some cases led to conflicting conclusions. But some conclusions were fairly firmly established:

Of the basic inputs for meeting basic needs, primary education consistently appears to be the most important according to all of the measures devised to test relative importance;

Nutrition and health care seem to be of significance, but less so than
  education, while water supply is of low priority;
The distribution of income (measured by the share of the bottom 40 percent) appears to be an important additional factor influencing basic
  needs, as is the ratio of female to total primary school enrollment; and
The size of the public sector and the level of urbanization do not seem to
  be related to basic needs fulfillment.

Naturally, all of these conclusions need appropriate qualifications:
they are based on inexact and perhaps inadequate measures of basic
needs inputs and outputs, and it is difficult to separate cause from effect.
However, one has to be impressed by the consistent power of education
(literacy) in explaining variations in life expectancy. Broadly, the priorities suggested by analysis of the country experience are borne out by the
cross-country statistical exercise. But country examples indicate that
basic needs can be met in a variety of ways: there are no iron laws that
must be followed. Looking at deviations from what would be expected at
different income levels, we find that Tanzania does extremely well for a
country of its income level in terms of literacy and water supply, but
does not rank high in terms of life expectancy. In fact, its actual life expectancy of 45 is about that expected for its income level (46) and
roughly similar to such countries as Zambia and the Ivory Coast, which
have much lower literacy rates. Tanzania illustrates the point that despite the generally high association between education and life expectancy, not all countries that have done well in education (as measured
by literacy) have necessarily done well on life expectancy. One possible
explanation, however, is that Tanzania's gains in education have come
recently, and there may be a lag with respect to their impact on life expectancy.
    Another interesting case is Egypt, which comes near or at the top of
the list of those countries doing above average in water supply, calorie
supply, and health care. Its life expectancy of 53, however, is only
slightly above its expected value of 49. The disappointing performance
on basic needs might in part be explained by the lack of substantial
progress in education; literacy in Egypt is estimated to be 40 percent,
only slightly above the expected level of 39 percent. Egypt appears to be
a case that confirms the importance of education in meeting basic needs.
    An important aspect is the role of women in meeting basic needs.
Strategies that improve the status of women in terms of their education,
income, and access to basic needs may be more productive than other
approaches, because of the role of women in child care, food preparation,
and education in the home. Water supply projects may provide safe water, but improper sanitation in the household can quickly lead to a loss of

potential health benefits. The greater benefit of water supply projects may, in fact, be in their impact in reducing the workload of women in hauling water. Almost all countries that have done well in basic needs have also done well in terms of making primary education available to women (or at least reducing the bias favoring males). The reverse, however, is not necessarily true, suggesting that female education is a necessary, but not a sufficient, condition for making progress on meeting basic needs. Studies indicate, furthermore, that improving the employment and productivity of women can have an important impact on basic needs, since it appears that women spend a larger share of their incomes on basic needs (food, health care) than men.

It appears difficult to identify properly worldwide priorities, although education does seem to have the edge. Sectoral priorities seem best determined at a country level, taking account of country objectives, resources, and past experience.[5]

## INTERNATIONAL COOPERATION

An important new light is thrown by the basic needs approach on the objective of narrowing the gap between rich and poor countries. In the past, this gap has usually been defined in terms of relative income per head. It is very doubtful whether it is either desirable or possible to close the income gap in the near future. But closing the gap in terms of basic needs fulfillment, as shown by such indicators as life expectancy, literacy rates, or nutrition levels, is more desirable, feasible, and worthy of international cooperation efforts. Life expectancy is biologically bounded to somewhere around seventy years. Literacy rates cannot be more than 100 percent. Adequate nutrition levels can be exceeded. Therefore, the aim of closing the basic needs gap is more sensible and appealing than that of closing the income gap. National and international policies aiming at this objective should mobilize wide consensus.

This is not to say that such efforts are separable from either concerns about national growth or flows of external resources. A basic needs approach is not antigrowth; in fact, growth (appropriately composed, distributed, and measured) is particularly important—indeed critical—for low-income countries in order to achieve basic needs objectives.[6] Furthermore, national and international efforts to pursue absolute improvements in life expectancy, health status, literacy, and the like must involve resource reallocations from (1) the developed countries to the developing countries exhibiting greatest basic needs disparities; (2) from higher income groups in the developing countries to lower income groups; (3) from tangential to critical sectors within developing countries; and (4) within each sector from nonbasic needs to basic needs objectives.[7]

## NOTES

1. International Bank for Reconstruction and Development, *World Development Report, 1979* (Washington, D.C., August 1979).
2. For further discussion of Sri Lanka, see Chapter 4.
3. For a further discussion of family planning, nutrition, and health, see Chapter 2.
4. Norman L. Hicks, "Sector Priorities in Meeting Basic Needs: Some Statistical Evidence," mimeo (Washington, D.C.: World Bank, 1979).
5. On basic needs as a planning framework, see Chapter 1.
6. See Chapter 3 on the issue of growth, distribution, and basic needs indicators.
7. See Chapter 5 on resource transfer allocations.

# Preface

As we enter the decade of the 1980s, the goal of reducing absolute impoverishment throughout the world seems as distant as ever. What progress has been made in past decades now seems threatened by the direct effects of oil price increases and the indirect effects thereof on the global economy.

It is perhaps unfortunate that the basic human needs (BHN) approach evolved into an acceptable conceptual exercise during the late 1970s. It has yet to gain the broad acceptance of the "growth with equity" approach of the 1970s; still, whether under the name of BHN or whether othewise disguised, the approach is having its effect on the policies of bilateral and multilateral donors and on developing countries.

This volume of essays written by economists involved in the early BHN debates presents a cohesive set of ideas that describe the potential contribution of the basic needs approach to development theory and practice.

*Danny M. Leipziger*
Washington, D.C.

# BASIC NEEDS AND DEVELOPMENT

*Chapter 1*

# Basic Human Needs: A Development Planning Approach

*Michael J. Crosswell*

## INTRODUCTION

In the past three decades, perceptions of development objectives have been increasingly refined. Early views of development included an underlying concern for improving the situation of the poor in developing countries, but focused largely on achieving more proximate objectives, such as high rates of growth in GNP, that eventually were to entail broadly based increases in standards of living. However, the links between higher rates of GNP growth and widespread improvements in well-being have proved to be more tenuous and elusive than expected, so that concern with these linkages has steadily mounted. The basic human needs (BHN) approach brings this concern to the forefront by directly focusing on patterns of growth and development in terms of their contribution to meeting basic needs on a sustainable basis.

The basic human needs approach was first put forth in an international forum by the International Labour Office (ILO) at its 1976 World Employment Conference and was subsequently elaborated by others at the World Bank, at the OECD, and within AID (see International La-

I would like to thank Constantine Michalopoulos, John Eriksson, and Danny Leipziger for their extensive, helpful comments on previous drafts. This chapter draws on AID Discussion Paper #38.

bour Office 1977; Streeten 1977; Burki and Voorhoeve 1977; Development Assistance Committee 1977; Crosswell 1977; Leipziger and Lewis 1977; Agency for International Development 1978). These various presentations of the basic needs approach have spawned a number of critical responses.

One reaction has been that the BHN approach is nothing new—that development efforts have been concentrating for some time on employment, income distribution, rural development, and the like, so that the basic needs approach is simply a different label attached to the same product. A second reaction is that the BHN approach is little more than a slogan that expresses a worthy intention but offers no concrete policy guidance. Accordingly, it may be of some use in generating political support but not in formulating development plans. A third reaction acknowledges that the basic needs approach has content, but views policies for meeting basic needs as inimical to growth. At the extreme, the view is that one dollar spent on meeting basic needs is one dollar less for productive investment and growth, so that the two objectives are in practice dichotomous. A corollary of this is the reaction that basic needs is ancillary to the overall business of development. Fourth, among the more political reactions, basic needs is perceived by some as an improper focus for a cooperative (donor/recipient) development effort. Instead, it is a matter of priorities internal to developing countries.

This chapter directly confronts the first three of these reactions and thereby offers some input for consideration of the fourth. According to the interpretation set forth, the BHN approach proceeds from the assumption that the ultimate objective of development strategies is to achieve sustainable improvements in the material well-being of individuals and establishes explicit links between this ultimate (but vague) objective and more proximate, concrete objectives that have more direct policy implications. It thus represents a step forward in providing a coherent framework that can accommodate the increasingly refined sets of development objectives that have evolved over the past thirty years and can systematically relate these objectives to various types of policies. The first section of the chapter sets out this framework and thereby highlights what is new in the basic needs approach—that it provides a better framework for development planning and policy.

The second section explores in a general way the policies that might be suitable in one setting or another for meeting basic needs. This section does not purport to represent an original discussion of new policy instruments—indeed, it should be emphasized that policies for meeting basic needs are on the whole quite familiar and that the problems and issues surrounding implementation of such policies remain difficult ones. Instead, this section seeks to demonstrate that the framework developed earlier is in fact a valuable tool for planning and organizing development policy in a coherent, internally consistent fashion.

These first two sections of the chapter refer to GNP growth in terms of its contribution to meeting basic needs on a sustainable basis and stress the importance of the *pattern* of growth—in terms of the composition of increases in output and employment and the distribution of increases in income—that underlies the aggregate rate of growth. However, given the widespread concern with GNP growth per se, it is important to explore the implications of a basic needs approach for growth rates of GNP (rather than vice versa). Accordingly, the third section of the chapter looks at the channels through which BHN policies would affect growth rates of GNP and examines arguments about whether these effects might be positive or negative.

## A FRAMEWORK FOR ANALYSIS

The framework described in this section attempts to order the elements of a BHN strategy in such a way as to facilitate planning and organization of the general policies entailed by a BHN approach and analysis of the relationship between BHN and growth. The key feature of the framework is that it attempts to order ends and means by establishing an explicit hierarchy of objectives, from ultimate objectives that have only vague policy implications to more immediate objectives that have quite direct implications for policy.

Ultimately, BHN objectives comprise the current and future well-being of individuals. There are many factors, tangible and intangible, that determine well-being. The more concrete objective of the BHN approach is to enable individuals to attain on a sustainable basis a minimum standard of living defined in material terms, which is a more or less necessary condition (though not sufficient) for attaining acceptable levels of well-being. That is, a BHN strategy focuses on the tangible necessities of life—food, water, clothing, shelter, health, education, and so forth—without which a person has little or no chance to lead a fulfilling existence.[1] The less tangible needs—a sense of autonomy, self-realization, and the like—are considerably more difficult to define, analyze, and satisfy. They are for the most part beyond the scope of this chapter, except for the caveat that policies providing for material objectives of a BHN strategy should be supportive of the more intangible goals. This provides one of several good justifications for stressing the importance of participation of the poor—those who cannot satisfy their basic needs—in decisions concerning the design and implementation of policies that enhance their capacity to meet these needs.

Of course, development strategies must provide for increases in overall GNP, including policies and programs that have a positive impact on living standards of those already able to satisfy their basic needs. The BHN approach per se does not purport to cover all aspects of development planning. However, it does provide a suitable basis for a planning framework in countries where absolute poverty is widespread, and a high priority is placed on achieving a pattern of growth that results in substantial alleviation of poverty on a sustainable basis.

Estimates of the proportion of the developing world's population that is in poverty range widely, depending importantly on the definition of poverty. Estimates published in the *World Development Report, 1978* (IBRD 1978) indicate that 52 percent of the population in low-income countries (1975 per capita incomes of $250 or less) are poor. The corresponding figure for middle-income developing countries is 17 percent, bringing the average for the developing world as a whole to 37 percent.[2] A second set of estimates for the developing world as a whole, prepared as background for the International Labour Office's World Employment Conference (1976), puts the percentage of poor at 84 percent, the percentage of seriously poor at 67 percent, and the percentage destitute at 39 percent (Richards 1976). The corresponding figures for many of the low-income countries—where most of the world's poor are located—would of course be even higher. Accordingly, any effort to raise earned incomes and living standards of the bulk of the poor in such countries would necessarily entail policies and programs that would have broadly positive impacts on overall GNP.

For purposes of economic planning and policy, it is useful to discuss minimum standards of living in terms of consumption levels of key goods and services.[3] The concept of minimum standard levels of consumption is in principle straightforward for goods such as food, clothing, water, and shelter. For education and health the concept is more difficult, but might embody years of education (however defined) and consumption of preventive health services—such as examinations and innoculations—as well as curative services as needed. The explicit target group of a BHN strategy is the poor—those whose current level of consumption is below the standard levels. The intermediate objective of a BHN strategy is to enable the poor to progressively (over time) narrow the gap between their present consumption levels and the minimum standard levels, as a means of achieving the more ultimate objective of enhanced well-being.

At this stage, BHN objectives have at least three dimensions—the number of poor, the types of essential goods and services, and time. The fact that BHN objectives comprise not only current but future consumption levels immediately and inevitably introduces the need to consider savings, investment, and growth, since savings commonly represents a decision to forego consumption now for the sake of investing and obtaining greater consumption possibilities in the future. Once this time dimension is considered, the aforementioned dichotomy that separates efforts to meet basic needs from efforts to achieve higher rates of growth is exposed as false dichotomy, and the role of growth in meeting basic needs over time becomes more evident. (This argument is developed in considerable detail in Crosswell and Michalopoulos 1979.) However, not only are the rates of investment and growth important, but also the pattern—that is, the composition of increases in output and the distribution of increases in income.

Second, the fact that BHN objectives are defined in terms of numbers of poor individuals now and in the future suggests a potentially important role for population policies that would retard fertility rates, which currently average 6.2 in low-income countries.[4] The volume of resources required to achieve increased satisfaction of basic needs will depend not only on the number of poor, but also on the composition by age and the implied dependency ratios. This rationale for population policies exists apart from the consideration of whether access to contraceptive methods and/or smaller family size is perceived to be a basic human need.[5]

Third, the definition of the goods and services that satisfy basic human needs suggests several important considerations. While the broad categories cited above are likely to be common to all countries, the specific goods and services and the levels of consumption would tend to vary across countries, and within countries, according to social, cultural, and geographic factors. Since what is perceived as needs depends in some measure on resource availability, there is also likely to be variation over time in the specification of a minimum standard of living. In this sense, basic needs are country specific and dynamic.[6]

The broad categories of basic needs also suggest the likelihood of important interdependencies in both production and consumption. For instance, shelter, water, and sanitation are likely to be closely linked in their provision. Second, the volume of health services required by a person declines as other needs are met, and food requirements diminish with reduced incidence of parasites, diarrhea, and other debilitating illnesses that interfere with nutrition. Accordingly, the sum of the resource costs of attaining each consumption target separately tends to overstate the cost of covering all consumption deficiencies together. These interdependencies suggest the need for an integrated approach, which in turn points to the usefulness of planning.[7]

Finally, while basic needs objectives have so far been described in terms of consumption levels of goods and services, much of this consumption is more accurately characterized as investment in human capital through better health, education, and nutrition. Such investment may be justifiable on pure efficiency grounds, apart from considerations of equity.[8]

So far, the ultimate objectives of a BHN approach have been described in terms of levels of well-being of individuals; a necessary condition or means of attaining these objectives has been discussed in terms of sustainable levels of current and future consumption of essential goods and services. In turn, there are two necessary conditions for achieving such consumption levels. First, there must be adequate overall production and supplies of the needed goods and services, distributed in forms and geographic areas so as to be widely accessible. Second, people must have enough income to be able to acquire these goods and services. These two intermediate objectives—sufficient income and adequate production—are highly interrelated but conceptually distinct, as for example in the national income and product accounts. They are interrelated in that certain policies can contribute to achieving both objectives simultaneously.

For instance, policies that enable people to better meet their dietary needs by growing more food would increase both income and output. Further, the adequacy of production and supply of essential goods and services will in general have an effect on prices, which in turn will help determine the sufficiency of a given level of income. At the same time, the distinctions between income and production objectives are crucial. For purposes of more completely satisfying basic needs, it does little good to achieve adequate overall food supplies, as many countries have, if people have insufficient income to obtain food. Similarly, it is of limited value to achieve higher income levels if there are no water or health facilities nearby or if rising food prices erode the purchasing power of that income. In this respect there are two sides to the problem of meeting basic needs. This integrated focus on both income and production—more specifically on the pattern of production and the distribution of income—distinguishes the basic needs approach from other development strategies that focus on employment and income distribution alone, without separate concern for the composition of output (for example, Chenery and Associates 1974).

The intermediate objectives of sufficient income and adequate production and supply of essential goods and services can in turn be broken down into public and private components. For purposes of a BHN strategy, there are two types of income—earned income and income transfers. Earned income can be defined as returns to labor and returns to productive assets, such as land. Transfers are customarily defined as payments for which no goods or services are received in return. Comparisons of the extent of poverty with overall resource availability in most developing countries suggest that policies directed toward achieving sufficient income must focus mainly on generating more productive employment.

These policies, which are described in more detail in the next section, would in general include expanding employment opportunities at wages sufficient to meet basic needs; increasing human capital; and increasing the stock of physical assets and resources available to the self-employed poor. However, for that group that can be neither productively employed nor supported by those who are, some form of transfers will be necessary if their needs are to be met. (Streeten [1977] mentions the figure of 20 percent of the poor.) Transfers might hypothetically take the form of direct supplements to financial income—for example, cash grants. However, for reasons discussed below, it is more likely that transfers would be in forms that more directly promote consumption of essential goods and services—for instance, food subsidies, building materials, and subsidized education and health.

On the production side, needed goods and services can be divided into those frequently provided publicly (though not necessarily gratis) and those available through private markets. For public services, the strategy calls for direct public production and distribution in forms and geographic areas that make them widely accessible. For goods that are typically produced privately (e.g., food), adequate supplies can in general be achieved through some combination of domestic production and imports. This may call for more or less direct public sector intervention, with the possibilities ranging from policies that affect profitability in key sectors to policies that more directly determine the pattern of private investment to direct public production.

Apart from its potential usefulness in relating concrete policy objectives to more ultimate development objectives having to do with well-being, this framework also suggests some of the targets and indicators that might be associated with a BHN approach. The framework elaborated above starts with the ultimate objectives of a BHN strategy—the current and future well-being of individuals. Well-being depends (in part) on achieving a minimum standard of living defined in terms of consumption of essential goods and services. Attaining consumption objectives calls for adequate production and supply of these goods and services and for income levels sufficient to acquire them. These can be accomplished via goals in terms of employment and income transfers on the income side and of production, supply, and distribution of certain public services and private goods on the supply side.

The targets and indicators suggested by this framework of objectives are first of all those relating directly to well-being. These might include, inter alia, indicators such as life expectancy, infant mortality, morbidity, and literacy where these measures are calculated with particular attention to the poor.[9] Insofar as low birth rates and fertility rates indicate a greater sense of economic well-being, these might also be useful indicators. A second set of targets and indicators might relate more directly to consumption and living standards—for instance, variables included in housing and nutrition surveys, school attendance, and consumption of health services. A third set of targets and indicators would measure income and employment among the poor and availability of essential goods and services, such as supply and productive capacity for food and housing; number and location of clinics, schools, and trained personnel; and sanitation and water networks.

## POLICIES FOR MEETING BASIC HUMAN NEEDS

The value of the framework elaborated above depends on how well it serves as a device for organizing and planning development policies. The policies mentioned in this section are quite general, cover a broad spectrum, and should be familiar to most readers. The specific mix of these policies would vary from country to country, depending on the scope and nature of poverty and the social and political institutions for dealing with poverty. The purpose of this section is to place the policy options in a coherent framework and to make explicit how these policies might contribute to meeting basic needs.

The policy discussion is organized around the four intermediate objectives of a BHN approach—those having to do with employment, transfers, public services, and private goods. There are two immediately apparent areas of overlap. First, some policies, such as land reform, may simultaneously promote the two objectives of increased food production and more productive employment of the poor. More generally, to the extent that shifts in the pattern of production toward essential goods and services entail increases in the labor intensity of production, both employment and supply objectives will be served. However, the objectives of employment and output are conceptually distinct, since achieving objectives in terms of output and supply will in general not generate enough jobs to meet employment and income objectives.[10]

A second area of overlap has to do with production and distribution of public services and transfers. Often health and education services are offered at subsidized rates or even gratis—a form of transfer in kind. Indeed, for some public services—for example, central water taps—there may be no efficient way of directly charging to cover costs. In other cases, such as health and education, public production and distribution may appear to be the most practicable way of effecting redistribution through transfers. Nonetheless, decisions and policies directed toward generating the capacity to provide public services are in principle distinct from policies that determine the rates charged for these services.

## Policies for Promoting More Productive Employment

There are several well-known sets of policies that developing countries might consider in their efforts to expand productive employment.[11] First, developing countries can implement policies that lead to changes in access to the existing stock of productive assets. Since most of the poor are located in rural areas, and most of these work in agriculture,[12] increased access to land and water is the most important example. The ILO (1977:61) has pointed out that "in many countries the implementation of the [basic needs] strategy is likely to have to begin with agrarian reform . . . agrarian reform is likely both to increase the supply of basic food and to ensure that it is distributed to some of those in greatest need." Policies that would increase the access of the poor to land include direct redistribution of land, changes in tenure arrangements whereby returns to land would accrue in larger degree to the poor, and development and settlement of new land. The feasibility of agrarian reform depends on the overall availability of land and the pattern of ownership. The political and administrative constraints on successful agrarian reform are formidable. Even where agrarian reform can be carried out, a necessary condition for success in terms of increased productivity is availability of complementary inputs, including seed and fertilizers; access to credit and technical assistance; other agricultural services such as marketing and storage; and, of course, water.

A second type of policy involves redirection of investment along patterns that would increase access of the poor to productive resources. This might involve widened access to tools or equipment for the self-employed poor—for example, farm implements and looms. Another policy would be to increase public investment in certain types of infrastructure and services that support productive activity carried out by the self-employed poor, such as rural public works, credit and marketing facilities, and research and extension. Rural public works are an example of the dual potential of generating considerable employment in their construction as well as creating assets that can facilitate the expansion of production and employment among the poor in a key sector (see Lewis [1978], who analyzes the problems and possibilities of public works as a proegalitarian policy instrument). Finally, investment in human capital in the form of more extensive education beyond basic needs requirements may further improve the productivity and skills of the poor.

A third type of policy would involve adjustment of the relative prices of capital and labor so as to encourage employment of the currently abundant resource—unskilled labor. This may call for changes in the structure of tariffs and the exchange rate(s) that currently encourage imports of capital equipment associated with capital-intensive technology and discourage labor-intensive exports. Further, there may be scope for policies affecting interest rates, credit allocation, and fiscal incentives in directions that will expand employment. Finally, minimum wage policies should take account of effects on total employment as well as on income of the employed. (This is analyzed in considerable depth in Little, Scitovsky, and Scott 1970.)

The success of policies affecting the relative price of labor depends on how well production techniques respond to such price changes. A fourth type of policy, therefore, would include measures that encourage and promote responsiveness of production techniques to relative factor prices and the underlying factor endowments in LDCs. Such policies would include efforts to develop and disseminate information on appropriate technology and techniques that are both labor intensive and efficient. They would also include policies to promote research and development activities that focus on technological improvements in labor-intensive activities and sectors (for more detail, see Singer 1977).

Finally, policies that directly influence the composition of output can promote employment by encouraging the production of goods that are labor intensive rather than those that are capital intensive. Aside from efforts to expand production in "core" basic needs sectors such as food and housing, which will have a positive employment impact, policymakers can offer a variety of incentives in sectors and activities that are suitably labor intensive. (These incentives are discussed below in the context of policies to influence production and supply.) In particular, policies aimed at export expansion will tend to generate employment insofar as the comparative advantage of many low-income developing countries lies in abundant labor.[13] Further, as income distribution becomes less skewed, reflecting increases in income levels of the poor, there is some evidence that the composition of final demand will in some measure shift in the direction of more labor-intensive goods and services.[14]

As generation of employment plays a key role in a basic needs strategy, this points toward a greater, but not exclusive priority on labor intensity in the general structure of production. This priority on labor intensity reflects considerations of both equity and efficiency. To the extent that labor is abundant and capital scarce and that relative prices do not reflect relative factor scarcities, policies that affect input prices and technology so as to induce substitution of labor for capital are likely to result in greater efficiency and output.[15] At the same time, there are some clear examples of appropriate capital-intensive production processes. For instance, the techniques associated with exploitation of certain natural resources may be exclusively capital intensive. Second, certain inherently capital-intensive goods and activities such as electric power generation usually cannot be imported and must be produced domestically. Finally, for some tradable goods, such as cement, transport costs may be so high that they are more cheaply produced domestically, even at prices reflecting relative factor scarcities.

Similarly, insofar as most of the poor in most low-income countries are in rural areas, the strategy points toward a greater but not exclusive weight in terms of policy efforts to rural development. Indeed, the problem of poverty in many developing countries has been exacerbated by an overallocation of resources to capital-intensive industry located in urban centers that is "modern" in the sense of replicating production patterns in capital-rich industrialized countries, but not in the sense of corresponding to current and future conditions in developing countries. (Lipton [1977] presents an extensive discussion of urban bias as a cause of persistent poverty in LDCs.) In many countries a basic needs approach would call for some redress of this imbalance. A focus on productive employment in rural areas will tend to reduce pressure on overburdened urban public services that has resulted from rural-urban migration. However, in some countries, particularly the "middle-income" developing countries, the problem of poverty is to a greater degree concentrated in urban centers, calling for employment policies that seek to raise productivity in the informal urban sector and expand employment more rapidly in the formal urban sector.

## Policies Regarding Income Transfers

Apart from the general role of transfers as a redistributive device, there are at least two rationales for income transfers in the context of a basic human needs approach. The primary rationale is that some of the poor cannot be productively employed, nor do they have access to incomes of productively employed individuals. These include some of the chronically ill, the aged, and children who are not provided for by families or other private sources. If the basic needs of these groups are to be met, then some type of transfer will be necessary. Typically, these transfers would be "in kind"—for instance, free food and health services. Transfers in kind are generally superior to transfers in cash when the goal of the transfer is to achieve target consumption levels of specific goods and services.[16]

The second rationale for transfers is more complex. In this case, the need for transfers arises from the possibility that a family may have sufficient income to meet basic needs (including access to public services) but may nonetheless allocate that income in ways that do not satisfy these needs, so that consumption deficiencies persist. For instance, lack of information and/or established tastes may steer food consumption toward items that are low in nutritional value. Second, the virtues of clean water, sanitation facilities, and preventive health measures may not be readily appreciated. Finally, there may be intrafamily distributional problems that prevent the needs of women and children from being met.[17]

It is extremely difficult to gauge the magnitude of these sorts of problems and even more difficult to determine appropriate policies. There are at least three broad, nonexclusive approaches, focusing on tastes and preferences, income, and prices.

The first approach includes efforts to accommodate existing preferences (e.g., nutritional additives to preferred but relatively unnutritious food) and efforts to change these preferences through improved information. In this respect, participation of the poor in the determination of basic needs and the policies for satisfying them can play a critical role. Participation is often mentioned as an important element in a BHN approach. Its importance lies not only in considerations of the more intangible aims of the strategy, but also in efficiency considerations. From the standpoint of efficiency, participation generates crucial information about the needs, preferences, and capabilities of the target groups that basic needs programs are meant to benefit as well as the environment in which these programs are carried out. At the same time, participation provides timely information to target groups so that they may fully take advantage of these programs. In terms of broader aims of the strategy, genuine participation enhances one's sense of individual autonomy, dignity, and self-respect.

The second possibility for overcoming such consumption deficiencies is to increase incomes beyond the minimum for meeting basic needs. For instance, while an income of $200 per capita per year may be just sufficient to satisfy nutritional and other basic requirements, an income of $300 may be the minimum income that actually results in choice of a diet that meets nutritional standards. More generally, as long as there is a positive preference for the goods or services in question, there is some level of income that will produce the desired consumption level. However, this tends to increase resource requirements for a given set of consumption targets, since target income levels are higher than the bare minimum.

A third possibility—which may be cheaper than the second in some cases—is to alter consumption patterns through transfers in kind and price subsidies. For instance, subsidies on nutritious types of food will tend to shift consumption patterns in the desired direction. Similarly, clean water may have to be offered virtually free of charge to persuade people not to use contaminated sources that are freely available and conveniently located. The obverse of these policies is to tax consumption of nonessential goods and services.

Transfer policies can be clarified somewhat by looking at specific components of basic needs. Transfers of health and education services are not uncommon. Transfers related to private goods such as food and housing are also frequent, but can be quite problematic, since they can entail disincentives to producers.[18] Further, opportunities for illegal transactions are plentiful, since there are private markets for these same goods.

In terms of the balance between transfer policies and employment policies in reaching income and consumption goals, it is apparent that the primary focus in most countries must be on generating more and better employment opportunities. Insofar as poverty reflects underemployment, primary reliance on transfers would be inefficient in that underutilization of labor resources would be perpetuated. Moreover, in most cases it would be infeasible in terms of political, economic, and administrative constraints. As far as political constraints are concerned, primary reliance on transfers would imply a substantial redistribution of current income in most countries, in forms and magnitudes that would probably be unacceptable. Economically, current average levels of per capita income in many countries are barely above levels that would satisfy basic needs, so that increased employment and growth will be necessary to provide sufficient output to meet basic needs. Finally, the administrative costs of a transfer approach in terms of manpower, managerial skills, and leakages would be substantial.

At the same time, the constraints facing employment policies are not to be underestimated. Policies involving land reform, redirection of investment, changes in the relative price of capital and labor, and adoption of appropriate technology will in varying degrees encounter stiff opposition from some groups. However, the virtue of this approach is that through better utilization of labor, growth of output and incomes can be enhanced. This will—for a given absolute income target—diminish the amount of income redistribution required, both in relative and absolute terms.

## Policies Regarding Private Goods

On the income side, the distinction between earned income from productive employment and unearned income in the form of transfers is analytically clear-cut. However, on the supply side, the distinction between those basic goods and services that are essentially private and those that are public is conceptually rather blurred. Public sector provision of a good or service is frequently justified by a substantial degree of joint consumption (the pure case being national defense, which everyone consumes jointly) and/or by technological considerations that provide for natural monopolies (e.g., urban water and sewerage facilities), although some natural monopolies are privately operated under public regulation (e.g., some utilities).

In theory, virtually all goods and services that meet basic needs could be efficiently produced privately, with public sector intervention in production limited to regulation in some cases and provision of a few essentially public inputs—for instance, agricultural research and extension services, infrastructure, and disease eradication measures. In practice, there is a mix between public and private production that varies from country to country, depending upon a variety of factors apart from those mentioned above.

This section deals with policies for achieving supply objectives for goods such as food, clothing, and shelter that are usually produced privately. Such essential goods have few if any external benefits associated with their consumption, and techniques for their production are such that they are not natural monopolies. Nonetheless, developing country policymakers may need to concern themselves to some degree with policies that ensure availability of some of these goods where they are not already available or likely to become available in sufficient quantities. Indeed, while attention to the composition of output is one of the key distinguishing features of the basic needs approach, the extent of intervention in private markets can range from near laissez faire to direct public production, depending on the general organization of production and the underlying political and social values, on how well markets might respond to increases in demand, and on the perceived importance of self-sufficiency in production of basic needs commodities such as food.[19]

Policies directed toward production in private sectors of the economy would in general focus not only on those sectors that produce essential final products such as food, housing, and clothing, but also on private sectors that supply material inputs such as seed and fertilizer, building materials, and intermediate textiles. From this standpoint (not to mention employment considerations), it is incorrect to view the basic needs approach as one limited to only a few sectors of the economy.

For private goods, supply generally is possible through some combination of domestic production and imports. (Even simple housing could hypothetically be imported, at least in nearly complete form.) An important political and economic issue, especially with respect to food, is the extent to which countries should strive for self-sufficiency in production of essential goods. From the standpoint of economic factors, this would depend in general on notions of efficiency and comparative advantage broadly conceived to include not only considerations of factor endowments (labor, capital, natural resources), technology, demand factors, and transport costs, but also other considerations such as the uncertainty surrounding foreign supplies of imports (and demand for exports), the vital nature of the commodities in question, dynamic factors such as technological change, and adjustment costs of changes in the composition of production. While self-sufficiency in food production is often mentioned in the context of basic needs, such a goal could be quite costly in economic terms.

A particularly important consideration in decisions about domestic versus foreign supply is the crucial role of employment in the overall basic needs approach. Fortunately, insofar as the abundant resource in most developing countries is unskilled labor, employment and efficiency considerations are likely to coincide. However, these considerations do not indicate a priori the degree of specialization and reliance on trade versus self-sufficiency. For instance, one scenario of extreme specialization could have the poor employed in sectors and activities that produce solely for export, with adequate supplies of essential private goods secured through imports. At the opposite extreme, a polar case would have each poor household become self-sufficient in producing its own food, clothing, shelter, and so forth. Third, a less extreme point on the spectrum would entail national self-sufficiency in production of essential goods, but specialization within the country—for example, some of the poor working in construction, others in textiles, others in sectors that produce nonessential goods. The important point is that each of these three examples, as well as intermediate cases, could be consistent with both employment and supply objectives in a basic needs strategy.

There is a wide range of familiar policy instruments appropriate in one country or another to ensure adequate production and supplies of basic goods in cases where the response of private markets to increased demands is inadequate. Various forms of price policies, such as subsidies to producers of essential goods and taxes on production of nonessential goods, are one possibility for affecting the pattern of production. Second, since investment within some sectors is constrained by internal sources of funds, there is considerable scope for intervention and improvement in credit markets to increase mobility of financial capital. (This point is emphasized in Pyatt and Thorbecke 1976). Third, production and certainly distribution in private sectors is dependent in varying degrees on various public services and infrastructure, so that public investment that provides or upgrades these services will promote increased output and influence the location and distribution of this production. Fourth, policy-makers can implement measures to improve the functioning of private markets by policies that promote competition and by regulation of industries that are natural monopolies because of economies of scale, limited markets, and the like. A final policy option is direct public production of essential goods.

For example, the scope for public policies to promote private sector food production is quite large and well recognized. There are significant investments to be made in areas traditionally reserved to the public sector owing to the difficulty of charging prices or because of the large fixed investment cost involved. These include agricultural research, extension, and infrastructure, but may also include marketing, storage, and credit facilities. Government pricing policies with respect to food are prevalent, but not always well conceived (see Lipton [1977: ch. 13] for an extensive discussion). For instance, in many developing countries, food prices have been kept artificially low, so that food production has been discouraged, and incomes and employment of the rural poor have been depressed. At the same time, however, consumption of an important commodity has been encouraged with favorable effects on the urban poor. In general, pricing policies (including minimum wage laws) can be expected to have mixed effects both on the allocation of resources and on the distribution of income—effects that need to be foreseen and taken into account.

In the area of housing, development of sites and public services for low-income housing, provision of credit and materials for housing improvements, and direct public production have become increasingly important, particularly in urban areas. The example of site development suggests the more general need for an integrated approach and planning capability to coordinate geographically policies having to do with employment and policies that affect production and distribution of both private goods and public services.

The implications of a basic needs approach for the overall pattern of production, in particular the relative weights to agriculture versus industry, depend on strategies for achieving income and supply objectives. These strategies can be expected to vary from country to country according to several factors. First, these weights will depend on the pattern of domestic production that underlies the securing of adequate supplies of core private commodities. Expansion of domestic food production or of general agricultural production and exports to finance imports of food obviously points toward an emphasis on agriculture. On the other hand, increased industrial exports to finance imports of food, expansion of construction of low-cost housing, and increased production of manufactured intermediate inputs indicate an important role for industry. Second, the larger the portion and absolute numbers of poor in urban areas that employment policies aim to affect, the greater will be the emphasis on industry as opposed to agriculture. Finally, within the rural sector, the emphasis on agriculture versus industry will reflect the particular policies implemented to achieve employment objectives. For instance, agrarian reform points to an emphasis on policies that encourage and promote agricultural productivity; efforts to employ the rural poor in nonfarm activities may point to industry.

The implications of the basic needs approach for investment priorities are similarly dependent on country-specific factors. Increased satisfaction of basic needs calls for policies that promote productive employment and ensure adequate supplies of goods and services that meet basic needs. The latter consideration immediately points to investment to ensure adequate capacity in core areas such as food and construction of low-cost shelter. It may also call for investment in production processes that provide material inputs and in activities directed toward export expansion to finance the import requirements for meeting supply goals in core basic needs sectors. Finally, investment in infrastructure to support production and distribution of these goods and services will also be required. Investment in these sectors should be in forms that promote efficient, labor-intensive production processes, in keeping with the employment objectives of the strategy.

As demonstrated earlier (see note 10), the expansion in productive activity that ensures an adequate supply of basic goods and services will generally not be sufficient to attain employment objectives. Accordingly, income objectives would call for investment in forms and areas that effectively promote productive employment among the poor. The types of policies chosen to achieve employment objectives will have direct implications for the pattern of investment.

Regarding implications for investment priorities central to more familiar development strategies, the question is not whether a basic needs approach calls for more or less effort in areas of infrastructure, export earning capability, or industrialization. Rather, the question is what kind of infrastructure, export activity, and industrialization in light of an expanded and refined set of objectives. A basic needs strategy focuses not just on the aggregate level of output, but on the composition and distribution of output and particularly on employment. It is in terms of such objectives that rates of return to various programs and projects must be evaluated and the optimal pattern of investment determined.

## Public Services

In general, not all of the goods and services essential to well-being will be produced privately. The considerations mentioned earlier do not clearly point to a need for public production of health, education, and water and sanitation facilities, and examples of private production in each of these spheres are readily apparent.[20] Nonetheless, provision of such services frequently entails production and distribution under public auspices. In such cases, the policy implications of this element of a basic needs strategy are straightforward, though novel in certain aspects compared with conventional health, education, and public utility policies. For instance, a frequently occurring problem is that facilities providing public services are in various respects inaccessible to the poor. This is not only a matter of location (reflecting the general imbalance of policy focus toward the central city, at the expense of outlying areas), but also of mismatching of the types of services offered with the needs of the poor and of insufficient information and communication. As an example of former, the poor probably cannot take advantage of advanced education and may find traditional primary education of little use in terms of information and skills that are taught. As an example of the latter, clean water may be physically accessible, without any appreciation of its importance for preventing disease. In this regard, the emphasis on participation of the poor is particularly crucial in planning, setting up, and maintaining the facilities that provide public services.

The provision of public services should reflect the priority on generation of productive employment that is an essential element of a basic needs approach. The importance of appropriate technology and efficient labor-intensive production methods extends to provision of these services. Use of local resources, especially relatively unskilled labor, to set up and maintain the services can economize on more expensive resources and also heighten awareness and involvement of the community in the service.

Important interdependencies and linkages among basic needs goods and services that should be taken into account in general are particularly evident in the provision of public services. For instance, clean drinking water and adequate diets will lessen the demands on health services. Educational services can impart information about the importance of nutrition and sanitation in maintaining health (see Brown and Burki 1978).

Some of the most important policy issues surrounding public services have to do with how these services are to be financed, including both set-up costs and recurrent costs. (For a good discussion of these issues see Curry 1978.) While some of these issues belong under the heading of resource requirements—a topic beyond the scope of the present chapter—a few comments should be made, particularly since the public service component of basic needs frequently raises the specter of stagnant economies in which high welfare costs perpetuate low levels of income by reducing savings, investment, and growth.

Setting up health clinics, schools, and other public services—including both construction and training of personnel—is no less a form of investment than building a factory that produces consumer and/or producer goods (say household appliances). In each case, the investment represents a gross addition to the capacity of the economy to produce valuable goods and services in the future. The productivity of such investment depends upon the value—net of variable production costs (i.e., recurrent costs)—of the ensuing stream of output. In the case of the factory, productivity of the investment would be determined by the net market value of household appliances produced by the factory. Abstracting from problems of divergence between shadow and market prices, it would be appropriate to undertake this investment if the net market value of the output were anticipated to exceed the interest and amortization payments associated with borrowing to finance the investment.

In the case of social services, these have a market value as indicated by the fact that people are generally willing to pay fees for such services. Further, this is likely to understate the social value because of the meritorious nature of such services, whereby consumers tend to underestimate their private value, particularly with respect to their investment components (e.g., many forms of education and preventive health services);[21] and because of external benefits in consumption, whereby one person's consumption of such services may have positive effects on the well-being of others.[22] Comparing the net value of output with costs of investment, there is no a priori basis for concluding that expenditures associated with building a factory are more productive than expenditures associated with building a school.

The means for financing investment and recurrent costs in the example of the factory is ultimately established by market prices. In the case of social services there are several nonexclusive sources of finance to cover recurrent and capital costs. If a basic needs approach is successful in generating more productive employment, higher incomes, and increased output among the poor, then more resources will be available to help finance these costs. An immediate possibility is employment of the poor in constructing and administering these services, a form of "taxation in kind." The second possibility is to generate employment for the poor that is sufficiently productive so that the poor can afford to pay direct fees to cover the costs of public services. However, for reasons mentioned earlier, such fees may be counterproductive in terms of promoting consumption of essential services, since the perceived private value of such services is likely to be less than actual private and social value. A preferable alternative may then be to directly tax some portion of the income or output associated with more productive employment of the poor and then use these revenues to finance services delivered at fees that are correspondingly less than costs.

These possibilities are based on simultaneous expansion of earned income among the poor and production and distribution of essential public services. To the extent that basic needs policies do not initially raise earned income of the poor, then the scope for financing expanded production and distribution of social services will depend on the extent to which the existing pattern of public expenditures can be changed (e.g., from military expenditures to health expenditures or, within health, toward delivery systems that are more responsive to basic health needs)[23] and/or on the extent to which new revenues can be generated (through increased fees or taxes paid by the nonpoor). As both of these options are essentially redistributive, they could be politically quite difficult. Accordingly, an important (and difficult) task is to coordinate the pace of expansion in supply of essential goods and services with the rate of increase in income and employment. The framework elaborated earlier in this chapter is designed to facilitate this task.


## THE IMPLICATIONS OF A BASIC HUMAN NEEDS APPROACH FOR GROWTH RATES OF GNP

The discussion so far has been concerned with ways in which growth of income, output, and employment serve the purpose of meeting basic needs. Insofar as growth is not an end in itself, but rather a means for achieving more ultimate objectives, this perspective was appropriate. Nonetheless, it is of interest to turn the question around and ask how a basic human needs approach will serve the purposes of achieving high rates of growth in GNP. This question can be addressed by looking at various sources of growth and asking how a BHN approach would work through each of these channels. These sources of growth include increases in stocks of productive resources in the economy, increases in the economic efficiency with which these resources are employed, and technological change.

Regarding increases in stocks of productive resources, the immediately apparent source of growth is savings and investment that lead to increases in the physical capital stock. Two broad considerations help determine decisions about savings and invesment. First, how much more consumption in the future is afforded by foregoing one unit of consumption now?—that is, How productive is investment? While many factors affect the productivity of investment, this is essentially a technical question. The second consideration is subjective—namely, How important is consumption now compared with consumption in the future (i.e., the rate of time preference)? A starving man faced with the two possibilities of one loaf of bread now and one loaf later or no loaves now and four later will tend to pick the first, however attractive the second may be on technical grounds.

The latter consideration suggests that a BHN approach will tend to lower the aggregate domestic savings rate (defined as the ratio of total domestic savings to total income or GNP), since the rate of time preference—the future return necessary to induce a person to forego one unit of consumption now—is likely to be higher among poor people, who by definition are not consuming enough to meet basic needs. According to this line of reasoning, taking the needs of these people more into account will result in higher current consumption and lower rates of savings and investment, leading to less growth in GNP. The conclusion reached is that a BHN approach is unadvisable for countries seriously concerned about economic development.

There are at least three critical questions that need to be answered before this line of reasoning can be accepted. First, will the rates of domestic savings and investment actually decline? Second, will the GNP growth rate decline? Third, does a lower rate of growth imply that a BHN approach is contrary to developmental interests? The answer to the first question is quite uncertain and depends on several considerations. First of all, considering provision of basic goods and services as essentially a matter of consumption, the effect on aggregate rates of savings and investment of meeting basic needs depends on the extent to which consumption rather than income is redistributed. As an extreme case, if all of the increase in consumption of the poor came at the expense of consumption (but not savings) of the nonpoor, then the savings rate would not decline. To some extent this can be achieved if current expenditures on public services are reoriented rather than expanded—for instance, toward services provided by rural clinics, primary schools, and central water taps and away from public expenditures that tend to correspond to nonessential consumption of the nonpoor.[24] Also, policy instruments such as interest rates and consumption taxes can be used to increase incentives (or reduce disincentives) to save and thereby affect savings propensities.

Further, a more careful analysis of what constitutes savings and investment indicates that many of the expenditures that might be associated with a BHN approach actually represent investment. A substantial part of the "current" expenditures on health, education, and improved diets will result in increases in the stock of productive assets available to the economy (i.e., labor).[25] Such increases are essentially investment, the productivity of this investment depending crucially on how effectively labor can be employed. Further, expenditures on housing and on water and sanitation facilities represent increases in the physical capital stock, since these expenditures produce durable assets that yield services on into the future. Increases in incomes of the poor that are allocated to these types of expenditures are more accurately classified as investment and savings than consumption.

Finally, while a skewed income distribution may result in a higher recorded savings rate, these savings are not necessarily translated into productive domestic investment. Wealthy savers may instead invest in financial or physical assets abroad or else in speculative domestic land transactions.[26] Such "investment" yields little or no return to the domestic economy in terms of increasing the stock of productive resources. Accordingly, a decline in the savings rate would not necessarily entail a concomitant decline in the rate of productive domestic investment.

Suppose, however, that rates of savings and investment properly measured do decline. Will this result in a lower rate of growth? In an economy operating at full employment, with resources efficiently allocated, the answer would tend to be yes. However, developing countries are generally characterized by underutilization of labor and misallocation of resources (see White [1978] and Krueger [forthcoming] for supporting evidence). A basic human needs approach that aims at increasing the income of the poor by generating productive employment will tend to use both labor and capital more effectively in sectors and processes more appropriate to the factor endowments of developing countries. To the extent that a BHN approach results in more effective and more complete utilization of resources, particularly labor, the result will be significant increases in GNP. This growth could even come about without any net increase in capital, insofar as the economy is using existing supplies of labor, capital, and land more effectively.[27]

The essential point is that an increase in the physical capital stock is only one of several possible sources of growth. Other sources include increases in the quantity and quality of other factors of production (labor, human capital, land) and improvements in the technical and economic efficiency with which these resources are employed. A BHN approach emphasizing more effective employment of labor is commendable not just from the standpoint of equity, but also efficiency. Such an approach, if successful in improving resource allocation, will tend to generate increases in GNP.

A final source of growth—technological change—needs to be considered. It may be that technical progress is most rapid in those sectors and processes that are capital intensive—those least suited to the factor endowments of developing countries. In this case there may be a conflict between static efficiency considerations, which point to expansion of production in labor-intensive sectors, and dynamic considerations that point to the opposite pattern of expansion. On the other hand, it may be that possibilities for rapid technical progress simply have not been exploited in labor-intensive processes, because there have not been sufficient priorities or incentives with respect to better utilization of labor.

Suppose, however, that with all things considered—savings, investment, employment, and technological change—a developing economy will grow faster following a capital-intensive pattern of growth than a labor-intensive pattern of growth that enables people to meet basic needs. Opting for the higher rate of growth will tend to result in a more skewed distribution of income, a high degree of underutilization of labor, a pattern of production ill-suited to meeting basic needs, and consequently, a pattern of growth with little direct impact in terms of reducing poverty. Furthermore, the political structure that would accompany such a concentrated pattern of growth would not likely generate fiscal mechanisms (e.g., taxes and transfers) that would redistribute the benefits of growth to the poor. At this point one would have to question the benefits of a higher rate of growth and ask why, indeed, is more rapid growth important?

## CONCLUSION

This chapter has attempted to represent the basic needs approach as a sound organizing framework for development planning in countries with widespread poverty. The crucial premise is that the development process should provide for sustainable improvements over time in the well-being of those currently too poor to satisfy their basic human needs. The basic needs approach establishes explicit links between this objective and more tangible objectives having to do with employment and income among the poor and with production and supply of essential goods and services. These objectives can be systematically linked to some general types of policies that are on the whole quite familiar. There is no presumption that all of these policies would be appropriate in all countries, but rather that any country concerned with satisfying basic needs on a sustainable basis could identify some subset of these policies that would be both effective and appropriate given its particular political and economic circumstances. This specific set of policies would in turn have implications for various measures that donors could undertake in support of developing country efforts to meet basic human needs.

A necessary, but not sufficient, condition for meeting basic needs in most developing countries is substantial growth in output and income. However, achieving basic needs objectives depends crucially on the pattern of growth in terms of the composition of increases in output and the distribution of increases in income. The BHN approach provides explicit criteria by which to evaluate alternative patterns of growth, according to their contributions to increased and more productive employment and to adequate production and supply of essential goods and services.

## NOTES

1. These broad categories are common to most discussions of basic needs, but do not exhaust the possibilities. Further, specification and quantification within these categories would vary from group to group and over time.
2. These figures are based on country-specific poverty lines equivalent in purchasing power to the income level of the fortieth percentile in India in 1975. Such a poverty line probably understates the income necessary to meet basic needs by a substantial margin. Estimates of percentages of population would be correspondingly understated.
3. For an illustrative example with reference to Bangladesh, see Khan (1977:73), who discusses the difficulties in defining minimum standards and concludes: "in reality a practical planner often finds it possible to define *a core* of basic needs that seems surprisingly robust. This is particularly the case in a situation of extreme poverty and deprivation."
4. This average holds for 1977 per capita income threshold of $300, $500, or $700. See *World Development Report 1979* (IBRD 1979).
5. While the economic rationale for these policies can be appraised in a straightforward way, political considerations often make them difficult. At the same time, more complete satisfaction of basic needs can lead to lower birth rates because of greater economic security and a higher probability that children will survive and remain healthy.
6. This does not preclude the possibility of some meaningful universal targets that correspond to standards common to or exceeded by all countries—for example, a certain level of calorie intake to be achieved (or exceeded) by all countries.
7. These interdependencies are systematically and comprehensively discussed in Brown and Burki (1978:i), who state that "achievement of any one of the core group of basic needs can be shown to be beneficial to achievement of each of the others, and conversely lack of any one has adverse effects on efforts to meet any other basic needs."
8. For examples, see Selowsky and Taylor (1973), who discuss the costs of malnourished children; and Wheeler (1980), who tests a simultaneous model of basic needs fulfillment and economic growth and finds that changes in the physical quality of life appear to have a strong effect on productivity of labor in poor countries. Ram and Schultz (1979:420) find that "data from India's agriculture provide fairly good evidence of the positive effect of health improvement, fall in mortality, and increase in life span on productivity and output."
9. Using the national average of life expectancy as an indicator has some of the same problems as using overall per capita income, in that distribution is ignored. These problems are less severe in that the range of variation for life expectancy is relatively limited compared with the range of variation for per capita incomes of various groups within a country.

10. There are two lines of reasoning underlying this claim. First, suppose that the BHN consumption bundle costs $200 per person, but that some of the direct or indirect value added embodied in that cost necessarily accrues to the nonpoor—for example, $100 for services of doctors, teachers, assets not owned by the poor, and so on. Then supplying the needs of two poor people ($400) would at best generate income (e.g., through value added by unskilled labor) to cover the needs of only one ($200). Therefore, an additional $200 of income would need to be generated by employing a poor person in some other activity (or in production that goes beyond BHN supply objectives). Second, it may be that an income of $300 is required to evoke a pattern of consumption that includes the basic needs bundle costing $200. (This possibility is discussed more thoroughly in the section on transfers.) Then even if all value added in production of essential goods and services accrued to the poor, expansion of employment and income would need to extend beyond that connoted by BHN supply targets.
11. For a more thorough exposition, see Chenery and Associates (1974), as well as Frank and Webb (1978). For a pioneering modeling effort that systematically appraises the effects of many of these policies, see Adelman and Robinson (1978).
12. Lipton (1977:16) states that over 80 percent of the "really poor" depend on agriculture for a living. According to the *World Development Report, 1978* (IBRD 1978), 82 percent of the developing world's poor live in countries with per capita incomes in 1976 at or below $250. For substantially the same group of countries, the *World Development Report, 1979* (IBRD 1979) estimates that over four-fifths of the group population live in nonurban areas and nearly three-quarters of the labor force are occupied in agriculture. Furthermore, these shares have diminished very little over the past fifteen years. It is safe to assume that the corresponding shares for poor populations are higher than for the population as a whole.
13. For an analysis of the relation between trade regimes, growth, and employment based on ten country studies see Krueger (forthcoming).
14. A critical review of some of the recent evidence that has tended to discredit this hypothesis, as well as some new findings in support of the hypothesis, are contained in Thirsk (1977).
15. See White (1978) for a comprehensive review of the evidence on factor proportions for manufacturing in LDCs. This evidence "suggests strongly that greater labor intensity in LDC manufacturing is feasible, and would be efficient" (p. 56).
16. Assuming consumers place some value on the good or service in question and assuming that there is limited fungibility—e.g., education services (see Mishan 1968).
17. Some of these issues relate to social choice and the role of government. These are discussed more fully in Leipziger and Lewis (1978) and Streeten (1977).
18. See Isenman and Singer (1977), who analyze the positive and negative contributions of food aid as well as policies that affect these contributions. They conclude that the deep concern about disincentive effects often expressed in the literature is unwarranted, while the increases in total supply of food brought about by food aid have several positive external effects on the recipient country's development.
19. Where self-sufficiency is perceived to be important (for instance, for political reasons, considerations of risk and uncertainty, etc.), public intervention might be necessary to raise production levels above those corresponding to purely private considerations.
20. See the preceding section. In particular, these are subject to the exclusion principle (see Buchanan 1968: ch. 4).
21. The general concept of merit goods is analyzed in Head (1974) and is applied to the basic needs approach in Leipziger and Lewis (1978).
22. Neither the merit good argument nor a concern with external benefits in consumption points to a need for public production (see Buchanan 1968: 65–72).

23. The 1978 IBRD (1978:36) review of world development suggests that only 10 percent of health budgets in developing countries are allocated to provision of basic health services.
24. The IBRD estimate cited earlier—that only 10 percent of public health expenditures go to basic health services—suggests considerable scope for such reorientation (IBRD 1978: 36).
25. Ram and Schultz (1979:419) note in their review of the literature that "in particular the conventional concepts of saving and investment that are used are very much in error because of the omission of human capital in the form of health and schooling." For empirical evidence on the contribution of investment in human resources to growth of GNP, see Hicks (1979,1980) and Wheeler (1980).
26. See Harburger (1978:260) who claims, "A factor of much more importance than labor migration, however, is that of capital. There can be little doubt that most wealthy people, in any less-developed country in the world, can and do find ways of having bank accounts and securities portfolios abroad."
27. Hans Singer, in an address to the International Development Conference in February 1978, estimated that current underutilization of labor in developing countries amounts to an unemployment rate of 25 percent.

## BIBLIOGRAPHY

Adelman, I., and S. Robinson. 1978. *Income Distribution Policy in Developing Countries.* London: Oxford University Press.

Agency for International Development. 1978. "A Strategy for a More Effective Bilateral Development Assistance Program: An A.I.D. Policy Paper." Washington, D.C., March.

Ahluwalia, Montek, Nicholas Carter, and Hollis Chenery. 1978. "Growth and Poverty in Developing Countries." Background Paper #6 for the *World Development Report, 1978*. Washington, D.C.: The World Bank, August.

Brown, Gilbert, and S. J. Burki. 1978. "Sector Policies and Linkages in Meeting Basic Needs." Basic Needs Paper #7. Washington, D.C.: IBRD, February.

Buchanan, James M. 1968. *The Demand and Supply of Public Goods.* Chicago: Rand McNally.

Burki, S. J., and J. J. C. Voorhoeve. 1977. "Global Estimates for Meeting Basic Needs: Background Paper." Basic Needs Paper #1. Washington, D.C.: IBRD, August.

Chenery and Associates. 1974. *Redistribution With Growth.* London: Oxford University Press.

Crosswell, Michael. 1977. "Analysis and Implications of a Basic Human Needs Strategy." Washington, D.C.: A.I.D./PPC, June.

Crosswell, Michael, and Constantine Michalopoulos. 1979. "Evolution of the Basic Human Needs Concept." Washington, D.C.: Development Coordination Committee Staff Working Paper, March.

Curry, Robert. 1978. "Public Finance Aspects of a Basic Needs Strategy: Some Research Issues." Washington, D.C.: A.I.D./IIA, June.

Development Assistance Committee, OECD. 1977. "Statement by DAC Members on Development Cooperation for Economic Growth and Meeting Basic

Human Needs." Annex to the Communique of the DAC High-Level Meeting. Paris, October.

Frank, C. R., and R. C. Webb, eds. 1978. *Income Distribution and Growth in the Less Developed Countries*. Washington, D.C.: The Brookings Institution.

Harberger, Arnold C. 1978. "Fiscal Policy and Income Redistribution." In C. Frank and R. Webb, eds., *Income Distribution and Growth in the Less Developed Countries*. Washington, D.C.: The Brookings Institution.

Head, J. G. 1974. *Public Goods and Public Welfare*. Durham, N.C.: Duke University.

Hicks, Norman. 1979. "Growth versus Basic Needs: Is There a Trade-off?" *World Development* 7, no. 10/11, November/December.

Hicks, Norman. 1980. "Economic Growth and Human Resources." World Bank Staff Working Paper #408. Washington, D.C., July.

International Labour Office. 1977. *Employment, Growth and Basic Needs: A One-World Problem*. New York: Praeger.

Isenman, Paul, and Hans Singer. 1977. "Food Aid: Disincentive Effects and Their Policy Implications." *Economic Development and Cultural Change* 25, no. 2 (January).

IBRD. 1978. *World Development Report, 1978*. Washington, D.C.: World Bank, August.

IBRD. 1979. *World Development Report, 1979*. Washington, D.C.: World Bank, August.

Khan, A. R. 1977. "Basic Needs: An Illustrative Exercise in Identification and Quantification with Reference to Bangladesh." In *The Basic-Needs Approach to Development: Some Issues Regarding Concepts and Methodology*. Geneva: International Labour Office.

Krueger, Anne O. Forthcoming. *Alternative Trade Strategies and Employment: Theory and Empirical Evidence*. Chicago: University of Chicago Press.

Leipziger, Danny, and Maureen Lewis. 1977. "The Basic Human Needs Approach to Development." Paper presented to the Western Economic Association Meetings, Honolulu, June.

Lewis, John P. 1978. "Designing the Public Works Mode of Anti-Poverty Policy." In C. R. Frank and R. C. Webb, eds., *Income Distribution and Growth in the Less Developed Countries*. Washington, D.C.: The Brookings Institution.

Lipton, Michael. 1977. *Why Poor People Stay Poor: Urban Bias in World Development*. London: Oxford University Press.

Little, I., T. Scitovsky, and M. Scott. 1970. *Industry and Trade in Some Developing Countries*. London: Oxford University Press.

Mishan, E. J. 1968. "Redistribution in Money and Kind: Some Notes." *Economica* 35, no. 138 (May).

Pyatt, G., and E. Thorbecke. 1976. *Planning Techniques for a Better Future*. Geneva: International Labour Office.

Ram, Rati, and Theodore Schultz. 1979. "Life Span, Health, Savings, and Productivity." *Economic Development and Cultural Change* 27, no. 3 (April).

Richards, Peter. 1976. "Poverty, Unemployment, and Underemployment." In *Background Papers*. Vol. 1. World Employment Conference. Geneva: International Labour Office.

Selowsky, M., and L. Taylor. 1973. "The Economics of Malnourished Children: An Example of Disinvestment in Human Capital." *Economic Development and Cultural Change* 22, no. 1 (October).

Singer, Hans. 1977. *Technologies for Basic Needs.* Geneva: International Labour Office.

Streeten, Paul. 1977. "The Distinctive Features of a Basic Needs Approach to Development." Basic Needs Paper #2. Washington, D.C.: IBRD, August.

Thirsk, Wayne. 1977. "Income Distribution and the Composition of Final Demand: Some New Findings for Colombia." Discussion Paper #79. Houston, Texas: Rice University, Fall.

Wheeler, David. 1980. "Human Resource Development and Economic Growth in Developing Countries: A Simultaneous Model." World Bank Staff Working Paper #407. Washington, D.C., July.

White, Lawrence J. 1978. "The Evidence on Appropriate Factor Proportions for Manufacturing in Less Developed Countries: A Survey." *Economic Development and Cultural Change* 27, no. 1 (October).

*Chapter 2*

# Sectoral Aspects of a Basic Human Needs Approach: The Linkages among Population, Nutrition, and Health

*Maureen A. Lewis*

## INTRODUCTION

The basic human needs (BHN) approach to economic development focuses on improving human welfare within the context of broad-based macroeconomic growth. As part of this emphasis, human capital considerations have achieved greater prominence as a means of generating and sustaining economic growth. Although not new, such an emphasis has fostered a reordering of development priorities, which has been reflected particularly in resource allocation decisions of foreign assistance donors.

Development targets have traditionally and explicitly been focused on GNP growth, while poverty alleviation and improved individual welfare have implicitly been of secondary importance. The basic human needs approach addresses both issues directly, by stressing improvements in the quality of life as well as growth strategies to achieve those objectives;

The author is an economist at the U.S. Agency for International Development in the Human Resources Division of the Bureau for Program and Policy Coordination. The views expressed here are those of the author and do not necessarily reflect those of U.S. AID.

I would like to thank David Dunlop, Theresa Lukas, and Alan Sorkin for reviewing the entire chapter, Carol Adelman for guiding the nutrition section, and Charlotte Leighton for reviewing the health section. All errors are my own.

the focus is on the absolute poor, the group often overlooked in economic development strategies.

This chapter places some critical components of a BHN approach in perspective—specifically, it addresses health, family planning, and nutrition (HPN). The interrelationships among these factors are emphasized, as are their mutually reinforcing nature and their role in meeting individual and national development objectives.[1] The intent is also to familiarize the reader with the rationale behind the current emphasis on human capital investments in development and their importance in meeting the basic needs of the poor.

The chapter is divided into four sections. The introductory section (1) introduces the BHN concept, briefly discussing major issues; (2) estimates the costs of service delivery (in population, health and nutrition); and (3) provides information on current resource allocations from national and donor sources for HPN. The subsequent three sections present the major issues associated with each of these critical sectors in a BHN framework, including discussion of measurement tools, determinants, consequences, and policy and program options.

## BHN CONCEPTS

The objective of development strategies in the 1950s and 1960s was to achieve high rates of aggregate growth, and the assumption was that human welfare would be enhanced over the long run as the benefits of development "trickled down" to those at the bottom of the income scale. Over the last decade the notion that distribution concerns should be pursued in conjunction with macroeconomic objectives has evolved from the realization that growth, although it encouraged development in some segments of the economy, left large portions of the population untouched. Thus it became apparent that growth and equity concerns must be pursued simultaneously if economic development and a more equitable distribution of the benefits of development are to emerge (Chenery et al. 1974).

The basic human needs approach to development was put forward by the International Labor Office in 1976 in an attempt to focus particular attention on the specific needs of the poor in developing countries (LDCs). Earlier, broadly consistent approaches were adopted by the World Bank and the Agency for International Development (AID), among other bilateral and multilateral donors, indicating the general acceptance of the notion that equity concerns do matter; by the late 1970s donor policies had evolved further and were explicitly or implicitly aimed at BHN objectives.[2]

Components of a BHN approach include: (1) minimum consumption of food, shelter, and clothing; (2) access to services such as safe water, sanitation, health, family planning, and public transportation; and (3) participation of people in decisions that affect them.[3] This chapter will address the critical sectors of health, nutrition, and population.

## Human Resources and Target Population

Resources in LDCs are generally scarce; natural resources may be few; capital and technology are inadequate; and labor, though abundant, is lacking in quality—by which we mean it is characterized by low productivity because of ill health, malnutrition, and inadequate training.[4] Thus human capital investments are efficient means of harnessing this large, untapped resource. Government investments in human capital provide the poor with the essential tools for improving their livelihood. These investments supplement incomes by subsidizing goods and services and enhance employment opportunities by increasing labor productivity. Investment in health, family planning, nutrition, and education are particularly relevant for enhancing human capital and contributing to the achievement of employment and income goals.

The investments in human capital that underlie basic needs raise labor's capability through improvements in nutrition, health, and education. Such improvements that raise productivity stimulate private sector demand for labor. A skilled, healthy worker is more employable and productive than is an unskilled, undernourished laborer; consequently, he is better able to generate income. The issue of employability is thus a central objective of efforts to meet basic needs and improve welfare, for it enhances income-earning ability.

A BHN strategy is aimed at the lowest absolute income group in a given country, those having inadequate purchasing power to satisfy their basic needs. This means reaching anywhere from 20 to 60 percent of the population. In a country like Sri Lanka, the target group would be close to 20 percent; in Nepal the proportion might exceed 60 percent. The International Bank for Reconstruction and Development (IBRD) estimates that roughly 700 million people in the developing world fall into this category.

Individuals lacking access to services and/or sufficient purchasing power to fulfill their basic needs constitute the specific target group. As a result, a BHN approach favors rural areas, where services such as health and family planning are less likely to be available,[5] over urban areas. The areas in which governments prefer to provide services may not reflect preferences of the target group. Providing health centers, family planning services, water and sanitation supplies, and schools may not now reflect local priorities, but in supplying these services at subsidized rates the government encourages use: for example, from witch doctor to paramedic, from folk methods to modern contraceptives, or from household employment to student.[6] Lower costs encourage use, providing an inducement for consuming new and unfamiliar services.

## Merit Goods

Merit goods are relevant for the discussion of HPN, and they serve to incorporate issues of minimum consumption, service access, and participation within that context. Clothing and transportation on the other hand are goods and services best provided by the private sector, as they are not characterized by the "jointness of supply" or "external economies" criteria of public goods, nor by the uncertainty or informational gap nature of merit goods (Head 1974).[7] Rises in absolute income and purchasing power are preferable means for stimulating private sector supply of these goods and services, although a role for government in transportation can be justified. Shelter fits the merit good criteria, but we will not address it here.

Government adoption of a BHN approach does not necessarily occur in response to public demand, but rather from a realization that the poor, especially in rural areas, will not be able to meet their basic needs without increased transfers and/or additional income. In providing transfers, governments feel obliged to impose constraints and encouragements to specific kinds of consumption; since certain goods and services are considered meritorious (merit goods), these are provided free or at highly subsidized rates to encourage use.[8] Provision of merit goods stems from government's perception that certain goods and services are underconsumed due to inadequate knowledge and/or information, and to high uncertainty associated with consuming unfamiliar and often costly services (Head 1974).

Although merit goods are encouragements to consume particular goods and services, it is not correct to say that the poor are consistently irrational in their decisionmaking. Possibly the best documented evidence of rational behavior is in nutrition, where increases in income have consistently lead to improvements in nutrition (Berg 1979; Pinstrup-Anderson and Caicedo 1978).[9] For those whose demand for modern health care, family planning, and nutrition services is below minimally acceptable levels, the BHN approach aims at making services accessible and affordable; subsidizing consumption should encourage changes in behavior and actual demand for such services. Once sufficient demand exists, as a result of income generation and learning, the private sector can more efficiently participate in providing some of these services.[10]

Thus governments are proposing substantial expenditures for a given period of time, with the expectation that demand for such services will evolve, allowing institutions of fees or private sector involvement, both of which reduce public sector subsidies.

## Costs

Efforts have been made to estimate the worldwide costs of providing adequate health and food to the poor in LDCs. Burki and Voorheuve (1977) have estimated the average annual capital and recurrent costs of health care (including provision of water and sewage disposal) and adequate food at $9.2 billion (1975 U.S. dollars) and $7.1 billion respectively. However, these aggregate figures are not particularly useful in designing country or regional programs.

Project design determines the extent of service outreach (essentially "rural house calls") and the range of health-related services to be provided, both of which contribute substantially to the costs of integrated health services. The greater the number of services provided, the higher the recurrent costs—those costs required to keep the program operating after the initial investment has been made. The fixed costs of building facilities, stocking clinics, setting up referral and supervision systems, and training personnel are large, one-time investments.[11]

Recurrent costs need special attention since they tend to become the long-term responsibility of the developing country; and, if recurrent expenditures are high and budgets constrained, programs have limited prospects for continuation and ultimate success.

In recent years a number of experimental service delivery/research projects have been completed, providing "soft" cost estimates of vertical and integrated health, family planning, and nutrition programs.[12] Table 2–1 lists the per capita costs of delivering various mixes of HPN services. Given the differences in project design and the wide variation in costs of living,[13] the costs basically only convey orders of magnitude. However, Gwatkin, Wilcox, and Wray (1979) contend that these figures are roughly comparable to LDC national per capita health expenditures. Health represents between 0.5 and 2.0 percent of per capita GNP in the selected countries in Table 2–1, which is well within the 0.5-to-3.0-percent range observed in many LDCs (Table 2–3). But, as the authors point out, since the national (and project) figures include only a small portion of the population, the actual per capita costs of extending HPN services to the unserved urban and rural areas will be different and possibly considerably higher than the figures in Table 2–1 imply.[14]

The costs of individual components of a health program are described in detail in Grosse et al. (1979) and Heller (1975) for Indonesia and Ma-

Table 2-1. Per Capita Costs of Integrated Service Delivery Experiments

| Location/Services Provided | Annual Per Capita Costs of Services (U.S. $) |
|---|---|
| Imesi, Nigeria MCH,N,NEd | $1.50 (1967)[a] |
| Etimesgut, Turkey H | $3.17 (1972) |
| Narangwal, India H,N | $1.80 (1973) |
| Rural Guatemala H,N (N costs not included) | $3.50 (1972) |
| Hanover, Jamaica N,NEd | $2.50/child (1974) |
| Kavar, Iran N,MCH,FP,HEd | $3.54 (1972) |
| Danfa, Ghana H,HEd,FP,N | $4.39 (1976) |

Source: Gwatkin, Wilcox and Wray (1979) and Danfa Project Final Report (1979).

Note: These costs are rough estimates of capital and recurrent costs. Also, it should be noted that each program contained a slightly different mix of services, inhibiting comparison of per capita service costs across experiments.

Legend: MCH = maternal and child health; H = health services; N = nutrition services; NEd = nutrition education; FP = family planning services; HEd = health education

[a] Dates in parentheses refer to dates of publication.

laysia respectively, and will not be covered here. However, the former project provides some interesting additional data on the relative costs and cost effectiveness of different interventions. Figure 2-1 provides data on the tradeoffs between crude death rate (declines) and five year per capita expenditures on health interventions in rural Indonesia. The graph presents an optimal program mix for a given budget level. Hence, the best mix at $5.00 per capita over five years (or $1.00 per capita per year) includes a main center (assumed for all six points), 25 village health workers, and immunizations; the 8.8 crude death rate associated with the $5.00 per capita expenditure represents the maximum benefit obtainable at that budget level [15] (Grosse et al. 1979). In each category the program mix represents the most cost-effective approach, the one that will have the greatest dampening effect on the crude death rate[16] for the investment. Such exercises are extremely useful tools in planning for integrated health services because they help maximize the use of resources.

An issue of critical importance in health planning and in cost estimation is the extent of demand for health care: Heller (1976) has measured demand for health in Malaysia—a country with a relatively high per cap-

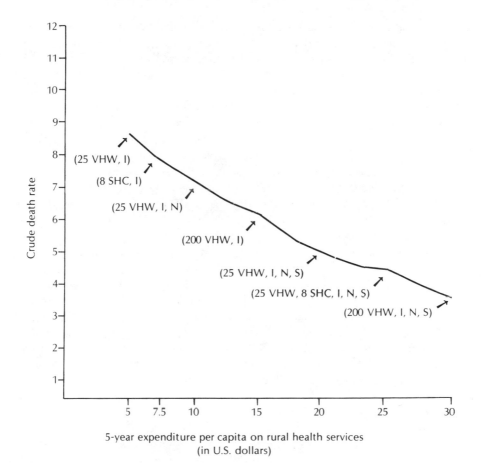

5-year expenditure per capita on rural health services
(in U.S. dollars)

Each rural health program plotted includes a health center
plus one or more of the following designations:

    25 VHW = 25 Village health workers
  200 VHW = 200 Village health workers
    8 SHC = 8 Subhealth centers
        I = Immunization
        N = Nutrition
        S = Sanitation

*Source:* Grosse et al. (1979).

**Figure 2–1. Preferred programs at seven budget levels.**

ita income and an established, nationwide health system. Although these factors distinguish Malaysia from other LDCs, Heller's analysis is instructive. He found that as incomes rise, households tend to shift their demand away from traditional practitioners toward modern medical facilities.[17] Travel time appears to decrease utilization, although time costs (e.g., waiting time) do not significantly affect consumption of health services. Most significant is the apparent inelastic demand for medical services, indicated by the fact that fees do not significantly deter utilization.

Heller's (1976) results imply that where sufficient demand exists, fees for services can be instituted, which can help reduce recurrent costs. But it also becomes clear that a critical minimum level of income must be attained before the shift in demand behavior can occur, either because health and health-related services become affordable or because attitudes and preferences change as income increases.

An integrated approach is particularly relevant in the BHN context, for such a strategy can most efficiently meet complementary needs and at the same time minimize costs. The need to provide merit goods may raise costs in the short run, but if income and demand rise as anticipated, fees can be introduced to cover some portion of service costs. The BHN approach should not be seen as a welfare dole, but as an investment in human capital that will produce a more productive population and will help meet the basic needs of the poor. Hence the cost of HPN services are essentially long-term investments in human capital.

## Resources

Assessing the actual cost burden of HPN services is difficult without knowing their relative claim on LDC government budgets. One reflection of government commitment is per capita government public health expenditures and the proportion of federal and local budgets devoted to health services. Table 2–2 provides both statistics, along with the percent of gross national product devoted to public health, for selected developing countries. The range is considerable. For example, health as a percent of total public expenditures ranges from 1.2 percent in Korea to 14.7 percent in Honduras. The gap in per capita resources is even greater, with India providing $.46 per citizen versus Singapore's $40.04 per citizen.[18] Nepal spends only $.79 per capita, but health represents a relatively high 6.7 percent of its national budget, indicating the relative importance of health in budget allocation and the extent of central responsibility for health.

However, these figures can also be misleading measures of government commitment to health care and the poor. First of all, it should be noted that "health expenditure" can mean anything from integrated services

## Table 2-2. Government Health Expenditures of Selected LDCs

| | Health Expenditures as % of Total Public Expenditures, 1976 | Public Health Expenditures as % of GNP, 1976 | Public Health Expenditures per Capita (U.S. $), 1976 |
|---|---|---|---|
| Ethiopia | 4.5 | 0.8 | .87 |
| Burma | 6.6 | 0.9 | 1.12 |
| Chad | 4.2 | 0.8 | .95 |
| Nepal | 6.7 | 0.7 | .79 |
| Zaire | 3.8 | 1.2 | 1.68 |
| India | 2.2 | 0.3 | .46 |
| Pakistan | 1.8 | 0.3 | .56 |
| Tanzania | 7.0[b] | 2.1[b] | 3.49[b] |
| Sri Lanka | 6.1[b] | 2.1[b] | 3.92[b] |
| Kenya | 8.2 | 1.8 | 4.24 |
| Yemen Arab Republic | 2.9[a] | 0.3[a] | .50[a] |
| Thailand | 4.3 | 0.7 | 4.39 |
| Bolivia | 8.0 | 1.3 | 5.06 |
| Honduras | 14.7 | 2.9 | 11.15 |
| Philippines | 5.0 | 0.7 | 2.86 |
| Zambia | 7.0 | 2.7 | 11.92 |
| Morocco | 3.3 | 1.3 | 7.05 |
| Guatemala | 8.4 | 0.9 | 5.60 |
| Ecuador | 7.2 | 1.0 | 6.58 |
| Korea, Republic of | 1.2 | 0.2 | 1.48 |
| Nicaragua | 4.1 | 0.7 | 5.11 |
| Dominican Republic | 8.9 | 1.5 | 11.44 |
| Peru | 5.8 | 1.0 | 7.69 |
| Tunisia | 6.6 | 1.9 | 15.75 |
| Malaysia | 5.7 | 1.5 | 13.15 |
| Turkey | 2.5 | 0.6 | 5.68 |
| Costa Rica | 5.6[a] | 0.8[a] | 7.07[a] |
| Mexico | 4.2[b] | 0.9[b] | 9.14[b] |
| Brazil | 6.0[b] | 0.3[b] | 3.37[b] |
| Uruguay | 3.8 | 0.7 | 10.00 |
| Iran | 3.3 | 1.2 | 23.16 |
| Venezuela | 4.9 | 1.4 | 37.15 |
| Singapore | 7.7 | 1.5 | 40.04 |

*Sources:* IBRD, *World Atlas,* 1977; IMF, *International Financial Statistics,* 1978; IFM, *Government Finance Statistics Yearbook,* Vol. 2, 1978.

[a] 1974.

[b] 1975.

with nutrition, health education, and family planning as components to vertical, curative health services for the elite.[19] Second, the amounts do not reflect an equal geographic distribution of resources; expenditures may be distributed across rural and urban communities of rich and poor or be concentrated in wealthy, urban centers. As such, expenditure levels represent the emphasis the government places on health services, but says nothing of the government's target group or their success in satisfying the basic needs of the poor.

As the BHN approach or some variant of it has been embraced by bilateral and multilateral donors, the relative and absolute budget levels devoted to PHN by donors has increased. Table 2–3 lists the resource levels devoted to health, population, and nutrition by the four largest donors: the U.S. Agency for International Development (AID), the United Nations Fund for Population Activities (UNFPA), the World Health Organization (WHO), and the International Bank for Reconstruction and Development (IBRD).

**Table 2–3. Health, Population, and Nutrition Resource Allocation by Major Donors (millions of U.S. dollars)**

| | AID | | | | | |
|---|---|---|---|---|---|---|
| *Fiscal Year[a]* | *Population* | *Health* | *Nutrition* | *HPN Subtotal* | *Total Budget[d]* | *Percent of Budget* |
| 1977 | 140.3[b] | 83.6 | n.a. | n.a. | 848.1 | n.a. |
| 1978 | 160.5 | 96.8 | 12.0 | 269.3 | 1,008.6 | 27 |
| 1979 | 185.0 | 133.0 | 11.0 | 329.0 | 1,147.2 | 29 |
| 1980 | 185.0 | 131.3 | 21.0 | 337.3 | 1,152.4 | 30 |
| 1981 | 238.0[c] | 159.2[c] | 30.5[c] | 427.7[c] | 1,409.2[a] | 30 |

| | IBRD | | | | |
|---|---|---|---|---|---|
| *Fiscal Year* | *HPN Subtotal[e]* | *Total Budget* | *HPN Percent of Budget* | *UNFPA[f] Total Budget* | *WHO Total Budget* |
| 1977 | 61.5 | 7,100.0 | .87 | 81.4 | 132.3 |
| 1978 | 55.0 | 8,400.0 | .66 | 100.3 | 165.0 |
| 1979 | 114.0 | 10,000.0 | 1.14 | 114.6 | 175.7 |
| 1980 | 143.0[c] | 12,000.0[c] | 1.19 | 136.0 | 192.7 |
| 1981 | n.a. | n.a. | n.a. | 159.0[c] | 232.3[c] |

*Sources:* IBRD, *World Bank Annual Report,* 1977–1979; AID, *Congressional Presentation,* 1977–1981; WHO, *Proposed Programme Budget,* 1974–1978; UNFPA, *Annual Report,* 1977–1979.

[a] The U.S. government and IBRD fiscal years were both July–June through 1976, when the U.S. shifted to an October–September fiscal year. WHO and UNFPA funding follow the calendar year.

[b] The family planning and health budgets were combined until FY 1978; the agriculture and nutrition budget are a combined category, and FY 1977 breakdowns are not available.

[c] Estimate.

[d] Includes development assistance only, and excludes the Sahel Development Program.

[e] These are committed funds for HPN.

[f] Includes all estimated obligations for activities funded under the regular budget and other sources for each fiscal year.

AID's emphasis on these areas and their perceived importance is apparent from the relative resource allocations listed in Table 2–3. Roughly 30 percent of AID's total development assistance budget has been devoted to HPN over the last few years, and the trend can be expected to continue.

The IBRD has only recently begun to (modestly) raise the proportion of its budget going to HPN, despite shifts in articulated policy emphasizing human resource investments. However, the establishment of a health programming sector in fiscal year 1979 and the themes of the recent annual *World Development Reports* bode well for future directions.

Although UNFPA ostensibly supports population activities exclusively, its mandate and activities are much more broadly defined. In 1982 almost 50 percent of the budget will go to family planning programs, many of which are aimed at providing maternal and child health (MCH) and pre- and postnatal care, as well as contraceptives. WHO is almost exclusively a health organization, although many of its programs have nutrition components.

These aggregate data incorporate a wide range of activities, including, among others: family planning clinics, health clinic construction, (tropical) disease research and eradication activities, water and sanitation installation, health and nutrition education, demographic data collection, and research on means of delivering service(s) and encouraging their use. The coverage is broad, and size of funding for subcategories tends to reflect regional and sectoral needs, as perceived by donors and host governments in the developing countries.[20]

The trend in the proportion of funding going to HPN by multisector donors appears to be on the upswing, despite high inflation rates in donor countries and stagnating real foreign assistance budgets. The need to address human resource issues is beginning to receive the rhetorical and financial attention it deserves, and budget allocations of the past few years reflect this shift in or reaffirmation of priorities. One hopes that this movement will continue, especially since the rapid growth in LDC populations in the next few decades will be adding service recipients at an increasing rate. The expected growth in population will require more resources just to maintain current, and admittedly inadequate, levels of service in nutrition, family planning, and health.

\*     \*     \*

The following three sections will outline the major issues associated with population, nutrition, and health, and their importance in the achievement of the basic needs objectives among the poor. The three areas are extremely broad and the issues chosen for discussion are somewhat arbitrary. The sources included in each section provide further references where more in-depth information is desired.

## POPULATION ISSUES

### Introduction

Rapid population growth has been perceived as a major economic problem since the time of Malthus; his predictions of doom have never been realized in the developed countries, but many of his worries have become very real issues for development and health planners in the developing countries. High population growth has negative implications for the rate of economic development, and both factors directly affect human welfare and the attainment of basic needs.[21] In the bulk of the developing world, rapid population growth is impeding economic progress and development; as Table 2–4 shows, although a number of less developed countries (LDCs) experienced advances in gross domestic product (GDP) between 1970 and 1976, their per capita income growth lagged.

The strain on national budgets of high fertility rates inhibits extension of services, including health, education, safe water, and transportation services, particularly to rural areas where the bulk of LDC populations live. (See Conroy and Folbie [1976] for a good survey of the literature; and Morawetz 1978.) Population pressures may well prevent LDC governments from providing essential services to their populations regardless of the intensity of their commitment to meeting the basic human needs of their people.[22]

High fertility is by no means universal in all developing countries, although it is a grave issue for many. A recent monograph by Tsui and Bogue (1978) reports a comprehensive drop in total fertility in the developing world. With few exceptions, they perceive a growing momentum toward smaller families worldwide, ostensibly based on national statistics. Although decreases in fertility have occurred in some countries, the generalization that fertility is experiencing a sustained downward trend in the LDCs is questionable. Fertility has been reduced in a number of LDCs, but the rosy predictions of Tsui and Bogue appear unlikely given recent experience and rising fertility in some areas, notably Africa.[23]

### Demographic Indicators

While the science of demography has spawned a wide range of measures relating to population size and distribution, in this discussion we will confine ourselves to those indicators that are most relevant in the devel-

**Table 2-4. LDC Population and GNP Growth Rates**

| | GNP per Capita (U.S. $), 1977 | Average Annual Growth of GNP per Capita (%), 1960–1977 | Average Annual GDP Growth (%), 1970–1977[a] | Population (millions), Mid-1977 | Average Annual Growth of Population (%), 1970–1977 |
|---|---|---|---|---|---|
| Low-income countries | 170 | 1.4 | 3.2 | | 2.3 |
| Bhutan | 80 | -0.2 | .. | 1 | 2.2 |
| Cambodia | .. | .. | .. | 8 | 2.5 |
| Bangladesh | 90 | -0.4 | 2.3 | 81 | 2.5 |
| Lao PDR | 90 | .. | .. | 3 | 1.1 |
| Ethiopia | 110 | 1.7 | 2.5 | 30 | 2.6 |
| Mali | 110 | 1.0 | 3.5 | 6 | 2.5 |
| Nepal | 110 | 0.2 | 2.8 | 13 | 2.2 |
| Somalia | 110 | -0.4 | 1.2 | 4 | 2.3 |
| Burundi | 130 | 2.2 | 1.4 | 4 | 2.0 |
| Chad | 130 | -1.0 | 0.8 | 4 | 2.2 |
| Rwanda | 130 | 1.0 | 3.9 | 4 | 2.9 |
| Upper Volta | 130 | 0.6 | 3.3 | 5 | 1.6 |
| Zaire | 130 | 1.1 | 1.9 | 26 | 2.7 |
| Burma | 140 | 0.9 | 3.7 | 32 | 2.2 |
| Malawi | 140 | 3.0 | 6.3 | 6 | 3.1 |
| India | 150 | 1.3 | 3.0 | 632 | 2.1 |
| Mozambique | 150 | 0.9 | -5.0 | 10 | 2.5 |
| Niger | 160 | -1.4 | 1.8 | 5 | 2.8 |
| Vietnam | 160 | .. | .. | 51 | 3.1 |
| Afghanistan | 190 | 0.2 | 4.5 | 14 | 2.2 |
| Pakistan | 190 | 3.0 | 3.6 | 75 | 3.1 |
| Sierra Leone | 190 | 1.3 | 1.9 | 3 | 2.5 |
| Tanzania | 190 | 2.6 | 4.5 | 16 | 3.0 |
| Benin | 200 | 0.2 | 2.0 | 3 | 2.9 |
| Sri Lanka | 200 | 2.0 | 3.1 | 14 | 1.7 |
| Guinea | 220 | 1.3 | 5.3 | 5 | 3.0 |

**Table 2-4** (continued)

| | GNP per Capita (U.S. $), 1977 | Average Annual Growth of GNP per Capita (%), 1960-1977 | Average Annual GDP Growth (%), 1970-1977[a] | Population (millions), Mid-1977 | Average Annual Growth of Population (%), 1970-1977 |
|---|---|---|---|---|---|
| | 170 | 1.4 | 3.2 | | 2.3 |
| Low-income countries | | | | | |
| Haiti | 230 | 0.1 | 3.8 | 5 | 1.7 |
| Lesotho | 240 | 5.8 | 5.2 | 1 | 2.4 |
| Madagascar | 240 | -0.2 | -0.3 | 8 | 2.5 |
| Central African Empire | 250 | 0.2 | 0.9 | 2 | 2.2 |
| Kenya | 270 | 2.5 | 6.2 | 15 | 3.8 |
| Mauritania | 270 | 3.6 | 2.3 | 2 | 2.7 |
| Uganda | 270 | 0.7 | 0.1 | 12 | 3.0 |
| Sudan | 290 | 0.1 | 5.0 | 17 | 2.6 |
| Angola | 300 | 2.3 | -10.4 | 7 | 2.4 |
| Indonesia | 300 | 3.3 | 7.7 | 134 | 1.8 |
| Togo | 300 | 3.8 | 3.1 | 2 | 2.7 |
| Middle-income Countries | 1,140 | 3.6 | 6.1 | | 2.6 |
| Egypt | 320 | 2.1 | 7.9 | 38 | 2.2 |
| Cameroon | 340 | 2.9 | 3.4 | 8 | 2.2 |
| Yemen, PDR | 340 | -4.8 | 5.1 | 2 | 1.9 |
| Ghana | 380 | -0.3 | 0.4 | 11 | 3.0 |
| Honduras | 410 | 1.5 | 3.5 | 3 | 3.3 |
| Liberia | 420 | 1.8 | 2.7 | 2 | 3.4 |
| Nigeria | 420 | 3.6 | 6.2 | 79 | 2.6 |
| Thailand | 420 | 4.5 | 7.1 | 44 | 2.9 |
| Senegal | 430 | -0.3 | 2.8 | 5 | 2.6 |
| Yemen Arab Republic | 430 | .. | 7.8 | 5 | 1.9 |
| Philippines | 450 | 2.5 | 6.4 | 44 | 2.7 |
| Zambia | 450 | 1.5 | 2.8 | 5 | 3.1 |
| Congo, People's Republic of the | 490 | 1.1 | 5.6 | 1 | 2.5 |
| | 490 | 3.4 | 5.0 | 3 | 2.4 |

| | | | | | |
|---|---|---|---|---|---|
| El Salvador | 550 | 1.8 | 4 | 5.1 | 2.9 |
| Morocco | 550 | 2.2 | 18 | 4.8 | 2.8 |
| Bolivia | 630 | 2.3 | 5 | 6.0 | 2.9 |
| Ivory Coast | 690 | 3.3 | 7 | 6.5 | 5.9 |
| Jordan | 710 | 1.8 | 3 | 7.0 | 3.3 |
| Colombia | 720 | 2.7 | 25 | 6.4 | 2.1 |
| Paraguay | 730 | 2.4 | 3 | 7.2 | 2.9 |
| Ecuador | 790 | 3.1 | 7 | 9.2 | 3.0 |
| Guatemala | 790 | 2.8 | 6 | 6.0 | 2.9 |
| Korea, Republic of | 820 | 7.4 | 36 | 10.4 | 2.0 |
| Nicaragua | 830 | 2.5 | 2 | 5.8 | 3.3 |
| Dominican Republic | 840 | 3.6 | 5 | 9.1 | 2.9 |
| Peru | 840 | 2.3 | 16 | 4.6 | 2.8 |
| Tunisia | 860 | 4.3 | 6 | 8.4 | 2.0 |
| Syrian Arab Republic | 910 | 2.3 | 8 | 7.0 | 3.3 |
| Malaysia | 930 | 3.9 | 13 | 7.8 | 2.7 |
| Algeria | 1,110 | 2.1 | 17 | 5.3 | 3.5 |
| Turkey | 1,110 | 4.1 | 42 | 7.4 | 2.5 |
| Mexico | 1,120 | 2.8 | 63 | 5.0 | 3.3 |
| Jamaica | 1,150 | 2.1 | 2 | (·) | 1.7 |
| Lebanon | : | : | 3 | : | 2.5 |
| Chile | 1,160 | 1.0 | 11 | 0.1 | 1.7 |
| China, People's Republic of | 1,170 | 6.2 | 17 | 7.7 | 2.0 |
| Panama | 1,220 | 3.5 | 2 | 3.5 | 2.7 |
| Costa Rica | 1,240 | 3.2 | 2 | 5.7 | 2.5 |
| Brazil | 1,360 | 4.9 | 116 | 9.8 | 2.9 |
| Uruguay | 1,430 | 0.8 | 3 | 1.6 | 0.3 |
| Iraq | 1,550 | 3.8 | 12 | 10.8 | 3.4 |
| Argentina | 1,730 | 2.7 | 26 | 2.9 | 1.3 |
| Iran | 2,160 | 7.9 | 35 | 7.8 | 3.0 |
| Trinidad and Tobago | 2,380 | 1.6 | 1 | 3.4 | 1.2 |
| Hong Kong | 2,590 | 6.5 | 5 | 8.2 | 2.0 |
| Venezuela | 2,660 | 2.7 | 14 | 5.7 | 3.4 |
| Singapore | 2,880 | 7.5 | 2 | 8.6 | 1.5 |

Source: IBRD (1979).

ª Excludes countries with populations under one million.

oping country context. In applying demographic principles to LDCs, a major constraint is data availability, and therefore one's choice of measure(s) is frequently dictated by data availability.

Although a few LDCs have experienced declines in birth rates, the average rate of population growth in LDCs exceeds 2.5 percent per year, implying a doubling of the population in less than thirty years.[24] Completed family size in many developing countries is over seven, and the average crude birth rate (CBR) is over forty per thousand population.[25] A less commonly used but perhaps preferable indicator of fertility change, because it takes age distribution into account, is the total fertility rate, defined as the average number of children a woman will have if she experiences a given set of age-specific birth rates throughout her reproductive life (usually considered between the ages fifteen to forty-nine).[26]

Table 2–5 shows aggregate data for all three indicators of population growth as well as the crude death rate (CDR) for the developed and developing countries. The overall discrepancy between developed and developing countries is acute. The population growth rate for the wealthy countries is well below 1 percent whereas the developing countries exhibit rates of about 2.5 percent. The similarity between the developed countries and the middle-income countries' (MICs)[27] death rates is striking, indicating a rapid decline in mortality as GNP rises.[28] The pattern between the middle- and low-income countries is mixed, for although the total fertility rates are very close, the other measures show considerable divergence. Essentially, differences in base populations and mortality account for the disparity; childbearing women have roughly the same number of children as indicated by the similar total fertility rates, but a

**Table 2–5. Fertility Indicators**

| | Population Growth Rate 1970–1978 | Crude Birth Rate 1978 | Crude Death Rate 1978 | Total Fertility Rate 1978 |
|---|---|---|---|---|
| Low-income countries | 2.4 | 45 | 19 | 6.2 |
| Middle-income countries | 2.5 | 35 | 11 | 5.0 |
| Developed countries | 0.7 | 14 | 10 | 1.9 |

*Source:* IBRD (1980).
*Note:* Indicators are based on unweighted averages for each category of countries.

much lower death rate explains the higher rate of population growth in the MICs.

The highest fertility is observed among the poorest segments of the population. The poor tend to have neither the means nor the motivation for smaller families. The former can be ameliorated by contraceptive availability, but the latter is extremely difficult, and the issues involved will be discussed below. But even where national rates appear to be dropping, this does not suggest lowered fertility among all income groups. Hence, it may well reflect selective economic progress rather than widespread reductions in poverty.

As Table 2–4 shows, population growth rates are highest for countries at the upper end of the low-income category and for some in the middle-income group, implying that as countries' incomes begin to rise, as is the case in the MICs, so does fertility. Because fertility and mortality are closely correlated, as mortality levels fall due to improvements in health care, education, an income, fertility rates rise concomitantly, although often with a considerable lag period.[29] This lag can result in a spurt of population growth, which is most common in those countries that have experienced a rapid rise in income and improved health status.

High fertility and falling infant mortality have been the major causes of the population surge in the LDCs since the end of World War II. Dramatic rises in population sap national resources by constraining per capita public expenditures, inhibiting investments in human capital, and thereby creating a high dependency ratio.[30] This issue is at the heart of government attempts to provide basic needs. The dependency ratio measures the burden of the nonproductive population on the productive members, indicating the extent of resources being channeled to the young, who are considered unproductive resources in an economic sense.[31] This moves resources away from economically productive and development-enhancing activities and simultaneously discourages savings and thereby investments (see Leff 1969).

The severity of the population problem as an impediment to economic development is a function of the rate of increase as well as the size of the base population. For example, in Table 2–6, Bangladesh, with a growth rate of 2.7 and a base population of 84.7 million, will have a population exceeding 160 million in twenty-five years; whereas Niger, with a similar growth rate of 2.8, will only have 10.0 million people by the year 2000. Similarly, in roughly thirty-five years India's population will double to 1.29 billion and Chad's population will exceed 9.0 million.[32]

These figures indicate the importance of the base population, for it is clear that India grapples with a problem of greater magnitude than, say, the Ivory Coast, which has a higher birth rate but a considerably lower population and thus greater land and resources per capita.[33] An even

**Table 2–6. Comparison of Base Population and Population Growth Rates for Selected Countries**

| | Population (millions), 1978 | Average Annual Population Growth Rate (%), 1970–1978 | Estimated Population in 2000 at 1978 Growth Rate (millions) |
|---|---|---|---|
| Bangladesh | 84.7 | 2.7 | 143.0 |
| Rwanda | 4.5 | 2.9 | 8.0 |
| Chad | 4.3 | 2.2 | 7.0 |
| Nepal | 13.9 | 2.2 | 21.0 |
| Zaire | 26.8 | 2.7 | 47.0 |
| India | 643.9 | 2.0 | 974.0 |
| Niger | 5.0 | 2.8 | 9.0 |
| Pakistan | 77.3 | 3.1 | 139.0 |
| Indonesia | 136.0 | 1.8 | 204.0 |
| Kenya | 14.7 | 3.3[a] | 32.0 |
| Egypt | 39.9 | 2.2 | 62.0 |

*Source:* IBRD (1980).

[a] Preliminary World Fertility Survey results and those of a recent Demographic Survey in Kenya indicate a growth rate over 4 percent.

more critical consideration than the base growth rate ratio is the amount of arable land per capita, particularly since the majority of the labor force in developing countries is involved in agriculture. The International Bank for Reconstruction and Development (IBRD) estimates that in 1970, 85 percent of low-income and 51 percent of middle-income countries' labor forces were employed in agriculture. Arable land influences the amount of food that can be produced for domestic consumption and the level of food exports;[34] as population increases, land, particularly arable land, becomes scarce, and as it is cultivated more intensively, the soil becomes depleted and less productive. Table 2–7 gives some indication of the gross land-population pressures in the developing countries. Of particular relevance for a BHN strategy would be disaggregation of land ownership by income group as an indication of the effect of arable land availability on poverty alleviation.

## Consequences of High Fertility

Excessive pressures on land have side effects that create a disequilibrium in the locational distribution of people and in the quality of the environment. As land is split up among children and as jobs become scarce, mi-

**Table 2–7. Population, Arable Land, and Hectares per Capita for the LDCs and Selected DCs**

| | Total Population, 1977 (000) | Total Arable and Permeable Crop Hectares (000) | Arable Hectares per Capita |
|---|---|---|---|
| Low-income Countries | | | |
| Bhutan | 1202 | 252[a] | 0.210 |
| Cambodia | 8349 | 3046[a] | 0.365 |
| Lao PDR | 3381 | 961[a] | 0.284 |
| Ethiopia | 28854 | 13730[b] | 0.476[b] |
| Mali | 5842 | 9800[a] | 1.678 |
| | | | |
| Bangladesh | 75529 | 9392[a] | 0.124 |
| Rwanda | 4362 | 939[a] | 0.215 |
| Somalia | 3258 | 1065[a] | 0.327 |
| Upper Volta | 5716 | 5613[b] | 0.982[b] |
| Burma | 31992 | 9996 | 0.312 |
| | | | |
| Burundi | 3863 | 1260[a] | 0.326 |
| Chad | 4016 | 7000[b] | 1.743[b] |
| Nepal | 12877 | 2024[a] | 0.157 |
| Benin | 3160 | 2950[a] | 0.934 |
| Malawi | 5035 | 2288[a] | 0.454 |
| | | | |
| Zaire | 25098 | 6150[a] | 0.245 |
| Guinea | 4527 | 4170[a] | 0.921 |
| India | 628834 | 168880[a] | 0.269 |
| Vietnam | 44412 | 5600[a] | 0.126 |
| Afghanistan | 19796 | 8535[a] | 0.431 |
| | | | |
| Niger | 4732 | 15000[b] | 3.170[b] |
| Lesotho | 1173 | 355[a] | 0.303 |
| Mozambique | 9461 | 3080[a] | 0.326 |
| Pakistan | 72859 | 19420[a] | 0.267 |
| Tanzania | 15872 | 6290[a] | 0.396 |
| | | | |
| Haiti | 4626 | 870 | 0.188 |
| Madagascar | 8263 | 2862[a] | 0.346 |
| Sierre Leone | 2840 | 4094[a] | 1.442 |
| Sri Lanka | 14282 | 1979 | 0.139 |
| Central African Empire | 1829 | 5910[b] | 3.231[b] |
| | | | |
| Indonesia | 139635 | 19418 | 0.139 |
| Kenya | 13701 | 2160[a] | 0.158 |
| Uganda | 11701 | 5380[a] | 0.460 |
| Yemen Arab Rep. | 5467 | 1570[a] | 0.287 |

**Table 2–7** *(continued)*

| | Total Population, 1977 (000) | Total Arable and Permeable Crop Hectares (000) | Arable Hectares per Capita |
|---|---|---|---|
| *Middle-income Countries* | | | |
| Togo | 2312 | 2285[a] | 0.988 |
| Egypt | 36292 | 2826[a] | 0.078 |
| Yemen, PDR | 1710 | 172[a] | 0.101 |
| Cameroon | 6571 | 7345[a] | 1.118 |
| Sudan | 15674 | 7495[a] | 0.478 |
| Angola | 6561 | 1830[a] | 0.279 |
| Mauritania | 1465 | 1005[a] | 0.686 |
| Nigeria | 64887 | 23840[a] | 0.437 |
| Thailand | 43490 | 17650[a] | 0.406 |
| Bolivia | 4639 | 3336[a] | 0.719 |
| Honduras | 2876 | 890[a] | 0.309 |
| Senegal | 5111 | 2404[a] | 0.470 |
| Philippines | 43468 | 8000[a] | 0.184 |
| Zambia | 5167 | 5008[a] | 0.969 |
| Liberia | 1594 | 336[b] | 0.211[b] |
| El Salvador | 4239 | 669 | 0.158 |
| Papua New Guinea | 2783 | 353[a] | 0.127 |
| Congo, People's Republic of the | 1380 | 662[a] | 0.480 |
| Morocco | 18038 | 7830[a] | 0.434 |
| Rhodesia | 6493 | 2480[a] | 0.382 |
| Ghana | 10161 | 2700[a] | 0.266 |
| Ivory Coast | 6878 | 9160[a] | 1.332 |
| Jordan | 2779 | 1365[a] | 0.491 |
| Colombia | 24453 | 5160[a] | 0.211 |
| Guatemala | 5678 | 1735[a] | 0.306 |
| Ecuador | 7319 | 5096 | 0.696 |
| Paraguay | 2724 | 1035[a] | 0.380 |
| Korea, Republic of | 35340 | 2238 | 0.063 |
| Nicaragua | 2396 | 1505 | 0.628 |
| Dominican Republic | 5291 | 995[a] | 0.188 |
| Syrian Arab Republic | 7490 | 5672 | 0.757 |
| Peru | 15777 | 3330[a] | 0.211 |
| Tunisia | 5893 | 4410[a] | 0.748 |
| Malaysia | 12454 | 6004[a] | 0.482 |
| Algeria | 16100 | 7110[a] | 0.442 |
| Turkey | 40908 | 27699 | 0.677 |

**Table 2–7** *(continued)*

| | Total Population, 1977 (000) | Total Arable and Permeable Crop Hectares (000) | Arable Hectares per Capita |
|---|---|---|---|
| Costa Rica | 2018 | 490[b] | 0.243[b] |
| Chile | 10441 | 5828[a] | 0.558 |
| China, People's Republic of | 6852565 | 129500[a] | 0.152 |
| Jamaica | 2058 | 265[a] | 0.129 |
| Lebanon | 2959 | 348[a] | 0.118 |
| Mexico | 61196 | 27790[a] | 0.454 |
| Brazil | 112890 | 37630[a] | 0.333 |
| Panama | 1725 | 595[a] | 0.328 |
| Iraq | 11453 | 5290[a] | 0.462 |
| Uruguay | 2827 | 1905[a] | 0.674 |
| Romania | 21446 | 10518 | 0.490 |
| Argentina | 25719 | 35000[a] | 1.361 |
| Yugoslavia | 21560 | 8005 | 0.371 |
| Portugal | 8804 | 3600[a] | 0.409 |
| Iran | 31880 | 15950 | 0.500 |
| Hong Kong | 4283 | 11[b] | 0.003 |
| Trinidad and Tobago | 1019 | 157[b] | 0.157[b] |
| Venezuela | 12575 | 5322[a] | 0.423 |
| Singapore | 2284 | 8 | 0.004 |
| *Industrialized Countries* | | | |
| United Kingdom | 56074 | 6975 | 0.124 |
| France | 52915 | 18730 | 0.354 |
| United States | 215118 | 188330[a] | 0.875 |

*Source:* FAO (1977).
[a] FAO estimate.
[b] Unofficial.

gration to urban areas accelerates; migration may be the only alternative to joblessness and rural poverty.[35] Urban drift refers to crowding in one or two urban areas where services are in short supply, migrants are generally unskilled, and job opportunities are few. Underemployment is common, and as the labor force continues to expand, the numbers of un- and underemployed will rise disproportionately if fertility rates continue at current levels[36] (see Sinha 1976). If indeed they do, efforts to upgrade the labor force through investments in health and education will be frustrated by the sheer numbers entering the labor force.

Growth in urban populations averaged over 4 percent per annum in the developing countries between 1970 and 1975, and the trend does not appear to be abating. The United Nations estimates that LDC urban growth rates will remain at around 4 percent for the next decade; compared with a 1.5 rate of population growth in rural areas, this implies continued urban migration (Findley 1977). These patterns of urbanization are particularly relevant to a basic needs approach because the 1980s may well witness a shift from rural to urban poverty in many LDCs, requiring refinements in strategy and a different target population.

The environmental effect of population pressure is also striking. Through the relentless felling of trees for fuel and construction (without reforestation) and the intense and suboptimal cultivation of the soil, the renewable resource base is deteriorating at a rapid rate.[37] Soil erosion and depletion, siltification of rivers, and dwindling firewood supplies can all be linked to the growth in population.

High population growth can undermine any development strategy by depleting resources rapidly and making human capital investments difficult. A BHN strategy that aims at improvements in individual welfare and advances in macroeconomic growth is impeded on both fronts by excessive rates of population growth. Depletion of available natural resources removes a necessary input to production on a household level and inhibits growth on a national level.

## Determinants of Fertility

Why couples choose to have large families is not entirely clear, but decisions are made as to (1) a minimum desired number of children and (2) "insurance" births to ensure the survival of a desired number.[38] Extra births that are not actively sought, but are either not avoided or are a result of a lack of misinformation about contraceptives, also help to determine family size. Large families, often a rational choice on a family level, can be costly on a national level.

A few LDCs have reduced their population growth rates (notably Taiwan, Korea, Singapore, Hong Kong, Costa Rica, and Colombia), and the experience has led to a considerable literature attempting to explain the phenomenon. (See Rich 1973; Mason and David 1971; McGreevey and Birdsall 1974; Birdsall 1977; Ridker 1976; and Cassen 1976 for surveys of the literature and synopses of issues.) Overall development obviously is an important factor, as evidenced by the particular countries experiencing a drop, but it is a more complex issue, for a number of countries (or areas within countries) have also achieved lower birth rates despite modest increases in aggregate economic growth.[39]

The factors most often associated with falling fertility rates are (1) status of women and female labor force participation, (2) education, (3) income, (4) economic value of children, (5) health care, (6) family planning programs, (7) biological phenomena, and (8) urbanization.[40] Where infant mortality rates are high, generally fertility is as well. Both behavorial and biological factors play a role in this phenomena. Improvements in health practices and nutrition encourage survival of mother and child, which in turn reduces the net costs to couples of many births. Parents assume a certain number of births will ensure survival of a desired number and may not respond to or perceive initial decreases in infant mortality. These positive effects on fertility are most apparent as mortality begins to fall. However, over the long run, fertility tends to be reduced as parents adjust to the reality that a greater number of infants survive (Shultz 1976).[41]

Women in many developing countries are entirely dependent on parents or husbands for economic support and social status, often being excluded from family decisionmaking and protected from influences outside the (extended) family. Education is not considered critical to child raising, and resources are commonly reserved for males (Germaine 1975; Dixon 1975). Analysis over the last decade or so has indicated the importance of women's education and labor force participation (Williams 1976; Shields 1980; and Standing 1978) in reducing fertility. As women become better educated, enter the wage economy, and control their earnings expenditures, their role in the family and the community is enhanced, and their ability to exercise influence in fertility decisions increases.

Education lowers fertility over the long run, but perverse effects have been observed with marginal increases, particularly when the educational attainment is restricted to the lower elementary grades. For example, a recent paper by Evenson, Rosenzweig, and Wolpin (1980) shows a small negative effect on fertility of increased female education among Indian women, but a much greater dampening effect among Philippine mothers. The marginal educational increases occurred at the lower elementary grades for Indian women, but in the Philippines the increments were in the later high school years. These results help to explain the confusing results between mother's education and fertility. This is consistent with available evidence that indicates that high school education in particular (especially for girls) negatively affects fertility, and tends to support the view that the relationship between education and fertility is nonlinear (Cochrane 1979).

Educational attainment and labor force participation are closely correlated, and employment, especially that which is incompatible with child rearing, raises the opportunity costs of raising children. Education acts to broaden women's horizons as well as their acceptance of new methods and ideas. Investments in a few children, use of family planning, and later marriage all appear to be more acceptable to women who have some education, and all are correlated with lower fertility.

The role of income in bringing birth rates down is a controversial topic in the fertility determinants literature. As discussed earlier, as aggregate income rises so does fertility, but the threshold where the trend reverses has not been pinpointed. Available information indicates a stronger relationship between improved income distribution and lower population growth than between absolute income increases and fertility declines (Repetto 1974; Kocher 1976). The former observed relationship is not easily explainable, but could be attributed to the income distribution variables acting as a proxy for socioeconomic change or availability of public services. If this is the case, it is an important finding for a BHN approach because it means that income gains alone, unless complemented with health and family planning services and education, will not serve to reduce population growth rates.

Children are desired for their lifetime earning potential, social security function, household labor, and obviously, for the joy and comfort they provide. The long-run, net economic benefits of children accruing to parents often do not outweigh the costs, but in societies where children are a major source of old age support and a cheap source of seasonal labor they are perceived as valuable commodities.[42] Little work has been done that satisfactorily clarifies these relationships, but they are perhaps the best explanations for why couples have large families, particularly in rural areas (Liebenstein 1974; Mueller 1976).

The role of family planning in fertility reduction is a controversial issue that has only recently approached a compromise.[43] The total supply of children is determined by biological limitations, social restrictions, and to some extent, contraceptive availability. Regardless of the high parity levels apparent in most developing countries, women generally do not achieve their maximum biological fertility potential (Bongaarts 1975). Part of the explanation is social. Sexual taboos on intercourse and explicit rules regarding behavior before, during, and after marriage—as well as age of marriage—impose regulations on frequency and timing of intercourse and thus on conception and births (Davis and Blake 1956). A woman's health and nutritional status determines her fecundability; the likelihood of sterility and spontaneous abortion; the ages of menarche, menopause, and death (Butz and Habicht 1976). Also inhibiting is postpartum amenorrhea (short-term postbirth sterility), which can be extended by breast feeding (see nutrition section).

The availability of modern contraceptives such as the IUD, the "pill," and sterilization, among others, has made the decision to restrict family size far easier. Some have attributed recent declines in fertility entirely to contraceptive availability (Brackett, Ravenholt, and Chao 1978). However, evidence on the causality among socioeconomic development, contraceptive availability, and fertility has demonstrated the close relationship between socioeconomic change and reductions in fertility (Mauldin and Berelson 1976).

Family-planning services and information can therefore be an important factor in reducing fertility, but its availability must occur in conjunction with other development factors (Freedman and Berelson 1976; Mauldin and Berelson 1976). When, where, and how family-planning services are introduced will also have a bearing on their effectiveness in individual country settings, and thus the stage of socioeconomic development is particularly critical for the success of family-planning efforts (Birdsall 1977). On the whole, country efforts in family planning have been programs aimed at making contraceptives available without firm evidence that it is a cost-effective means of controlling fertility.[44] However, family-planning services are a necessary component for reducing fertility. The question is when, what, and how services should be made available, and how much emphasis should be placed on family-planning delivery in a given context.

There is a clear discrepancy between urban and rural fertility; those who migrate to urban areas generally exhibit lower fertility either because of the characteristics of the people who elect to move (selectively) and/or because of their adoption of urban norms (adaptation). Children are also more costly in urban settings, and their productivity is less valuable. It is difficult to separate out the effect of urbanization in couples' family size decisions, but it appears to have a dampening effect on fertility (Findley 1977).

Thus there are a multitude of factors that operate jointly in perpetuating high fertility. The relative importance of each is culture and country specific. What is critical is the realization that fertility levels are a function of a number of socioeconomic variables that are not intuitively linked to birth rates.

## Policy Implications

The brief survey above outlines some of the salient ongoing discussions on the determinants of fertility, but little of these research endeavors have provided policymakers with firm guidance. The patterns that emerge do not allow an easily adaptable framework for controlling population and, more importantly, introduce considerable uncertainty with regard to what kinds of programs will indeed reduce fertility levels.

The highest rates of population growth occur in the middle-income LDCs; there, mortality rates have fallen (due largely to improvements in public health and to increased availability of health services), and birth rates have largely remained at levels in keeping with earlier mortality rates.

Countries and income groups at the bottom end of the income scale are generally not the major sources of high population growth, although birth rates are highest in this group (see Tables 2–4 and 2–5). High mortality and poor maternal health and nutrition—both correlated with poverty—contain population growth at low levels of national income. If BHN policies are to be successful in improving the health and nutrition status of the lower income groups, the result will be an increase in population growth, unless simultaneous efforts are made to encourage smaller families. And it is the poor who suffer most from high parity, as high fertility and low income combine to reinforce existing poverty. Such an emphasis on the poor is in keeping with BHN objectives to improve the well-being of the lowest income cohorts.

Embracing a BHN approach requires particular attention to questions of employment and income if people are to satisfy their basic needs through means other than transfers. Any attempt to redistribute land, to increase farmer's incomes, or to generate off-farm employment must take into account the size of the labor force and thus by implication the growth of population. Thus, controlling population growth is a vital concern in encouraging economic growth and enhancing welfare, but the actual means for mitigating its impact are far from clear. Differing socioeconomic contexts, levels of development, and resource availability determine what methods and policies are required to reduce fertility, and as in any development strategy, a blueprint approach is only applicable in a general sense.

Population issues are closely intertwined with other sectors, and programs to encourage reductions in fertility must be designed to fit into the larger BHN scheme. To minimize development of conflicting policies, especially across sectors, and to allow realistic (long-run) planning, it is essential that fertility concerns be incorporated into a cohesive plan to improve well-being. BHN strategy relies on a complementary approach, emphasizing interdependence among sectors in achieving welfare and growth objectives.[45] Hence, population issues must be effectively integrated into the BHN strategy with a clear understanding of how fertility reduction fits into the overall strategy[46] (Family Health Care 1979).

Designing sensible approaches to reducing fertility requires consideration of a wide range of factors, both because fertility behavior responds in different ways to changes in socioeconomic factors and because a BHN strategy involves activities in numerous sectors that may conflict with fertility reduction objectives in the short run. Programs must also reflect sensitivity to the level of development and the specific cultural milieu. Successful programs in Asia (such as Taiwan and Korea) may prove meaningless in the Middle East, where women's status, income levels, and social structure work to discourage smaller families. And by the same token, countries at different stages of development respond differently to policy initiatives. Policies to elicit change in, say, farming methods are far different in Mexico than in Nepal, since new methods, literacy, formal learning, and transportation are far more common in the former, and our grasp of the national context allows the development of a sensitive approach to behavior change. To a great extent, the fact that the objective of this policy is to modify behavior implies that a country-specific approach must necessarily be designed; even within countries, diverse tribal groups may suggest the development of various approaches.

Attempts to slow fertility directly through government programs and regulations is a slow process with dubious outcome, precisely because the means to elicit behavior change are not known. Providing safe, accessible, and affordable family-planning services is of considerable importance since motivation is only one component of a population policy. Encouragements to reduce family size are necessary but not sufficient; the means for controlling fertility must also be acceptable and obtainable if we are to expect women to be able to limit their fertility. Innovative approaches to delivering family-planning services deserve greater exploration; for example, outreach workers in water and sanitation or agriculture could conceivably deliver family-planning information and contraceptives. Particularly where health services are inaccessible or ineffective (in health and/or family planning), these mechanisms could play a major role in motivation and delivery.

Improving employability (through provision of health care and education) and increasing employment opportunities, especially for women, also work to reduce population growth over the long run, because they encourage women to use contraceptives. Women with high opportunity costs tend to exhibit lower fertility rates; and women with more education are more likely to demand a greater role in family decisionmaking, including fertility decisions. Hence, raising the status of women contributes to lower demand for children, especially in the long run.

Incentives such as extension of social security programs will probably have the greatest impact, since it is in the household's economic interest to reduce family size when attractive alternatives are available.[47] The provision of free contraceptives is only one form of incentive. Measures such as those used in Singapore, where low fertility couples receive preferential treatment in housing and some other public services and high fertility couples are penalized through the tax system, may be called for in some instances, but such schemes are country specific and need to be carefully conceived and implemented. And as mentioned earlier, incentives must be designed in tandem with other programs so as to not present conflicting incentives.

The importance of unchecked fertility growth in the BHN context has largely been ignored, but attainment of basic needs requires careful consideration of population issues, specifically fertility. To devise and implement a successful growth strategy and extend public services to the poor, population growth must be slowed—for both objectives may prove impossible otherwise.

## NUTRITION ISSUES

### Introduction

Nutrition is possibly the most serious welfare problem facing the developing countries. Because nutrition status affects health, labor productivity, learning capacity, and thus income, malnutrition also has significant implications for economic development as well as for population growth. It is estimated that roughly 1130 million or 74 percent of the developing world's population in 1965 consumed below the minimum FAO–WHO daily calorie requirements (Reutlinger 1977); recent projections for 1975 show a potential deficit for somewhere between 1073 and 1373 million people, or 55 to 71 percent of developing country populations (Reutlinger and Selowsky 1978).

Nutrition problems in the LDCs resemble those of the health sector in many ways. Aside from the synergistic relationship between health and nutrition outlined in the section on health, the determinants of nutrition encompass most of the factors determining a population's health. Uncontrollable events such as weather, fertilizer availability, and the whims of international trade and finance play a large role in determining nutrition status, and by influencing nutrition status, these factors also affect health—but the initial and primary impact is on nutrition.

Malnutrition involves deficiencies in the quality of food consumed as well as in food quality and variety. Although sufficient food intake is a biological necessity, nutrient composition has profound implications for morbidity (illness) and mortality. The adverse consequences of poor nutrition (as opposed to undernutrition, the consumption of insufficient calories and proteins)—such as blindness, lethargy, and chronic disease—point up the need to examine the specific causes of malnutrition. To accomplish this, measures of intrahousehold consumption are required, and such information is not widely available and is costly to collect.

Means to reducing malnutrition range from direct food subsidies to disease control and income supplements. On a macroeconomic level, governments can ensure adequate supplies and distribution of food during shortages and have a role in promoting adequate nutrition through pricing policies and welfare measures. On the household level, however, government's role is less well defined. Major problems associated with both national and household-directed nutrition programs include (1) defining the malnourished population; (2) designing efficient programs to reach only the target groups; and (3) addressing needs in other areas that bear indirectly, yet significantly, on nutrition.

The most severely and most chronically malnourished are the poor, especially infants, children, and mothers. Malnutrition is primarily a consequence of poverty, but at the same time it aids in perpetuating poverty. Poor nutrition impedes learning and reduces productivity, and it inhibits attempts to raise income and increase employment through acquisition of new skills. The basic human needs approach, with its stress on improving individual welfare, cannot overlook nutrition issues, both because it is related to sufficient food intake and because it is a major determinant of health status. If a BHN strategy is to prove successful, nutrition must form a central component, for it is a major factor in determining welfare in developing countries.

This section will concentrate on the major issues affecting malnutrition and its consequences for the LDCs. Health-related topics will only be touched on, as these have been covered to some extent in the section on health.

## Measurements of Malnutrition

Malnutrition is defined as a pathological state resulting from inadequate or excessive consumption of one or more essential nutrients. Undernutrition and specific deficiency, both forms of malnutrition, stem from inadequate food (or food energy) consumption over time and lack of individual nutrient(s), respectively (Jelliffe 1966). Malnutrition in developing countries results directly from both undernutrition and specific deficiency.

Kwashiorkor and marasmus, severe forms of protein-calorie malnutrition in children, are perhaps the most widely recognized nutrition problems in developing countries,[48] although their incidence is considerably below the milder forms of malnutrition associated with chronic morbidity and debility, which are more difficult to determine. A wasted, apathetic child exhibits clear signs of severe malnutrition, but signs of milder forms of malnutrition are not as easily attributable. Nutritional problems are mostly due to deficiencies in a number of specific nutrients that impede straightforward diagnosis. Often manifestations of malnutrition in adults are not severe enough to warrant the time and attention necessary for diagnoses and treatment. In children symptoms such as slow growth may not serve as a warning if malnutrition is a chronic community affliction. Hence, motivation and diagnosis can pose major impediments to diagnosing and controlling malnutrition.

Malnutrition can be identified and measured in a number of ways, none of them totally satisfactory and many of them unsuitable in rural settings. Primary tools include (1) clinical examination, (2) anthropometric measures, (3) biochemical tests, and (4) indirect methods.

Clinical examinations provide the simplest and least expensive method of assessing nutritional status (Jelliffe, 1966). Careful, superficial examination and identification of malnutrition symptoms form the basis of clinical diagnoses. Clinicians must distinguish the physical signs of malnutrition from a well-nourished standard,[49] and major difficulties arise in differentiating nutritional deficiencies from diseases with identical symptoms. Application of supplementary techniques such as those described below may be mandatory if confusing symptoms are observed. Clinical tests are ideal in some circumstances, and their low cost and simple technology make them particularly appropriate in rural areas and LDCs.

Growth is determined by a number of biological and environmental factors, nutrition being among the most important. Nutrition influences physical dimensions, and anthropometric measures of body size (height), weight, and composition (degree of fat and muscle) have proven to be useful tools in determining the existence and extent of malnutrition.[50]

Properly executed anthropometric techniques are generally reliable indicators of nutrition status.[51] Comparing measurements at various ages is highly desirable, especially with children. But age is often unknown, and the normal nutritional standards of height and weight become difficult to apply in developing areas where malnutrition inhibits both measures.[52]

Biochemical examination tests measure the adequacy of dietary intake and identify lack of specific nutrients. Such tests pose difficulties in developing and applying standards and in the collection, storage, and transportation of specimens and analysis. These and the high cost make their use somewhat impractical in rural areas.[53] Small sample analysis probably is the most sensible application of this technique.[54]

Nonmedical or indirect methods for assessing aggregate nutrition status include the infant mortality rate, aggregate figures on food production, income distribution, health status, educational attainment, and household-specific information on food distribution and consumption. These proxies for nutrition are used extensively in the economic development literature, being particularly useful for cross-country comparisons.

However, they are imperfect measures of nutrition status. But for want of preferable, standardized measures, they are heavily relied upon for determining national nutrition needs.

Infant mortality rates (IMR) provide reasonably good indicators of overall malnutrition in childbearing women and infants, since it essentially reflects poor maternal nutrition: undernourished women produce low birth weight babies, who traditionally suffer high risk of death in the first year of life. Variations in infant mortality often indicate disparities in food availability or distribution and, as mentioned earlier, generally reflect health status (see Table 2–5). Food scarcity has been shown to raise mortality, as seen by the rapid rise in infant mortality experienced by Sri Lanka during the 1974 food deficit year.

The comparative review by Gwatkin, Wilcox, and Wray (1979) indicates the importance of health and nutrition programs in lowering infant mortality. Evidence from integrated programs in Imesi, Nigeria; rural Guatemala; Narangwal, India; and Jomkhed, India; and from a food supplement program in northern Peru reveal infant mortality reductions of between 20 and 100 percentage points over the course of the programs.[55] The IMR was also correlated directly with medical measures of malnutrition. Though admittedly a crude indicator of nutrition status, the IMR is a useful tool for conveying orders of magnitude and comparing malnutrition across countries.

Per capita daily calorie consumption estimates and requirements have been developed by the Food and Agriculture Organization (FAO) of the United Nations and widely adopted by the international community as indicators of national per capita nutrition status. Table 2–8 presents data on calorie consumption, requirements, and deficits for LDC regions. The variation among regions is substantial, and that observed inter- and

**Table 2–8. Per Capita and Gross Calorie Deficits by Region, 1965.**

| | Daily per Capita | | | Gross Daily Calorie Deficits (1000 millions of calories) | |
| --- | --- | --- | --- | --- | --- |
| | Calorie consumption | Standard calorie requirements | Calorie deficit (consumption requirements) | Regional average | Country average |
| Latin America | 2,472 | 2,390 | 0 | 0 | 19 |
| Asia | 1,980 | 2,210 | 230 | 202 | 213 |
| Middle East | 2,315 | 2,450 | 135 | 19 | 32 |
| Africa | 2,154 | 2,350 | 196 | 48 | 50 |
| Total | | | 561 | 269 | 314 |

*Source:* Reutlinger and Selowsky (1978).

intracountry is even greater. For instance, although Latin America registers a zero nutrition deficit, Bolivia, Ecuador, and El Salvador exhibit daily calorie consumption levels well below 2390 calories (Reutlinger and Selowsky 1978). This distributional phenomena also exists within countries where "pockets" of poverty and malnutrition occur despite respectable national averages.[56] Such distortions limit the usefulness of the data, but they are acceptable measures of calorie requirements for lack of more realistic statistics. In addition, such measures are rough indicators of aggregate nutritional deficits.

Official food supply statistics generally exist, but are imperfect measures of nutrition as they neglect production of subsistence agriculture and, again, implicitly assume an even distribution of food supplies. Subsistence farming characterizes low-income LDCs, and food availability/affordability is highly skewed toward higher income families in most countries. Often calorie and protein supply figures are given as a percentage of (biological) requirements, indicating something about "national" nutrition status. In the absence of preferable measures, food production data can give rough estimates of protein and calorie supplies, but they should be taken as means of unknown distributions.[57]

Household level measures of nutrition include consumer expenditure surveys (CES) and food consumption surveys (FCS). Both are difficult and costly to conduct, but constitute the only effective methods for collecting accurate information on family nutrition (other than direct medical examinations). The CES estimates malnutrition through information on calories and nutrients purchased; however, the role of cooking methods, intrafamilial food distribution, and general health status in reducing the full energy nutrient values of household food supplies is not taken into account. The FCS, on the other hand, records the food content and quality consumed by each household member, in order to provide a description of family nutrition. The time and detail of such studies restrict them to small samples, and their visible intrusion into family life may introduce a Hawthorne effect.[58] Further difficulties in selecting a representative sample and an unbiased time period (e.g., with regard to harvests) combine to make such studies somewhat rare, especially FCS. Though both survey methods pose major difficulties, they provide some insight into food consumption and expenditure patterns and are a useful means of assessing potential sources of malnutrition.[59]

These foregoing measures of malnutrition relate to individual and household nutrition status and as such are of limited use in comparing the nutrition of populations. Their usefulness as indicators of national malnutrition is limited to those instances where samples cut across all income groups and geographic areas. More aggregate estimates of national per capita daily calorie and protein requirements are needed.

## Sources of Malnutrition

Nutrition status derives from a wide range of factors determined by national and household level decisions, and both must be considered in a BHN approach. The quantity of food available obviously has a direct bearing on nutrition, but less apparent and equally important to nutrition status are household food preparation and distribution patterns, family health status, literacy, and probably most critical, income levels and land ownership.

**Food Production.** In 1975 the food deficit LDCs as a group experienced food shortfalls of about 37 million metric tons. By 1990 the International Food Policy Research Institute (1977) projects a major staples shortfall of between 120 and 145 million metric tons for these countries. The bulk of these shortages occur in those countries with GNPs below $300 (in 1975 terms) and rapid rates of population growth (International Food Policy Research Institute 1977). Food shortfalls mean that food quantity not only declines, but that traditional distribution patterns biased against the poor tend to be reinforced. Net food importers are particularly hard hit by world food deficits (Isenman 1980). Favorable food policies can help mitigate dependence on food imports by raising domestic food production. However, the prospects for alleviating malnutrition through national increases in food production alone appear dim, since simply increasing output, although necessary, does not guarantee improved nutrition as consumption is affected by other factors (Reutlinger and Selowsky 1978).

Income, preferences, and tradition play a major role in determining household consumption and nutrition. Coarse grains and roots form the basis of the diet of the poor, and increased production of these crops will have a greater probability of enhancing the diets of the poor specifically. However, considerable controversy exists as to the acceptable minimum calorie and protein needs of children and infants, making production requirements difficult to determine. The FAO-WHO standards are considered to be highly unreliable, partly due to the noncomparable sample of children used to develop these standards.

An additional and fundamental issue under dispute is whether an acceptable protein-calorie balance already exists in the diet of low-income groups, making the problem, therefore, merely one of quantity of food. Graham (1979) believes the mix to be neither optimal nor complete and points out specific deficiencies in typical diets, particularly those of children. A further point is the bulk of the diet, which inhibits consumption of adequate calories and/or protein. Graham points to this as the major contributing factor of "marasmic" malnutrition among poor children.

The counterargument, largely of nonnutritionists, assumes an adequate protein-calorie balance in the poor's diet: hence, the emphasis of nutrition interventions should be on increased calorie production (and consumption), particularly in high calorie foods such as cassava and corn (Pinstrup-Anderson 1976; Berg 1979; Fleuret 1979; Brown and Parisier 1975).[60]

Although the potential community effects are disputed, the need to expand the food supply of the poor is not. Increasing the output of protein and expensive grains tends to supplement the diets of the adequately nourished, as these costly and unfamiliar foods are generally beyond the purchasing power of the poor. A number of studies have shown that stimulating production of indigenous bulk crops specifically will have a greater impact on the diets of the calorie deficit poor[61] (Pinstrup-Anderson 1976; Berg 1979). And although alone it is not an optimal program and can have detrimental effects,[62] emphasizing increased calorie production (and consumption) may provide the only realistic approach to improving the nutrition of the lowest income groups through macroeconomic food policy.[63]

Traditional food preparation and disribution patterns within the household also affect nutrition and need to be considered explicitly by those attempting to implement policies to achieve BHN nutrition objectives. Overcooking and discarding of nutritionally valuable food, as well as taboos on certain kinds of food (such as meats in Hindu societies), inadvertently reduces the nutrient content of food consumed. Intrafamilial food distribution patterns favoring men and boys also contribute to malnutrition, particularly among women and young children (Taylor, Newman, and Kelly 1976). These detrimental practices are grounded in social custom and are thus highly resistant to change, but they must be addressed as part of the nutrition problem in LDCs if malnutrition is to be alleviated. For this reason an aggregate or mechanistic approach to nutrition and the costing out associated with it is not sufficient to address the problem.

**Health and Fertility.** Health, fertility, and education are influenced by and contribute to adequate nutrition. A recent review of nutrition, health, and population programs in developing countries by Gwatkin, Wilcox, and Wray (1979) points to the importance of integrating these sectors in order to improve nutrition. In seven country experiments (Guatemala, India, Iran, Jamaica, Nigeria, Turkey, and the United States), the effectiveness of nutrition and health interventions were evaluated. Although particular approaches, such as nutrition supplements for pregnant and lactating women and nutrition monitoring of children, seemed especially appropriate, the role of health services was of considerable importance. In fact, health care appeared to be as important or more important than nutrition interventions among older children and adults in the INCAP (Institute of Nutrition of Central America and Panama) program in Guatemala and the Narangwal program in India.

Much of the explanation for the importance of health and family planning interventions is essentially biological. Poor health impedes absorption of food nutrients, implying a need for more food without increased nutritional benefit. But ill-health has its greatest impact on maternal nutrition. Malnutrition during pregnancy can cause permanent damage in the mental and physical development of the fetus and proves deleterious to a woman's long-term health[64] (Caldwell, Campbell, Dunlop, and Fiedler 1978; WHO 1965).

Lactation is reduced in quality and may be diminished in quantity by poor maternal nutrition. The extent of immunity passed to infants from mothers decreases, and the amounts of fat, calories, and protein in mother's milk is lessened when the special dietary needs of lactating women are unmet.[65] The consequences of the latter lead to increased malnutrition and mortality among infants and children (Jelliffe and Jelliffe 1978; Baumslag, Kinsey, and Sabin 1978).

Evidence from Guatemala (Lechtig 1975) and India (Parker et al. 1978) indicates that the most efficient and cost-effective method of raising birth weight and improving child nutrition is through supplementing maternal diets. In the Guatemala project, a daily 1000 calorie supplement was given to pregnant women, which resulted in a 3 to 5 gram increase in birth weight. A halving of the infant mortality rate was attributed to women taking over 20,000 supplementary calories during pregnancy.

Fertility and nutrition are also closely linked. Nutritional status plays a role in determining fecundability (ability to produce children), since it is positively correlated with the incidence of spontaneous abortion and miscarriage and negatively associated with completed pregnancy (Austin and Levinson 1974). However, recent evidence shows that a good deal of confusion exists on this issue and that further research is essential (Zeitlin et al. 1980). Repeated pregnancy raises and broadens nutrition requirements that remain largely unmet, causing or exacerbating malnutrition among women and children. If improved nutrition does result in higher fertility, it will place increased food demands on the household as it expands,[66] and infants and younger children in large families often bear the brunt of the growing family food burden (Puffer and Serrano 1975), which can have implications for future productivity and income generation. In order to minimize these perverse effects, emphasis needs to be placed on education as a component of nutrition programs.

**Education.** Level of educational achievement in both the formal and informal sectors has a decided impact on nutrition status. Concurrently, raised child nutrition improves mental concentration ability and is associated with reduced absenteeism in school. Evidence by Florencio and Smith (1969) indicates that better educated parents are more adept at preparing a nutritious diet with a given income, since purchase, preparation, and intrafamilial food distribution are more efficiently accomplished by those with more education. Education's effect on fertility and health also works to improve nutrition status through reduced pregnancies and better resistance to diseases (Caldwell, Campbell, Dunlop and Fiedler 1978).

In an encouraging finding related to food production, Lockheed, Jamison, and Lau (1980) show that education is related to improved output. In a careful review of case studies, they found that in thirty-one of the thirty-seven cases, both formal and nonformal education had a significant positive effect on productivity. Their regression results indicate that these effects are further enhanced by modernization.

**Income.** Income is necessary but not sufficient for acquiring and maintaining an adequate diet. Malnutrition is associated with poverty on a national as well as houshold level, but its importance varies according to other economic circumstances.

On a community level, research has repeatedly found a significant relationship between low income and malnutrition (Fleuret 1979). The direction and strength of the causal relationship, however, is unclear. A few rigorous analyses of the effect of changes in income on nutrition have been undertaken. A recent study on data from Candelaria, Colombia, by Heller and Drake (1976) shows a small positive effect of increasing income on nutritional status and a positive relationship between family income and children's nutrition status (weight for height). The same study also yields an income elasticity of food expenditure (the percentage change in the amount of food purchased for a percentage increase in income) of .496, implying that food expenditures do not increase equiproportionally with income.[67]

The latter finding is in keeping with Berg's (1979) contention that calorie intake rises less than half as rapidly as income. Household expenditures, as well as other goods and services, rise with income; food does not claim even the bulk of the increase. Furthermore, households often purchase more expensive and potentially less nutritious foods as their incomes rise—for example, when polished rice replaces coarse grains and sugar enters the diet. However, families do tend to increase their consumption of animal protein and vegetables as their purchasing power grows.

On a more aggregate level, the relationship between malnutrition and GNP is consistently shown to be negative. Belli (1971) and the author find a positive correlation between protein supplies and income; more rigorous analysis by Correa (1975) and Correa and Cummins (1970) support these findings. The effect of income distribution on nutrition is less well examined. Belli (1971) attributes uneven income distribution to malnutrition because of the reduced learning ability and lowered productivity associated with an inadequate and unbalanced diet; and Leipziger and Lewis (1980) find a positive correlation between nutrition (protein per capita) and income distribution (Gini coefficient) in countries with per capita incomes above $550 GNP, but a negative relationship below $550 GNP. The evidence on this issue is too meager to draw any succinct conclusions, but income distribution does appear to be correlated with nutrition status, although per capita GNP levels may determine how much of an effect income distribution will have on the nutrition sector.

Berg (1979) and Pinstrup-Anderson and Caicedo (1978) have estimated the level of economic growth required if income alone were to solve the nutrition problem in LDCs. Table 2–9 illustrates the needs projected by Berg for Bangladesh, Brazil, India, Morocco, and Pakistan and by Pinstrup-Anderson and Caicedo for Colombia. With the exception of Colombia, the twenty-year growth requirement figures in column 2 assume a distribution of income growth favoring the calorie deficit population. The 0.9 figure for Colombia measures the amount of income growth needed if the total income increase were distributed to the lowest decile of the population. The income growth needed to alleviate malnutrition in the lowest decile category assumes an equal distribution of income across income groups.

The data on income growth requirements for the six sample countries imply that the proportion of poorly nourished in each country is unrelated to income distribution measures. Requirements for Brazil, with the highest Gini coefficient, are identical to Pakistan's, the nation with the lowest Gini coefficient in the sample. Without considering distribution, growth in GDP promises elimination of calorie deficits in twenty-two to seventy-nine years, assuming no other measures are taken to reduce malnutrition. Hence, countries interested in raising nutrition status can either distribute the benefits of income growth to the poor or design programs to directly improve their nutrition. The time required to eliminate calorie deficiencies is a long one for most countries with either approach, even under the optimistic assumptions in Table 2–9.[68]

The determinants of nutrition thus encompass a wide range of issues; resolving them requires changes in national food policies, household food habits, and food production. The prospects for positive change vary with

**Table 2–9. Current Growth and Income Distribution Indicators and Required Growth Rates for Eliminating Calorie Deficits in Selected LDCs**

| | Income Growth Required to Eliminate Calorie Deficit in 20 Years | GDP Growth Rate (1970–1976) | Income Growth Required to Eliminate Calorie Deficit in the Lowest Decile in Number of Years[a] | Percentage of Income Going to Lowest 40% of Income Earners (1970) | Gini Coefficient (1970) |
|---|---|---|---|---|---|
| Bangladesh | 2.5 | 1.6 | 1.5 (79) | 19.9 | .33 |
| Brazil | 2.2 | 10.6 | 4.8 (31) | 9.5 | .57 |
| India | 2.1 | 2.7 | 2.6 (30) | 13.1 | .47 |
| Morocco | 2.2 | 4.8 | 4.2 (22) | n.a. | n.a. |
| Pakistan | 2.2 | 3.6 | 3.1 (22) | 20.4 | .32 |
| Colombia[b] | 0.9[b] | 6.5 | 18.6 (91) | 10.4 | .54 |

*Sources:* Jain (1975), IBRD (1979), Berg (1979), and Pinstrup-Anderson and Caicedo (1978).

[a] These figures assume constant food prices over time.

[b] The income growth requirements for Colombia are calculated for an instant elimination of calorie deficiency; the 0.9 figure assumes all proceeds from economic growth go to the lowest decile. Only the Colombia data are from Pinstrup-Anderson and Caicedo (1978).

circumstances and thus by country, but it is unreasonable to expect dramatic changes in nutrition status in the short run. Even embracing a BHN approach will not produce an adequately fed population in the short term. However, as in health, the close (synergistic) relationship between nutrition and its determinants will work to maximize positive externalities generated by improvements in other sectors. The BHN approach is thus an ideal mechanism for enhancing nutrition because it attempts to make the linkage and externalities explicit.

## Economic Consequences and Implications of Malnutrition

The consequences of malnutrition were touched on in the previous section; however, the mental and economic effects of prolonged malnutrition bear special mention. A vast literature on the mental and physical damage caused by (grossly) inadequate diets, with particular reference to young children, has been generated over the past few decades.[69]

Severe protein-calorie malnutrition among infants and children has a direct negative effect on physical growth, as indicated by the preponderance of low height for age and smaller than normal brain circumferences evidenced among malnourished children.[70] Results from a number of nutrition studies in Peru (Graham 1967), Mexico (Cravioto and DeLicardie 1968), Jamaica (Birch and Richardson 1972), and Colombia (McKay, McKay, and Sinisterra 1973) point to lower height and smaller overall size among children receiving inadequate amounts of protein and/or calories (see section on nutrition measurement). Reduced intellectual ability and impaired cognitive development due to malnutrition and/or environmental factors has been even more thoroughly examined and with few exceptions indicates clear positive relationships.

While growth retardation and lowered intellectual capacity are expected outcomes of severe malnutrition, controversy persists as to the importance of age in determining long-term effects. The dispute centers on the duration of the "critical period" of brain development in infants and children. Adequate pre- and postnatal nutrition are essential to proper brain development. Low birth weight infants—associated with nutritionally deprived fetuses—exhibit an abnormally high incidence of mental impairment (Birch 1972).[71] Pryor (1975), Graham (1967), and Winick (1970) show that the earlier in life malnutrition occurs, the more severe and the more permanent the detrimental effects; duration beyond four months during the first year or so of life tends to intensify the negative effects of malnutrition and to inhibit reversal.[72] Work by Hertiz et al. (1972) disputes these findings; their results imply no association between age and severity of malnutrition effects. However, experts seem generally to concur that although inadequate diet early in life may not prove permanently detrimental, insufficient nutrients can impair physical and mental development. This indicates a need for concentrating on maternal nutrition programs in a BHN strategy as an efficient means of investing in human capital in the long run.

Mental deficiencies and physical debility from malnutrition severely hamper children in formal and nonformal (social) learning. Studies have shown a positive correlation between mental ability, measured by IQ scores, and learning ability and productivity (Scrimshaw, Taylor, and Gordon 1968) and between IQ and productivity (Selowsky and Taylor 1973). The work by Selowsky and Taylor indicates a strong causal relationship between IQ levels and learning differentials. Low intelligence is traced to early malnutrition, which retards learning abilities (IQ), thus producing a poorly educated wage earner of subnormal intelligence. The effect of childhood-infant malnutrition on income is substantial: a 6 to 7 percent increase in wage earnings is predicted for a 10 percent rise in IQ (Selowsky and Taylor 1973). These studies imply that nutrition programs can make future education expenditures more rewarding in a national sense, since returns to educational investments receive a higher return when learning ability is improved.

The discussion on productivity in the section on health applies to nutrition as well; productivity loss is attributable to inadequate diet as well as to poor health. Gains in productivity due to improved nutrition have been documented in both the developed and the developing countries; greater output per man has been observed in a number, if not all, settings when diets were increased and improved.[73]

Measuring nutrition's effect on national development has been attempted by Correa (1975), Correa and Cummins (1970), and Belli (1971), with a consensus view emerging that nutrition contributes significantly to economic growth and development.[74] Malnutrition (inadequate calories per capita) helps perpetuate the poverty of low-income groups by inhibiting earnings ability. Consequently, neglecting nutrition is essentially a disinvestment in human capital, reinforcing skewed income (and wealth) distribution patterns and slowing broad based economic growth.

Nutritional deficiency appears to affect the rate of development and economic growth. Belli (1971) shows a strong association between per capita protein supplies and individual income, and Correa and Cummins' (1970) regressions for nine Latin American countries indicate that nutrition (increased calorie intake) has almost as great an effect on GNP growth as does education.[75]

An examination of these disaggregated results suggests that the poorer the country, the greater the scope for increased calorie consumption to effect economic growth, both absolutely and relative to education. These results are consistent with our theoretical view of the economic structure of low-income LDCs: at lower income levels increased productivity is more dependent upon improved physical output; hence, increased calorie consumption tends to have a stronger effect on economic growth in poorer LDCs. Those countries with higher national incomes tend to benefit more from educational improvements. Correa and Cummins (1970) substantiate these findings, and the correlation analysis of Leipziger and Lewis (1980) complements them. In the latter analysis, countries with a per capita GNP below $550 exhibited a somewhat significant positive relationship between growth (per capita income) and nutrition (per capita protein consumption), but no relationship emerged between income distribution and nutrition. The correlation for LDCs above $550 per capita GNP indicates a strong positive relationship between improved income distribution and nutrition, but none between growth and increased protein consumption. Hence, income distribution appears to be significantly correlated with nutrition at higher levels of income, whereas growth is associated with improved nutrition in the poorest LDCs.

Prolonged malnutrition exacts a high personal and social cost over the long run, and unless policymakers are willing to intervene decisively, the cycle of poverty, undernutrition, reduced educability and productivity, and low income will continue. The following discussion on policy will explore the possible interventions for mitigating this scenario.

## Policy Implications

Nutrition considerations are at the heart of efforts to improve welfare under a BHN strategy. Achieving minimally acceptable levels of food consumption and adequate health status requires careful consideration of nutrition problems.

As discussed earlier, estimated national food supply needs are highly imperfect and are often misleading indicators of malnutrition. National level data often belie prominent nutritional deficiencies among certain segments of the population.[76] Projected national food needs convey nothing of intracountry food distribution, country- and region-specific nutrient deficiencies, or household level habits—all of which impede attainment of a nutritionally adequate diet. Although such data allows gross comparisons, it is not particularly helpful to policymakers on a national level, and it can encourage maldistribution of international food supplies. The issue, then, is not only how much food is required to meet minimal nutrition standards, but more importantly, how the national population can achieve and sustain an adequate diet.

A BHN strategy is focused on the lowest income group, where malnutrition is most prevalent. Berg (1979) points out that although all those suffering from malnutrition are poor, not all poor people suffer from calorie or nutrient deficiencies. Nonetheless, the target population is the (chronically) malnourished poor. Attempts to reach this group have taken various forms and have met with mixed success.

National nutrition policies aimed at particular income groups or age cohorts essentially try to improve or prevent malnutrition through reductions in the costs of some (nutritionally desirable) foods and through food supplement programs. Although problems arise with such programs, they present the only sensible mechanism for reaching the very poor. Institutionalization of food subsidies for income groups is often difficult to curtail, and assistance often continues beyond the period of financial need because it is politically unfeasible to end food subsidies. Limiting food distribution to those who are actually undernourished and discouraging substitution of supplemental feeding for meals pose additional problems. The latter has occurred frequently in school-clinic feeding programs for children, implying a need for nutrition education as a component of these programs to minimize potential detrimental effects.

A further complication of food programs is the possible negative incentive for agricultural production (Isenman 1980). Relying on food imports for adequate supplies is a dangerous practice and can prove disruptive during food shortfall periods. Hence, encouraging growth in domestic food supply is essential if good subsidy programs are to survive. And government efforts in stabilizing food supply on an annual and seasonal basis may be required to improve market efficiency and to minimize price variability. The government thus must encourage increased food production while providing free or subsidized food to low-income consumers. The need for carefully balanced policies is obvious and is impossible to dictate, given wide variations in circumstances (Berg 1979).

Despite these problems, target-oriented nutrition programs have become acceptable means of addressing the nutrition problem. Furthermore, food supplement and subsidy are politically palatable approaches for both donors and national governments. Where politicians cannot condone direct income transfers to the poor, feeding hungry people is seen as a humanitarian gesture worthy of public funds. Such food transfers are even more appealing from a political standpoint.

School feeding programs, widely adopted in the LDCs and the developed countries, have in some instances been shown to decrease child mortality and morbidity (U.S. Congress, 1976) and have had a positive effect on attendance and attentiveness of students; however, their nutritional impact is inconsistent. Supplementary school feeding programs have faced numerous difficulties: the logistics of food distribution have presented major stumbling blocks, especially in rural areas, and as mentioned, the incentive for families to substitute supplemental feedings for meals at home is quite strong and not uncommon.

Health clinics and food for work programs also serve as food supplement distributors. The major drawbacks with these are the inaccessibility of those who do not attend school, do not have access to or a perceived need for health care, and are ineligible for or inaccessible to food for work programs. In short, target populations, those who are chronically undernourished, often are not within the purview of supplementary feed programs (Singer and Maxwell 1978; Berg 1979).

Programs lowering the cost of food to the target population through availability of subsidized food or through the distribution of food supplements have exhibited a clear positive effect on welfare. Although formidable distribution and cost problems occur with such programs, they have proven to be the single most effective means of reaching the malnourished poor. Analysis of the Sri Lankan experience, where food subsidy and ration programs have existed for some time, shows a strong inverse relationship between food subsidy programs and death rates (Isenman 1980). Food subsidy and ration efforts (along with supplementary feeding) have contributed substantially to relatively equal food grain distribution practices, leading to reduced malnutrition and im proved welfare.[77]

The success of Sri Lanka's extensive food ration program was due in part to complementary efforts in education and health care.[78] The "package" approach, successfully attempted by Sri Lanka (and Kerala, India), provides reinforcement for the notion that a strategy aimed at BHN objectives that includes efforts in multiple sectors is a potentially efficient method of improving welfare.

The drawbacks of Sri Lanka's policies are equally noteworthy. Although the rice ration program supplied roughly 20 percent of the calorie intake of the lowest income group, it essentially formed an income supplement for higher income groups. And it required 16 percent of the government's total budget (Berg 1979).[79] In 1974, food import costs rose substantially, forcing curtailment of the ration program and contributing to a rising death rate. Directing programs to the needy (particularly childbearing women and children) appears to be the most cost-effective means of improving the nutrition status of the poor. Both the Sri Lanka and Kerala experiences and the theoretical study of Reutlinger and Selowsky (1978) substantiate this view. Further tailoring by subsidizing the low cost coarse grains commonly consumed by the poor can also cut costs without harming the diets of the target groups.[80]

Reutlinger and Selowsky (1978) have measured costs and cost-effectiveness of target group versus general food subsidy programs. They estimate that the cost of target group programs is roughly one to two times the price of the food, whereas general price subsidies run ten times the cost of the food. Food stamp programs appear to be the most cost-effective means of meeting nutritional needs, followed closely by price subsidies. General price subsidies are shown to be roughly five times less cost effective than either of the target group programs mentioned.

The role of household income and economic growth has been discussed in the previous section, and available evidence indicates that in the long term, income and development will have a major impact on nutrition. How development is pursued will determine how and when malnutrition will be considered. A BHN strategy aims at mitigating nutrition and health needs directly in the short run, thereby enhancing income-generating potential and enhancing growth prospects. But to remain financially viable, as well as to maximize results, nutrition interventions should be part of a "package" approach geared to meeting the nutrition and health needs of the poor.

## HEALTH ISSUES

### Introduction

Health status is a good indicator of physical well-being and is an acceptable measure of overall national welfare. Attaining an acceptable health status for the population involves activities in a variety of sectors, in recognition of the complex of factors affecting health. Many of these determinants include the BHN objectives described elsewhere in this chapter. In a sense, an inherently healthy population may indicate that people's basic needs have been met, at least on a minimal level.

A healthy population requires adequate consumption of food, shelter, health care, and education, for all are jointly responsible for good health. The synergistic relationship between health and other factors makes attempts to upgrade health status dependent on improvements in complementary areas. Endogenous factors, such as fertility, health care, education, and housing, can all affect health status directly, but exogenous factors of climate, topology, and social custom determine the extent to which any of these factors contribute to poor health. However, so little detailed information exists on the costs and benefits to health of individual sectoral programs, that we do not really know how critical any particular intervention is to achieving and sustaining adequate health levels. General evidence is available, however, that shows that all these factors can be important and that neglect of a complementary intervention may undermine the effectiveness of specific efforts to ensure a healthy population (Grosse and Perry 1979).

The rationale for investing in health status improvements is both humanitarian and economic. The former is well accepted and is increasingly seen as inextricable from the latter for two reasons. First, health is an investment as well as a consumption good. Health as a consumption good improves the quality of life; as an investment it is an effective means of upgrading productivity. Second, a labor force that is uneducated and undernourished is less skilled, less motivated, and less productive. The quality of the labor force is a function of health status, and given the importance of labor force productivity to economic growth and development, labor force quality emerges as a major issue in the attainment of basic needs (Balassa 1977; ILO 1976).

Because improvements in health status require involvement on a number of fronts, implementing strategies require either costly sectoral programs satisfying a range of needs bearing on health status or programs emphasizing an integrated approach to health care. The very fact that multiple factors determine health status and that health affects other objectives highlights the need to pursue the latter approach of addressing health within a broader BHN development context rather than as a self-contained sector. This is particularly relevant in developing countries where resources are scarce and a substantial level of unmet need exists.

In order to cover the diverse issues related to health, we expand the measures, determinants, and consequences categories used elsewhere in this chapter. The section includes discussions of health problems and of current approaches to delivering health care in rural settings. The additional detail is meant to clarify the importance of and difficulties associated with supplying health care services to the poor in developing countries, for many of the relevant interventions have either been dealt with elsewhere in this chapter or are too complex to discuss in sufficient detail here.

## Measures of Health Status

Health status is a difficult concept to define and equally difficult to measure. Ironically, the most available and relevant measures of health relate to mortality, specifically life expectancy and infant mortality. Morbidity (illness), particularly chronic disease, is difficult to quantify, and systematic measures are not readily available. Other indexes such as per capita calorie consumption and health personnel and facilities per capita are indirect measures of health status, but are less reliable. Although crude, such health statistics as life expectancy and mortality rates provide the only information for determining the extent and magnitude of the (national) health problem in developing countries. Re-

gional, age, and income breakdowns of these data improve their usefulness in a policy context, since such specificity enables the design of policies and programs aimed at those in greatest need. However, as is the
case in most sectors, such data are rarely available in developing countries.

The infant mortality rate (IMR)—the proportion of deaths of children
from birth to age one per 1000 live births—has been widely used as a
proxy for health status because data requirements are minimal, compu-
tation is straightforward, and the magnitude of national health problems
is reflected. Child mortality rates supplement the IMR and often provide
more accurate statistics, as undercounting is less common with children
than with infants.[81]

Causes of high infant and child mortality in developing countries are
associated with inadequate nutrition, unavailability of clean water and
sanitation, and inadequate housing as much as with lack of health care
per se. A child's environment can either foster or discourage survival, and
a newborn infant placed in unhealthy surroundings has not developed
sufficient immunity to ward off disease. Consequently, death rates reflect the condition of the immediate environment and thus indirectly indicate something about household living standards and income.

The crude death rate (CDR)[82] is related to but is less concise than the
IMR because it disregards age-specific mortality reflected in infant and
child mortality rates. Table 2–10 contains infant and crude death rates
for a number of countries. Among the countries in Table 2–10 the CDR
ranges from eight in Thailand to twenty-two in Upper Volta. The range
is small due to a number of factors. The death rate in the United States
is relatively high since a large proportion of the population is concentrated in the older age groups where mortality is high. In developing
countries life expectancy is relatively short, and the populations are
younger. For instance, in Malawi or Chad, a high rate of death in infancy
is balanced by a young, hardy population that has survived infancy and
experiences relatively moderate death rates. On the hand, countries like
Sri Lanka and Thailand have both low infant mortality and young populations (due to previous high rates of population growth) and hence exhibit the lowest death rates. Death rates have fallen substantially since
World War II in all countries, but especially in the LDCs, where adoption of public health measures and introduction of modern medicine (at
least in urban areas) has led to fewer deaths in the younger age groups,
where LDC populations are concentrated.

The lower IMRs in Table 2–10 suggest relatively higher levels of national welfare. In general the IMR is a better indicator of well-being
than the CDR, because as noted above, it takes age distribution into account to some degree and reflects living standards and the level of pre-

**Table 2–10. Rural-Urban Infant Mortality Rates for Available Developing Countries.**

| Countries (IMR Date) | IMR Rates per Thousand | | | 1977 Crude Death Rate per Thousand |
|---|---|---|---|---|
| | Total | Urban | Rural | |
| *Africa* | | | | |
| Chad (1964) | 160 | I34 | 162 | 21 |
| Guinea (1954–1955) | 220 | 190 | 220 | 21 |
| Liberia (1971) | 159 | 126 | 171 | 18 |
| Malawi (1970–1972) | 142 | n.a. | 151 | 20 |
| Rwanda (1970) | 127 | 113 | 128 | 19 |
| Upper Volta (1960–1961) | n.a. | n.a. | 263 | 22 |
| *Asia* | | | | |
| Bangladesh (1969–1974) | 153 | 127 | 156 | 18 |
| India (1970) | 127 | 90 | 136 | 14 |
| Thailand (1974–1975) | 56 | 10 | 64 | 8 |
| *Latin America* | | | | |
| Bolivia (1971–1972) | 161 | 133 | 178 | 15 |
| Dominican Republic (1970–1971) | 99 | 94 | 103 | 9 |
| Honduras (1971–1972) | 117 | 86 | 127 | 12 |
| *Near East* | | | | |
| Afghanistan (1972–1973) | 220 | 143 | 232 | 22 |
| Jordan (1972) | 86 | n.a. | n.a. | 13 |
| Morocco (1972) | 162 | n.a. | n.a. | 13 |

*Source:* U.S. Bureau of the Census (1980); IBRD (1979).
n.a. = not available

and postnatal care available to the high risk groups of childbearing women and infants.

Life expectancy is another commonly used indicator of health status that utilizes age-specific death rates. Life expectancy estimates are derived from complicated life table calculations, which project the probability of survival at any age based on a fixed, artificial population (Shryock and Siegle 1975). In effect, a life table outlines a probable mortality schedule, and the life expectancy calculation simply conveys the average chances of survival.

Life expectancy varies dramatically across countries and age groups due to differences in environment and changes in susceptibility to disease and disability over the life cycle. Disparities in national socioeconomic conditions and health care quality and accessibility produce a range of overall and cohort death rates that can be clearly reflected in life expectancy figures if indicators are provided separately for rural and urban populations—a rarity anywhere.

**Table 2–11. Expectations of Life at Specified Ages for Each Sex[a]**

| Country | Year[b] | 0 | | 1 | | 5 | | 10 | | 15 | | 20 | |
|---|---|---|---|---|---|---|---|---|---|---|---|---|---|
| | | Male | Female | Male | Female | Male | Female | Male | Female | Male | Female | Male | Female |
| Bangladesh | 1970–1975 | 35.8 | 35.8 | | | | | 56.1 | 58.7 | 51.2 | 54.2 | 47.0 | 49.7 |
| Bolivia | 1970–1975 | 45.7 | 47.9 | | | | | 31.0 | 37.0 | | | 26.0 | 32.0 |
| Brazil | 1960–1970 | 57.6 | 61.1 | 34.0 | 40.0 | 60.6 | 63.4 | 56.2 | 62.2 | 52.0 | 57.4 | 47.3 | 52.7 |
| Chad | 1963–1964 | 29.0 | 35.0 | | | 34.0 | 40.0 | 31.0 | 37.0 | | | | |
| Chile | 1969–1970 | 60.5 | 66.0 | 64.9 | 70.1 | 61.4 | 67.0 | 56.2 | 62.2 | 52.0 | 57.4 | 47.3 | 52.7 |
| Colombia | 1970–1975 | 59.2 | 62.7 | | | | | | | | | | |
| Egypt | 1960 | 51.6 | 53.8 | 56.2 | 59.9 | 60.5 | 66 | 56.6 | 62.0 | 52.2 | 57.5 | 47.7 | 52.9 |
| El Salvador | 1960–1961 | 56.5 | 60.4 | 60.7 | 63.9 | 60.8 | 64.2 | 56.8 | 60.2 | 52.2 | 55.6 | 47.9 | 51.2 |
| Gabon | 1960–1961 | 25.0 | 45.0 | 34.0 | 52.0 | 38.0 | 52.0 | 36.0 | 48.0 | | | 29.0 | 41.0 |
| Ghana | 1960 | 37.1 | | 48.0 | | 45.5 | | 43.4 | | 39.4 | | 35.8 | |
| Guatemala | 1963–1965 | 48.3 | 49.7 | 52.5 | 53.6 | 54.4 | 55.8 | 51.3 | 52.8 | 47.2 | 48.6 | 43.2 | 44.6 |
| Haiti | 1970–1975 | 49.0 | 51.0 | | | | | | | | | | |
| India | 1951–1960 | 41.9 | 40.6 | 48.4 | 46.0 | 48.7 | 47.0 | 45.2 | 43.8 | 41.0 | 39.6 | 37.0 | 35.6 |
| Indonesia | 1960 | 47.5 | 47.5 | | | | | | | | | | |
| Jordan | 1959–1963 | 52.6 | 52.0 | 58.2 | 58.2 | 56.7 | 58.5 | 52.7 | 54.4 | 48.2 | 50.1 | 44.1 | 46.0 |
| Kenya | 1969 | 46.9 | 51.2 | 52.6 | 56.6 | 53.8 | 57.1 | 51.0 | 54.1 | 46.7 | 49.1 | 43.0 | 45.7 |
| Liberia | 1971 | 45.8 | 44.0 | 52.1 | 52.7 | 52.1 | 53.7 | 49.0 | 50.3 | 44.3 | 46.9 | 40.8 | 42.7 |
| Malawi | 1970–1972 | 40.9 | 44.2 | 47.9 | 49.2 | 60.8 | 57.6 | 59.9 | 58.0 | 55.0 | 54.9 | 51.9 | 54.5 |

| | | | | | | | | | | | | | |
|---|---|---|---|---|---|---|---|---|---|---|---|---|---|
| Malaysia | 1975 | 65.4 | 70.8 | 66.8 | 71.8 | 63.6 | 68.7 | 59.0 | 64.0 | 54.2 | 59.2 | 49.5 | 54.5 |
| Mauritania | 1971–1973 | 60.7 | 65.3 | 63.8 | 68.0 | 61.3 | 65.8 | 56.5 | 61.1 | 51.7 | 56.3 | 47.0 | 51.6 |
| Morocco | 1970–1975 | 51.4 | 54.5 | | | | | | | | | | |
| Nepal | 1970–1975 | 42.2 | 45.0 | | | | | | | | | | |
| Niger | 1970–1975 | 37.0 | 40.1 | | | | | | | | | | |
| Nigeria | 1965–1966 | 37.2 | 36.7 | 44.5 | 43.2 | 49.3 | 47.3 | 46.6 | 44.7 | 42.9 | 41.2 | 39.2 | 38.1 |
| Pakistan | 1962 | 53.7 | 48.8 | 60.6 | 53.9 | 60.8 | 54.8 | 56.9 | 51.7 | 52.25 | 47.2 | 47.7 | 42.8 |
| Philippines | 1970–1975 | 56.9 | 60.0 | | | | | | | | | | |
| Rwanda | 1970–1975 | 39.4 | 42.6 | | | | | | | | | | |
| Singapore | 1970 | 65.1 | 70.0 | 65.6 | 70.3 | 62.0 | 66.6 | 57.1 | 61.8 | 52.3 | 56.9 | 47.5 | 52.0 |
| Sri Lanka | 1967 | 64.8 | 66.9 | 67.4 | 68.9 | 65.0 | 66.8 | 60.5 | 62.4 | 55.8 | 57.7 | 51.2 | 53.0 |
| Togo | 1961 | 31.6 | 38.5 | 36.4 | 47.9 | 40.01 | 48.2 | 37.4 | 44.3 | 33.8 | 40.4 | 30.3 | 37.8 |
| United Kingdom (England and Wales) | 1974–1976 | 69.6 | 75.8 | | | | | | | | | | |
| United States | 1975 | 68.7 | 76.5 | 68.9 | 76.6 | 65.0 | 72.8 | 60.0 | 67.9 | 55.4 | 63.0 | 50.8 | 58.1 |
| USSR | 1971–1972 | 64.0 | 74.0 | | | | | | | | | | |
| Uruguay | 1963–1964 | 65.5 | 71.6 | 68.0 | 73.7 | 64.4 | 70.1 | 59.5 | 65.2 | 54.6 | 60.3 | 50.0 | 55.5 |
| Zaire | 1970–1975 | 41.9 | 45.1 | | | | | | | | | | |

Source: United Nations (1977).

" Life expectancy is the average number of years of life remaining for persons at each age.

[b] The year(s) upon which the life expectancy figure is based vary but nonetheless provide a rough estimate of life expectancy. Given the general poor quality of the underlying data, this discrepancy should not have a substantial effect on the country's relative position.

Table 2–11 provides an indication of the changes that occur in life expectancy over the life cycle. Of particular note is the consistent rise in life expectancy for all countries from age zero (birth) to age one, implying that surviving the first year of life increases an individual's long-term prospects. Life expectancy drops around age ten in LDCs as children become exposed to new debilitating diseases and continues to fall as people age in both developed and developing countries.[83]

Additional health status indicators are available for some countries—such as population per physician or nursing person, population per hospital bed, and hospital bed occupancy rate. More useful in the developing country context is population per primary health worker, but these figures are available for only a few countries, and definitions of "primary health worker" vary widely. The latter are measures related to hospital care, which caters largely to the upper-income groups that are able to afford the time and fees involved. And the number of per capita health personnel is meaningless unless their distribution is known. From these figures we have no clear idea who is receiving care or if national health status is improving in a given LDC. Hence they are not of particular value unless the health care system is largely hospital and physician based.

Death rates in general, and infant and child mortality rates (CMR) in particular, are the basic measures of health status in developing countries. Comparable data are available for most countries, sometimes supplemented by life expectancy figures. Life expectancy and the IMR and CMR not only are generally reliable indicators of socioeconomic status but are also acceptable substitutes for one another. The CMR is closely related to both life expectancy and infant mortality. Correlations between the CMR and the latter two variables for 1970, using data from twenty-nine developing countries, exhibit coefficients of .91 and .92, respectively. The strongest association between life expectancy and socioeconomic variables using the same sample of LDCs was literacy with a correlation coefficient of .81.

Similar efforts by Grosse and Perry (1979), Berg (1979), and Hicks (1979) substantiate this relationship, as indicated in Table 2–12. These statistically significant, simple correlations point up the substitutability

Table 2–12. Correlations of Life Expectancy and Literacy

| Life Expectancy | Literacy |
| --- | --- |
| Lewis | .81 |
| Grosse and Perry (1979) | .88 |
| Berg (1979) | .91 |
| Hicks (1979) | .96 |

among the health measures and their importance and relevance as indicators of socioeconomic status in developing countries. Taking this one step further, health indicators seem to accurately reflect advances in areas that indirectly touch on health; hence, they reflect living standards as well as health status.

**Data Problems.** Although the health statistics described in Table 2–12 are heavily relied upon for a range of purposes, their accuracy is open to question. These measurements only convey orders of magnitude, because collection of complete and accurate statistics is rare even in developed countries, and vital registration is generally incomplete in LDCs. A major drawback of LDC statistics in general is lack of rural-urban breakdowns and other distributional indicators. For although national health status may appear sound, regions or pockets may belie the national statistics. Sample surveys have shown rural areas to have lower life expectancy levels and considerably higher infant mortality rates than their urban counterparts, and since data collection efforts are often concentrated in the more accessible and affluent urban areas, upward urban biases are not uncommon.

Rural people are by and large outside the public health system and have neither the desire nor the incentive to report births and deaths.[84] Even those who do have access to services neglect to report deaths and often overlook the need to report births, particularly if the baby is stillborn or if infant deaths are a common occurrence. In short, there is no incentive to register births or deaths,[85] and consequently, vital statistics are of questionable validity.

The only reliable means of determining health is on a community basis, but such an approach is extremely costly and hence somewhat uncommon. Some microlevel anthropological studies have been undertaken that provide insights into comunity health, but the results tend to be location specific and to involve small samples.

## Health Problems in LDCs

Morbidity (illness) is a way of life in much of the developing world. Parasitic and other tropical infectious diseases are common, and simple illnesses such as blindness from Vitamin A deficiency or dehydration and death from common bacterias or cholera are equally visible. The complex and simple exist simultaneously, often causing long-run chronic conditions that debilitate but do not cause death.

A number of LDC-specific factors inhibit preventive measures, facilitate disease transmission, and retard prompt, effective medical solutions.

Poverty, squalid living conditions, unsanitary personal habits, limited public health programs and services, and ignorance all contribute to an unhealthy environment. A clear understanding of disease transmission provides a starting point for understanding how and where preventive and curative programs should be established.

The World Bank (IBRD 1975) has broken disease transmission into four categories:

1. Fecally transmitted—typhoid, intestinal parasites and diarrheal diseases;
2. airborne—tuberculosis, pneumonia, diphtheria, meningitis, measles;
3. waterborne—infectious and parasitic disease; and
4. vector-borne (animal or insect transmitted)—malaria, trypanosomiasis (sleeping sickness), onchocerciasis (river blindness), schistosomiasis.

Prevalence of these diseases and disease categories shows an irregular pattern geographically due to varying environmental conditions and social customs. Salient examples are discussed below within the context of specific disease categories.

The World Bank estimates that fecally borne diseases[86] are the most prevalent in developing countries and frequently represent a major cause of mortality among young children and of chronic infirmity and debility among adults. Communities lacking safe water supplies or sanitation facilities commonly experience a high incidence of these diseases, susceptibility being enhanced by substandard housing and unsanitary habits. These conditions are exacerbated by insufficient incomes and inadequate information and education on disease transmission.

Airborne diseases also show a high prevalence and incidence in developing countries[87] and are associated with cramped and unsanitary housing, lack of public health services (particularly immunizations), and poor personal hygiene practices.

Water- and animal-borne disease prevalence is geographically determined; some areas suffer severely, while others are left untouched.[88] Where they occur, vector-borne diseases present severe problems in terms of high morbidity and mortality. Susceptibility to animal-borne diseases is associated with substandard living conditions (for example, absence of screens on dwellings in tropical climates), proximity of breeding grounds to human communities, and limited means of prevention. Infested areas are difficult to control and involve substantial costs. Costs are particularly high as infested regions are often rendered uninhabitable by man or beast (see Taylor and Hall 1967).[89]

## Determinants of Health

A number of factors seemingly unrelated to health status combine to determine health status. Most sources of disease in LDCs can be traced to factors directly associated with poverty: cases in point are the lack of sanitation facilities and substandard housing common in most low-income LDCs.

The linkages observed between behavior patterns and ill-health can be traced to low achievement in other areas—notably to lack of education, high fertility, malnutrition, and an unhealthy environment. The interrelationships among most of these factors are discussed extensively elsewhere in this chapter, but their specific relationships to health are discussed here.

**Education.** Uneducated in the causes and control of disease and illiterate, the LDC poor are ill equipped to deal with their own health problems. General education helps to dispel socially grounded (superstitious) beliefs in the causes of disease and encourages experimentation with new health services and, through increases in literacy, dissemination of written material to improve health knowledge and practices (Bryant 1969).

Functionally designed education programs (i.e., to health) are useful in improving habits that promote health.[90] Health outreach programs are particularly relevant for the poor, whose lack of knowledge and low incomes perpetuate poor health (and nutrition), which in turn has implications for income generating ability.

**Fertility.** Fertility bears directly on health through the ill effect of constant pregnancy on the health and mortality of childbearing women and their children. High parity (number of births) is associated with abnormally high levels of maternal mortality.[91] Numerous closely spaced births deplete a woman's strength, endangering her and her children's health and jeopardizing future pregnancies. Furthermore, lack of pre- and postnatal care increases the incidence of infant mortality and contributes to high parity (see population section). In order to encourage smaller families, family-planning programs have been established to make contraceptives available. Dissemination of family-planning services has traditionally been accomplished via the health system, and the absence of health care infrastructure inhibits effective dissemination of contraceptive information and services (Butz and Habicht 1976).

**Nutrition.** Malnutrition is a major contributor to morbidity and mortality, especially among children. For instance, Puffer and Serrano's (1971) work in Latin America showed malnutrition to be a major direct and/or contributing cause of mortality among children. Table 2–13 indicates the percent of deaths among children under age five attributable to malnutrition both as a primary and associated factor. According to the data in Table 2–13, malnutrition poses a more serious threat in rural areas and is generally an associated rather than a primary cause of death among children. Neither is surprising given lower incomes and erratic (seasonal) food supplies in rural (and semiurban) areas, Furthermore, mortality from severe malnutrition is less common than the milder, debilitating forms of malnutrition that underlie the "associated causes" of death in Table 2–13 (see nutrition section).

Inadequate quantities of food and insufficient nutrient intake combine

**Table 2–13. Malnutrition as Primary or Associated Cause in Deaths of Children under Five, Selected Latin American Countries, 1971**

| Area | Percent of Deaths Caused by Malnutrition | | |
| | Primary Cause | Associated Cause | Primary or Associated Cause |
|---|---|---|---|
| Argentina | | | |
| San Juan Province | | | |
| San Juan | 3 | 37 | 40 |
| Suburban | 9 | 39 | 48 |
| Rural | 8 | 39 | 47 |
| Brazil | | | |
| Recife | 6 | 60 | 66 |
| São Paulo | 6 | 45 | 51 |
| Ribeirão Preto | 2 | 67 | 69 |
| Colombia | | | |
| Cali | 16 | 40 | 56 |
| Cartagena | 15 | 44 | 59 |
| Medellin | 11 | 51 | 62 |
| Jamaica: Kingston | 6 | 32 | 38 |
| Bolivia: La Paz | 4 | 41 | 45 |
| Mexico: Monterrey | 4 | 48 | 52 |
| Chile: Santiago | 6 | 39 | 45 |
| El Salvador | | | |
| San Salvador | 9 | 49 | 58 |
| Rural | 14 | 44 | 58 |
| Average of all areas | 8 | 46 | 54 |

Source: Pan American Health Organization (1971).

to create severe nutrition and health problems, but the direction of causality is not well understood. Morbidity, particularly infection, prevents the absorption of sufficient nutrients; at the same time malnutrition weakens the body's defenses against disease. Consequently, mortality is far more common among malnourished children, and nutritional deficiencies are correlated with disease incidence. The effect of malnutrition among adults is less well understood and has been explored in the section on nutrition. However, malnutrition cannot be overlooked in provision of health care, for quantity and quality of food figure prominently in determining health status in LDCs.[92]

**Environment.** The environment in which people live determines to a great extent their susceptibility and exposure to disease. And custom or ignorance can reinforce the detrimental effects of the environment. For example, water infested with bacteria and parasites is rarely if ever boiled; food is left to sit uncovered, often accessible to animals and insects; and personal cleanliness is a problem, particularly since water is often hauled from distant locations and used sparingly. Furthermore, ramshackle housing allow mosquitos, flies, and other disease carriers easy access to their human victims; lack of sanitation facilities encourages transmission of fecal-borne disease; and unhygienic personal habits heighten the probability of acquiring these diseases.

Hence, custom, environment, and low income and education combine to encourage high disease prevalence. Efforts to improve health must address the multiple sectoral determinants as well as the unhealthy environmental conditions of the poor.

In sum, ill-health is attributable to numerous interrelated factors that encourage disease incidence, the most salient causes of morbidity being high fertility, malnutrition, and unsanitary conditions. From the discussion above, the role of unsanitary conditions emerges as probably the major factor in the spread of disease. Low incomes (and unemployment) exacerbate the situation; and little education, poor health education (including family planning and nutrition information), and lack of clean water and sanitation facilities make interventions to reverse the pattern of high morbidity and mortality extremely difficult and costly (IBRD 1976; Barlow 1979; Correa 1975).

## Economic Consequences of Health Investments

Mitigating human suffering is a worthy basis for providing health care, but a high incidence and prevalence of chronic disease has clear economic implications as well. Research in developed countries indicates a substantial loss in productivity due to chronic disease (see Barlow 1979: esp. 56–58). In the LDCs the effect is less documented if more obvious.

Mushkin (1962) has summarized the effects of illness on productivity into three categories—(1) deaths (loss of workers), (2) disability (loss of working time), and (3) debility (loss of productive capacity while at work). All three are common in developing societies, and health promotion serves to mitigate the prevalence of all three.

Studies in LDCs have produced conflicting results on the effect of debility and disability on productivity. Part of the discrepancy is due to differences in samples, methodologies, and disease prevalence. However, it is clear that chronic disease and malnutrition inhibit both working and learning capacity among children and adults (see section on nutrition). For example, the high absenteeism associated with chronic illness negatively affects children's academic performance and labor's productivity (Caldwell et al. 1978). Thus, the indirect evidence in developing countries points to a heavy cost in terms of human capital when health needs are neglected. Further evidence of the importance of preventive health measures on economic output comes from assessments of public health programs, which have consistently shown a propensity to improve productivity in a cost-effective manner in both developed and developing countries (Hill and Sanders 1960; Feldstein, Piot, and Sunderesan 1973).

The generally poor productivity performance of the labor force in developing countries stems largely from low skill and education levels and poor health. The extent to which potential productivity becomes actual is a function of the availability of technology and capital and other inputs. Nonetheless, improvements in income and welfare are seriously hampered by low productive capacity and substandard learning ability.

How much of an effect improved health status has on productivity is difficult to measure. Ram and Schultz (1979) have found that in India roughly 28 percent of agricultural productivity (or output increases) can be explained by reductions in mortality (which reflect improved health), and a 1 percent drop in mortality results in a 0.3 percent increase in labor productivity or output. Although crude, this study represents one of the few attempts to quantify the direct relationship between health and productivity.

Documented experiences of industrialized countries and results from research in LDCs indicate firm linkages between health and productivity and between increased productivity and macroeconomic growth. It seems likely, despite contradictory findings, that eradication of chronic, debilitating diseases will have a positive effect on productivity, welfare, and economic growth.[93] And although we know that health does have a positive effect on development, the extent of the effect, particularly relative to other inputs (such as technology or training), has not been quantified.

High costs of debility in terms of lost household resources also exist. Lack of health care encourages high fertility (with high child mortality parents often overcompensated to ensure survival of the desired number of children), leading to short birth intervals associated with inhibited physical and mental development (Caldwell et al. 1978). High fertility also implies stretching income further, perpetuating the cycle of low nutrition, poor health, and high fertility. Investment in a large number of children, a high proportion of whom die, is a waste of physical and capital resources. Furthermore, a malnourished child requires more food than does a well-nourished child to reach and sustain similar growth and development levels. These factors constitute a waste of household resources, implying a reduction in welfare of the family and, in the aggregate, of the society.

Productivity concerns extend the need for health-augmenting activities beyond humanitarian criteria. At the heart of decisionmaking is whether investments in human capital through various mechanisms that bear on health status (health, education, sanitation) make economic sense. The economic effects of not investing in health include (1) loss of labor and labor productivity; (2) reduction in land resources due to infestation by animal vectors of disease; (3) inhibited learning abilities and impeded skill acquisition; and (4) waste of economic resources through unproductive investments in children who die and expenditures on children and adults who consume beyond their normal needs because of disease. Health care—broadly defined to include basic health services (especially for mothers and children), family planning, nutrition and health education, and information—can be instrumental in mitigating these economic losses.

Low health status impedes achievement of basic needs objectives both as a component of core needs and as a mechanism for upgrading human capital. If learning and working are inhibited by poor health, agrarian and industrial labor productivity and incomes are affected. Hence, the link between health (and nutrition) and productivity is of fundamental importance in efforts to improve welfare and spur economic growth.

## Primary Health Care Delivery Experience

Possibly the most critical determinant of health status in LDCs is income. As outlined in the introductory section, the concept of primary health care (PHC)[94] as an acceptable health priority in LDCs is a relatively recent one. In the early 1960s, donors and governments alike became aware of the total absence of reliable health care in rural areas, where the bulk of the poor live. This lack of facilities and trained health workers was particularly critical in low-income LDCs where poor communications and transportation virtually isolated rural people from health care deliverers (i.e., physicians). Furthermore, health complaints of the (rural) poor tended to be concentrated on a few relatively simple medical problems. Hence, high cost physician-based care appeared inappropriate on social as well as economic grounds. Development of the primary health care concept was a response to these realizations.

Efforts over the last decade or so to deliver PHC have highlighted the preferred means for delivering health care and the necessity of including particular kinds of services in the PHC package. Less information has been garnered on the cost effectiveness of various PHC approaches and on realistic evaluation methods.

Evidence from health care programs in Narangwal, India; Lampang, Thailand; and rural Guatemala, among many others, indicates the necessity of delivering a range of integrated services, including basic preventive and curative care as well as family planning, nutrition, and health education services. It has also become clear that nurses, midwives, community health aides, and other paraphysicians are best suited for delivering most primary health care services. Doctors are in short supply and are overqualified for most of the services required in rural areas.[95] For as discussed earlier, the bulk of LDC health problems are simple ailments stemming largely from ignorance, poverty, and the environment.

A hierarchical system of health care providers and facilities has come to be accepted as the most efficient method of delivering PHC. Paraphysicians generally deliver services on the village level, often covering a number of communities and providing essential preventive and curative care.[96] These entail immunizations, family-planning services (depending on local and national sensitivities), basic maternal and child health care services, nutrition information, and diagnoses and treatment of diseases common to the locale, as well as simple illnesses such as diarrhea and dehydration (a particularly common complaint especially among infants and children). Complicated illnesses that the paraphysician cannot diagnose and/or treat are referred to a health center where a doctor is either in residence or available at certain times. The kingpin of this hierarchical referral system is a regional hospital serving a number of health centers.

A major component of local care is outreach services, achieved in various ways—periodic home visits, scheduled rotation of clinics, or health promoters scattered in small communities to encourage use of health care.[97] The overall importance of establishing a PHC outreach program varies, but it has proven to be essential for encouraging consumption and for overcoming fears of the unfamiliar health care services.

Implementation of PHC is still under experimentation, and although practices such as those described above are becoming more common, a recipe approach is unrealistic. The sociocultural milieu and economic constraints of individual countries and regions dictate how a program should be structured, and country-specific experiences only provide guidelines and highlight potential pitfalls. Opportunities for replication of PHC programs exist, but only to a limited degree, since local and national circumstances vary so considerably.

## Policy and Financing Implications

Health status is thus determined by a multitude of factors, and policy development must recognize and respond accordingly. The array of factors involved and the extent of unmet need in terms of geography and subpopulation in the LDCs makes policy design a formidable task. However, adoption of a BHN strategy provides an ideal mechanism for promoting health, especially if an integrated approach is chosen, because of economics of scale in implementation and linkages in planning and policy activities.

The need for government involvement in promoting health is evident. Rural areas of LDCs are sparsely (if at all) served by health care. Private sector involvement[98] in providing modern health care is minimal since profit potential is limited, although even in most developed countries, health care is a joint public-private responsibility. Public health measures such as immunizations and sanitation (particularly in urban areas) are campaigns normally initiated and funded by government, mainly because of the externalities[99] involved. Immunizations benefit communities as well as individuals; water supplies and sanitation are usually public due to the indivisibility in consumption. And since vector control is a costly venture that benefits entire populations, it is a cost that governments must absorb, for individuals are reluctant to invest in programs that allow "free riders" [100] (Mushkin 1962).

The previous sections briefly outlined the major problems facing the LDCs in attempting to provide their populations with adequate health care. A package approach delivering low cost[101] primary health care is the preferred means to delivering health services, particularly in rural settings of developing contries. The essential components of a PHC system include (1) basic preventative and curative care that can be delivered by community health workers; (2) delivery of integrated services, including nutrition, environmental sanitation, family planning, and health education at a minimum, preferably with some outreach services; (3) careful health planning and evaluation to ensure efficient allocation of resources and maximization of access; (4) sound management and supervision; and (5) community participation.

Government commitment to PHC is of critical importance to successful program implementation, particularly given the relatively weak positon of most ministries of health. The WHO Conference on Primary Health Care in Alma Ata, USSR, in 1978 saw a pledge by donors and LDC governments to renew efforts to provide health care to all citizens. The adopted slogan—"health for all by the year 2000"—is admirable, if impossible, but the conference served to reconfirm and highlight the importance of primary health care in developing countries and provided a forum for exchanges of experience and ideas on delivery systems. In addition, the conference emphasized the importance of addressing health within the context of nonhealth programs, thereby reaffirming the BHN concept and broadening the approach to improving health.

Progress on implementation has been substantial over the past decade or so and will no doubt be extended in the 1980s. However, issues of efficiency have been inadequately addressed, specifically those related to evaluation, costs, and planning. Building evaluation and cost analysis into planned programs can allow adequate assessment of the individual health care delivery program. With few notable exceptions (Lampang, Thailand; Narangwal, India; rural Guatemala; and Danfa, Ghana being obvious examples) current programs are ill equipped to produce useful feedback. Those that have generated useful information have been high cost pilot endeavors, which limits their replicability.[102] Analytic approaches are few and are generally geared to developed country data and technology (i.e., sophisticated computers requiring highly trained programmers). Simple recording of fixed and variable costs—excluding research costs—would be an important first step. Evaluation can take a number of forms, but has persistently focused on supply factors, largely ignoring questions of demand, increased access, community impact, and cost effectiveness.

Planning efforts bear some similarity to evaluation: generally little planning is undertaken, but where it exists it is done on an elaborate scale. Methodology in the developing country context is minimal, although work by Grosse et al. (1979) appears promising for developing appropriate means for rigorous health planning. Planning, though, is a difficult task, one many developed countries are still grappling with. But some level of evaluation and planning is essential to efficient financing and effective use of primary health care.[103]

Financing of "low cost" primary care is a substantial burden for many LDCs, particularly those at the bottom end of the income scale. Table 2–2 provides comparisons of per capita expenditure and percent of the budget devoted to health, but as discussed, they are poor indicators of health care quality and the equity of access. Expenditures may reflect costs of sophisticated urban care rather than basic nationwide health services used by the poor, and it is unclear whether investment or recurrent costs are involved in the computations. Country-by-country examination is requried to obtain this kind of specificity.

Donors have been particularly active in assistance for development of health care systems and construction of necessary infrastructure, but substantially less involved in financing recurrent (operating) costs. As costs rise, service quality and quantity suffer without support from donors. The burden of recurrent costs has recently been recognized as a development problem in general, and it is to be hoped that efforts to help countries alleviate some of the mounting annual costs will emerge as a result. An encouraging aspect of external finance is the growing emphasis on health within the basic human needs context. Donors embracing BHN strategies (ILO, AID, IBRD, for example) have increased health budgets. The World Bank has recently established a specific health program, supplementing its health-related activities in family planning and nutrition. The U.S. Agency for International Development has consistently increased its health budget over the past few years, although overall budget levels have experienced only modest increases. (See Table 2–3 for recent budget levels of donors.)

Increased commitments to health, spurred by Alma Ata and BHN considerations, bode well for future funding of health care, but issues of total cost, as well as the cost effectiveness of particular approaches, persists. Continued progress in smoothing bottlenecks in delivery can be expected, and increased access for the poor should also occur. But the complex issues determining health clearly pose an impediment that will inhibit even concerted efforts to improve health. The basic needs framework is particularly useful, and as a BHN strategy evolves, some of the interrelationships can be more effectively addressed. The issue of how health status can be upgraded most efficiently and effectively remains a challenge to LDCs and donors alike.

## NOTES

1. Education as a sector has been excluded due to space constraints; however, its importance in achieving improvements in welfare has been addressed within the context of each of the included sectors. It should be stressed that education is of paramount interest in encouraging health and nutrition improvements and family size reduction. In addition, increases in education, either formal or nonformal (such as education, health, agricultural or family planning delivered by outreach workers) is one of, if not the most important factor in achieving basic needs.

2. In 1973 the U.S. Congress enacted the "New Directions" legislation, requiring A.I.D. to focus its efforts on helping the LDC poor more directly. Amendments to the Foreign Assistance Act in 1978 called for a "program in support of countries which pursue development strategies designed to meet basic human needs and achieve self-sustained growth with equity." See the IBRD's 1980 *World Development Report* for a restatement of the World Bank's objectives.
3. These are essentially the basic needs put forward by the ILO, with the addition of family planning.
4. We shall use the terms "training," "instruction," and "education" interchangeably, as all represent education in the broadest sense, all are in short supply in LDCs, and all are of equal importance to development objectives.
5. Urban areas are rapidly attracting rural migrants, swelling the "urban poor" population, and placing increasing pressure on existing services. Although urban poverty is, and will continue to be, a pressing development issue, services are far more likely to be available there than they are in rural areas. Furthermore, existence of greater demand will encourage governments to provide services; such leverage is rarely possible in rural areas.
6. Demand for these services differs across countries, incomes, and cultures. For example, if schooling is a high family priority, parents will send their children to school, and may be willing to finance books and supplies; if education is not perceived to be a priority, even free schooling will not be consumed. It cannot be said that low-income groups don't demand any of these services; many do, but it cannot be taken for granted.
7. Jointness of supply, implying that a given unit is indivisible, and external economies, where exclusion of any individual (citizen) is impossible, characterize public goods. See Head (1974) for a detailed explanation of public goods and related topics.
8. A good example of a merit good in the developing country context are food supplement programs that encourage consumption of more nutritious foods. See Leipziger and Lewis (1977) for a discussion of merit goods in a BHN context.
9. In rural areas, perverse effects can occur where increased output of nutritious food is sold and the family subsists on inadequate, low-nutrient foods. In effect, the opportunity cost of consumption is too high and consequently nutrition suffers. As discussed below, however, a considerable proportion of, but not all, additional income is used for food.
10. We are also assuming here that BHN investments will eventually generate the income to enable families to purchase services, and that public provision of many services can be phased out. An exception is health services which generally is a joint public-private effort.
11. Traditionally, planners have largely limited their concern to the fixed costs, since these required considerable external funding and technical assistance. However, in the past decade the potentially enormous burden of recurrent costs has been realized and is beginning to be addressed. See Heller (1978).
12. A recent paper by Gwatkin, Wilcox, and Wray (1979) reviews the completed health field experiments in eight countries.
13. A major factor in cost of living is the medical doctor's salaries. See Robinson (1979) for relative physician pay scales in LDCs.
14. A major limitation of the project figures concern economies of scale; e.g., a project for the whole country will require a substantially greater investment since it is done on such a large scale that the economies made possible by a relatively small, regional program are no longer applicable.

15. Underlying the selected optimal interventions is extensive analysis that identified the most efficient mix of services. Unfortunately, family planning has not been included in the analysis. See Grosse et al. (1979) for further discussion.
16. See the nutrition and health sections for discussion of the importance of the crude death rate as an indicator of well-being.
17. However, this phenomenon may be due to factors associated with rising incomes rather than the income increases themselves. As discussed later, uneducated, poor families tend to have greater trust in traditional healers, and they are reluctant to embrace "modern" medical care without justification. One of the more compelling incentives for using public facilities is low fees; hence subsidized services should work to encourage usage at lower levels of income.
18. Some of the discrepancy, particularly in the case of India, is due to local (or state) responsibility for the financing of health care.
19. See health section.
20. One particular population trend in AID's population policy, for example, is the deemphasis on census and vital statistics data collection, and the shifting of funds toward improving motivation for and delivery of family planning services. This response to changing circumstances is indicative of the kinds of policy changes made by decision-makers in responding to changing LDC needs.
21. Although a high rate of population growth may impede economic growth, it can reflect a rational choice on a household level.
22. In Kenya, where roughly 30 percent of the national budget is allocated to education, the education requirements of a population growing at 4 percent per year will stymie government's attempt to increase the minimum amount of free schooling available to all children. Even if an increase were accomplished, quality as well as other competing services might well suffer.
23. See Demeny (1979) for an excellent critique of this "new" trend in fertility decline.
24. Rate of population growth is defined as the rate of national increase adjusted for net immigration and emigration.
25. Crude birth rate is defined as the number of live births per year per 1000 of population.
26. A related measure is age-specific fertility, the number of live births per age cohort of women over a given time period.
27. Middle-income countries are countries with annual per capita income above U.S. $300 in 1977 (IBRD 1979).
28. Even among the MICs, there is considerable disparity in CDRs. Those above $700 GNP per capita tend to have CDRs closer to the developed countries. Those at the lower end are closer to the low-income country average.
29. Decreases in mortality in LDCs mean primarily a drop in infant mortality, as life expectancy tends to respond more slowly than mortality to development advances. Infant mortality rate is the annual deaths of infants zero to twelve months per 1000 live births during the same year. Though often used, this measure tends to be an extremely rough estimate since many infant births and deaths are underreported in LDCs, particularly in rural areas. (See section on health for further elaboration.)
30. The dependency ratio is defined as the number of persons of fourteen years or under, plus sixty-five years or over (largely a nonissue in most LDCs, as life expectancy is usually below age sixty-five), divided by the productive population, defined as those between age fifteen and sixty-four years.
31. The age at which children become a net bonus to the family, particularly in rural areas, varies, but an accepted rule of thumb is fourteen years. Prior to that age children often help around the house, but they consume more than they produce.

32. Population doubling is approximately 69 (log 2) divided by the population growth rate.

33. The extent of a nation's population problem is also an inverse function of natural resource endowments. For example, those countries with extensive mineral deposits will be less constrained by high rates of population growth than will those with limited resources. Hence, a high rate of population growth in Chad may pose more serious difficulties to development than a high base population in a resource-rich country like Indonesia.

34. A food-exporting country like Nepal will soon be importing food as the population increases and forces consumption of previously exported rice. Kenya, with a population growth rate of 4 percent in 1979, will double its population in less than eighteen years. All available arable land is under cultivation, and farmers are moving into arid and semiarid regions of the country where yields are lower and the soil more fragile. Kenya cannot escape importing food (and therefore placing additional strains on foreign exchange earnings, leading, ceteris paribus, to reduction of other imports) in the near future, for land will simply not feed the rapidly expanding population.

35. See Richard Rhoda (1979), Findley (1977), and Findley and Orr (1978) for good surveys of the literature and Todaro (1969) for the classical economic rationale for migration.

36. This effect can be mitigated through concurrent LDC government policies stressing labor-intensive growth strategies. This has not necessarily been the case in the past; however, the BHN approach may encourage greater emphasis on labor force development, thus making labor-intensive investments a more attractive option.

37. Fertilizers have mitigated this problem somewhat in some countries, but the use of fertilizers is not a viable long-run solution given oil price increases and the scarcity of other fertilizer inputs. Other means will have to be found to regenerate or preserve agricultural land. High yield crops have reduced land pressure, but this requires additional capital that may not be available.

38. There is not a clear distinction among these factors, however. Births are the result of an implicit (or explicit) decision based on these kinds of considerations.

39. Of particular note are Kerala (state of India) and Sri Lanka, both of which have population growth rates below 2 percent. India's national population growth rate is above 2 percent, and countries with per capita incomes comparable to Sri Lanka's tend to exhibit much higher population growth (see Table 2–4).

40. The order in which the variables are listed bears no relationship to their individual importance, since different variables tend to exhibit greater causality in different settings and under application of different analytic techniques.

41. This phenomena is often referred to as the "infant survival hypothesis."

42. This implies that families may have an economic cost-benefit ratio that is unfavorable, but this ignores certain qualitative benefits.

43. Briefly, the controversy centers around the relative benefits of supply (contraceptive availability) and demand (behavior/attitude toward contraceptive use) factors. Supply proponents believe contraceptive inundation to be the only means to reduce fertility; the demand side of the debate asserts that only development factors affect fertility levels (see Mauldin and Berelson [1978] for discussion of this complex issue).

44. A few studies have attempted to estimate the costs of births averted through family programs; most notable is the work of Enke (1966).

45. A good example is manpower planning, which relies heavily on accurate information on population growth and national health and nutrition status to ensure learning capability and to effectively meet long-term labor force needs. The size of the dependent

population (those under age fifteen) will determine if adequate health and education services can be supplied; in the event that population growth outstrips government resources, manpower needs may well go unfulfilled and unemployment among the unskilled develop or persist.

46. Abuses have occurred in the past, such as the much heralded forced sterilization program in India in the later 1970s. Elimination of health services in the interests of controlling population growth has been suggested by some policymakers. But, both approaches generally prove detrimental in the long run; such proposals stem from narrow, short-run perspectives that focus on reducing fertility per se, rather than on enhancing social and individual welfare.

47. Little hard evidence exists on the actual impact of incentives, but the few studies that do exist imply a strong relationship between incentives and lowered fertility (see Muscat and Ridker 1973; and IGCC 1976, for examples of incentive schemes).

48. Kwashiorkor occurs primarily in infants and children and is primarily associated with a diet low in protein; generally other factors are involved, including infections, which exacerbate nutrition deficiency. Marasmus stems from a grossly inadequate diet and exhibits itself in severe wasting of muscle and subcutaneous fat and stunted growth (Jelliffe 1966).

49. Specifically, clinical assessments look for abnormalities in hair quality and color, facial form and pigmentation, eye and teeth conditions, skin texture, muscle mass, and skeletal formation. However, it is extremely difficult to diagnose certain illnesses, due to the fact that different standards are applicable in different settings. Standards are generally measures based on a given, but not necessarily a representative, population. "Standards" are often inapplicable to the population under analysis, and symptoms can be misleading or not apparent to the clinician.

50. Anthropometric measures to determine nutritional status vary on the basis of physical size and composition at a given age. Weight is a straightforward technique, but accuracy in measurement is essential. Linear measurements use body length (height) and circumference of head and chest as indicators of growth and development. Substandard height and weight in children reflect current and/or chronic protein-calorie malnutrition. Small head circumference implies a history of malnutrition. The soft tissues (muscle and fat) vary most with current protein-calorie deficiencies. A tricep skin fold is commonly used to measure the degree of subcutaneous fat on the body; arm circumference size identifies poor muscle development or muscle wasting.

51. In rural areas a string has been used to measure arms, chest, and head circumference as a simple means of determining past or present malnutrition.

52. The prevalence of malnutrition among children leads to considerable nutritional disparity among children of a given age, making diagnosis almost impossible, especially for chronic malnutrition, where height for age is the principle measure.

53. Biochemical measures are useful in diagnosing protein, iron, and iodine deficiencies, but are often of limited usefulness since they cannot account and adjust for body stores.

54. This section has drawn heavily on Jelliffe (1966), a detailed source on all topics covered here.

55. Control groups also exhibited drops in infant mortality, but by small amounts. One drawback of these studies is their generally small sample size. However, it does illustrate the applicability of the IMR as an indicator of nutrition status.

56. An additional problem is the variation in nutritional needs. The amount of energy expended determines calorie requirements, but this cannot easily be taken into account in national level data.

57. These data do not take into account issues of storage capacity, intra- and inter-country transportation facilities, and household level factors such as health status and food preparation methods, all of which affect the usefulness of agricultural output.

58. Hawthorne effect refers to changes in subject behavior when under observation, implying unrepresentative information.

59. Both CES and FCS have been conducted on community and national levels in various LDCs. The ILO has been instrumental in the collection of income and consumption data in conjunction with their efforts to construct consumer price indexes for various countries. These surveys have been largely urban based and have stressed expenditures rather than food quantity, although the latter has not been totally neglected. In cooperation with national governments, the Food and Agriculture Organization has conducted a few FCSs; notable among them are recent surveys in Brazil and Tunisia.

60. The problem with this logical approach relates to Graham's (1979) concern with the difficulty in digesting these high bulk crops.

61. Another reason for this emphasis is cost of production; protein consumed by an undernourished individual is converted to calories in the body, and the beneficial effect of the protein is lost. Such use of expensive protein for bulk (calories) is therefore a costly misallocation of resources.

62. Increased calorie production can result in stunted, overweight children, due to a "balanced" deficit of protein and calories caused by the bulkiness and poor digestibility of their diet (Graham 1979).

63. Other national policies affecting nutrition include food supplement subsidies, ration programs, and school feeding programs, which have had a generally positive effect on nutrition status. These policy issues are discussed later in this section.

64. Premature aging among high parity women is extremely common in the LDCs, due to poor health care, malnutrition, and repeated childbearing.

65. Breast-feeding practices are also strongly influenced by behavioral factors, which affects fertility since breast feeding acts as a natural contraceptive. High market demand for female labor (increased value of a woman's time), easily available contraceptives and weaning foods, and a ready supply of substitutes for breast feeding tend to negatively affect breast-feeding practices (Butz 1977).

66. As mentioned earlier, this tends to be a short-run phenomena. The effect of prolonged lactation and the long-term realization of increased child survival will work to offset improvements in fecundity (Delgado et al. 1978).

67. The usefulness of this figure is primarily indicative, since elasticities undoubtedly vary by expenditure item and by income group; hence, the regression results merely provide orders of magnitude.

68. The projections in Table 2–9 assume a constant rate of income growth, disallowing setbacks and ignoring the effects of external shocks such as worldwide recession and/or excessive oil price increases. The figures also presume adequate, domestic supplies of food that will keep pace with population increases.

69. See Jane Rubey (1976) for an extensive annotated bibliography on "Malnutrition, Learning and Behavior" that covers the major findings of this multidisciplinary field.

70. Small head circumference is associated with a past incidence of malnutrition; current malnutrition is indicated by stunted growth.

71. Learning impairments and poor education performance stem from (1) high absenteeism, general apathy, and lack of motivation toward learning; (2) interference with critical periods of learning and mental development; and (3) personality change (Cravioto and DeLicardie 1973). Apathy is symptomatic of an inadequate diet, and the

morbidity attributable to poor nutrition contributes to poor school attendance (Birch and Richardson 1972; Freeman et al. 1977).

72. Reversibility of physical and mental stunting is related to duration and timing (age), partly because malnutrition at "critical periods" impairs full brain development, which results in fewer brain cells.

73. See Sorkin (1976) for a review of some rather dated but still relevant studies on the effect of nutrition on worker productivity.

74. These analyses are plagued by poor data and statistical problems, but represent the best existing information on the subject.

75. Nine Latin American countries (Argentina, Brazil, Chile, Colombia, Ecuador, Honduras, Mexico, Peru, and Venezuela) were included in the analysis; similar results for ten developed countries indicates no effect on GNP growth from improvements in nutrition.

76. These estimates are particularly misleading in countries that show adequate food supplies. "Pockets" of malnutrition in food surplus countries can (and often do) reach 40 percent of the population. This is especially relevant in the middle income LDCs (Reutlinger 1977).

77. Isenman (1980) notes that sharp curtailment of food supplies and concomitant price increases in the world food shortfall year of 1974 resulted in a significant rise in mortality.

78. Sri Lanka had a literacy rate of 78 percent in 1974 and an infant mortality rate of forty-five per thousand in 1975. Both are closer to rates reported by middle-income LDCs.

79. For comparative purposes, Berg (1979) reports that the fraction of budgetary expenditure allocated for food subsidies is 21 percent, Egypt; 19 percent, Korea; and 12 percent, Morocco. However, the only other food subsidy program to be carefully analyzed is that of Kerala, India. Thus, hard evidence is unavailable on potential decreases in government food expenditure.

80. The selection of foods outside the diets of the upper and middle classes is in keeping with meeting basic needs through provision of merit goods (Leipziger and Lewis 1977).

81. The child mortality rate is the proportion of deaths of children aged one to five per 1000 population. A high proportion of births go unreported in LDCs, particularly stillborn infants and those who die in the first month of life (neonatal mortality).

82. The crude death rate is the number of deaths divided by the total population, per thousand. Cohort death rate is the death rate of a given age group or cohort.

83. Figures for the United States, the United Kingdom, and the USSR are included in the table for comparative purposes, highlighting the considerable discrepancy in life expectancy between the LDCs and the developed nations.

84. Unequal distribution of health facilities and services leads to considerable discrepancies in quantity and quality of data. Traditional medicine is far more common in rural areas of the developing world than are the national or private Western-oriented health services that systematically collect morbidity and mortality data. In some countries public health services are essentially competing with traditional deliverers of health care—druggists, injectionists, midwives, magicians, and "medicine men." Modern medicine must prove itself as a reliable alternative in these circumstances.

85. The only exception to this is school enrollment. In most countries, a birth certificate is required to enroll in school; however, this encourages late registration and does not capture children who die before school age.

86. It is estimated that a quarter of the world's population is infected with round worms (Van Zijl 1966).

87. For example, according to an IBRD report on Latin America, 19 to 29 percent of reported deaths in Bolivia, Guatemala, and Chile were traced to airborne diseases. The extent of illness caused by these diseases is unknown. Preston (1980) estimates that 45 percent of LDC mortality decline can be attributable to reductions in airborne disease. Increased immunization has been the major factor in the decline.

88. For example, the Niger River basin has developed into a breeding ground for the black flies that carry onchocerciasis, which has forced families to relocate to uninfested but less fertile areas. Efforts by the Club des Amis du Sahel and other donors are attempting to reclaim the land by destroying breeding areas.

89. Prevention is best accomplished through vector control measures (until new, resistant strains are introduced)—chemical spraying of breeding grounds and measures to inhibit areas from becoming conducive to vector reproduction (Taylor and Hall 1967). Human prevention through immunization is in its infancy for most vector-borne diseases, as is the development of curative drugs. Ongoing research is sparsely funded, since most vector-borne diseases are virtually unknown in the developed world. Prevention through modifications in behavior, lifestyles, or housing constuction are difficult in the short run, often being alien to local custom. Current prevention centers on outmigration from infested areas.

90. For instance, knowledge about optimal breast-feeding and weaning practices can significantly reduce malnutrition among infants and young children. Increasing the length of breast feeding and introducing proper food supplements at the appropriate time improves the quantity and quality of infant and child diets (Zeitlin et al. 1980).

91. High mortality among females in the childbearing ages (roughly ages fifteen to forty-nine) is a phenomena unique to developing countries and is due primarily to poor maternal health and nutrition, both seriously exacerbated by repeated pregnancies (see Shryock and Siegle [1975] for discussion of this point).

92. For evidence on these issues see Puffer and Serrano 1971; Scrimshaw, Taylor, and Gordon 1968, and Puffer and Serrano 1973.

93. See Sorkin (1976: 43–57); Barlow (1979); and Correa (1975: 39–53) for discussions of these and other relevant issues and analyses on health and productivity in developing countries. The section on nutrition reviews the linkage between health-nutrition and macroeconomic growth, and available evidence points to a positive relationship between improved nutrition and productivity.

94. Primary care is defined as "basic or general health care which emphasizes the point when the patient first seeks assistance from the medical care system and the care of the simpler and more common illnesses." Use of community health aids and other paraphysicians is called for, and community participation is an important ingredient (U.S. Congress 1976).

95. Doctors are often newcomers to the community, which discourages use of health facilities. Paraphysicians chosen from the community and trained and sent back to their residents tend to have greater acceptance.

96. Training varies by program. Some PHC programs have major, project-specific training programs. Others draw on the existing skills of nurses and midwives. Retraining often can be the most effective means of ensuring a well-trained, competent cadre of health workers. Improving postpartum care methods, for example, can easily be accomplished by retraining midwives in hygienic care of mother and child and encouraging them to abandon potentially harmful practices.

97. The preferred outreach approach is a function of custom and social structure as well as manpower availability. No program can be said to be "best" in all contexts.

98. The definition of private sector excludes the nonprofit private voluntary organizations (PVO) that implement a number of health programs for bilateral and multilat-

eral donors. PVOs generally run discrete, local projects rather than national programs.

99. An externality is a (social) good that involves (external) consumption effects by more than one individual. Hence, an immunization not only keeps the individual healthy, but protects the community from the incidence and spread of disease.

100. The "free rider" concept in economics refers to someone who consumes but does not pay for benefits. It was originally associated with the notion of driving to work: If I sacrifice by taking public transportation, my neighbor can drive with less traffic, and he benefits but I don't (necessarily). By the same token, if I am immunized, I protect my neighbor and I bear the pain, time, and costs. His costs are nil unless he too is immunized.

101. The goal of low cost health care is a relative concept, for per capita health costs will be high regardless, but basic care delivered by paraphysicians is far less costly than extending the present delivery system, which is comprised of high technology, physician-based hospital care.

102. The Thai government is currently developing a national program based on the Lampang experience, but it is necessarily pared down to fit available financial resources.

103. Evaluation and planning are particularly critical in the provision of merit goods such as health care. By definition, there is inadequate demand for merit goods without the government's involvement in their provision, and thus supply decisions rely on cost effectiveness rather than exhibited demand information for guidance in determining funding and program levels.

## BIBLIOGRAPHY

Austin, James, and James Levinson. 1974. "Population and Nutrition: A Case for Integration." *Milbank Memorial Fund Quarterly* 52, no. 2 (Spring): 169–184.

Balassa, Bela. 1977. "A Stages Approach to Comparative Advantage." World Bank Staff Working Paper Number 256 (May). Washington, D.C.

Barlow, Robin. 1979. "Health and Economic Development: A Theoretical and Empirical Review." *Research in Human Capital and Development* 1: 45–79.

Baumslag, N., C. Kinsey, and E. Sabin. 1978. "Breast Is Best: A Bibliography on Breastfeeding and Infant Health in Developing Countries," mimeo. Washington, D.C.: Department of Health, Education and Welfare.

Baumslag, Naomi, and Edward Sabin. 1978. "Perspectives in Maternal-Infant Nutrition," mimeo. Washington, D.C.: Department of Health, Education and Welfare.

Behrman, Jere, Barbara Wolfe, and Tunali Insan. 1979. "Women's Earnings in a Developing Country: Double Selectivity, a Broader Definition of Human Capital," mimeo. AID/otr-c-1571, December. Madison, Wisconsin.

Belli, P. 1971. "The Economic Implications of Malnutrition: The Dismal Science Revisited." *Economic Development and Cultural Change* 20(October): 1–23.

Berg, Alan. 1973. *The Nutrition Factor*. Washington, D.C.: The Brookings Institution.

———. 1979. "Nutrition, Basic Needs and Growth," mimeo. Washington, D.C.: IBRD.

Birdsall, Nancy. 1977. "Analytic Approaches to the Relationship of Population Growth and Development." *Population and Development Review* 3, nos. 1 and 2 (March–June): 63–101.

Birch, H. G., and S. A. Richardson. 1972. "The Functioning of Jamaican School Children Severely Malnourished During the First Two Years of Life." In *Nutrition, the Nervous System and Behavior.* Scientific Publication No. 251. Washington, D.C.: Pan American Health Organization.

Birch, H. 1972. "Functional Effects of Fetal Malnutrition." *Annual Progress in Child Psychiatry and Child Development.* New York: Brunner-Mazel, Inc.

Bongaarts, John. 1975. "Why High Birth Rates Are So Low." *Population and Development Review* 2 (December): 289–296.

Brackett, James, R. T. Ravenholt, and John Chao. 1978. "The Role of Family Planning in Recent Rapid Fertility Declines in Developing Countries." *Studies in Family Planning* 9, no. 12 (December): 314–323.

Brown, N., and E. Parisier. 1975. "Food Science in Developing Countries." *Science* 88: 589–593.

Bryant, John, M.D. 1969. *Health and the Developing World.* New York: The Rockefeller Foundation.

Burki, Shahid, and Joris Voorheove. 1977. "Global Estimates for Meeting Basic Needs: Background Paper." Basic Needs Paper No. 1. Washington, D.C.: IBRD. August.

Butz, William. 1977. "Economic Aspects of Breastfeeding." In Henry Mosley, ed., *Nutrition and Reproduction.* New York: Plenum Publishing Corporation.

Butz, William, and Jean-Pierre Habicht. 1976. "The Effects of Nutrition and Health on Fertility: Hypotheses, Evidence and Interventions." In Ronald Ridker, ed., *Population and Development, the Search for Selective Interventions.* Baltimore: Johns Hopkins University Press.

Caldwell, H., C. Campbell, D. Dunlop, and J. Fiedler. 1978. "The Dynamics of Human Capital Formation in the African Context: A Review of the Relationship between Health, Nutrition, Education and Population Change," mimeo. Nashville, Tennessee: Vanderbilt University. Fall.

Cassel, John. 1971. "Health Consequences of Population Density and Crowding." In *Rapid Population Growth,* Volume 2, 462–479. Baltimore: The Johns Hopkins University Press.

Cassen, Robert. 1976. "Population and Development: A Survey." *World Development* 6, no. 10/11: 785–830.

Chenery, Hollis, Montek Ahluwalia, C. L. G. Bell, John Duloy, and Richard Jolly. 1974. *Redistribution with Growth.* London: Oxford University Press.

Churchill, Anthony A., and Margaret A. Lycette. 1979. "Basic Needs in Shelter," mimeo. Washington, D.C.: IBRD.

Cochrane, Susan H. 1979. *Fertility and Education.* Baltimore: The Johns Hopkins University Press.

Conroy, Michael E., and Nancy R. Folbie. 1976. *Population Growth as a Deterrent to Economic Growth: A Reappraisal of the Evidence.* The Hastings Institute of Society, Ethics and Life Sciences, Occasional Population Paper. New York. February.

Correa, Hector, and Gaylord Cummins. 1970. "Contribution of Nutrition to Economic Growth." *American Journal of Clinical Nutrition* 23, no. 5 (May): 560–565.

Cravioto, J., and E. R. DeLicardie. 1968. "Intersensory Development of School-age Children." In N. S. Scrimshaw and J. E. Gordon, eds., *Malnutrition, Learning and Behavior,* Cambridge, Massachusetts: MIT Press.

———. 1973a. "Nutrition, Behavior and Learning." In M. Rechcigl, ed., *Food, Nutrition and Health, World Review of Nutrition and Dietetics,* vol. 16. Washington, D.C.: Karger, Basel.

———. 1973b. "The Effect of Malnutrition on the Individual." In A. Berg, N. S. Scrimshaw, and P. L. Call, eds., *Nutrition, National Development and Planning.* Cambridge, Massachusetts: MIT Press.

Danfa Comprehensive Rural Health and Family Planning Project. 1979. Final Report. Los Angeles: UCLA School of Public Health. September.

Davis, Kingsley, and Judith Blake. 1956. "Social Structure and Fertility." *Economic Development and Cultural Change* 4, no. 3 (April): 211–235.

Delgado, H., M. Lechtig, E. Brineman, and R. Klein. 1978. "Nutrition, Lactation and Post Partum Amenorrhea." *The American Journal of Clinical Nutrition* 31 (February): 322–327.

Dema, I. 1969. "Nutrition and Agriculture." In *Proceedings of the Eastern African Conference on Nutrition and Child Feeding, Nairobi,* pp. 201–205.

Demeny, Paul. 1979. "On the End of the Population Explosion." *Population and Development Review* 5, no. 1 (March): 141–162.

Dixon, Ruth. 1975. "Women's Rights and Fertility." *Reports on Population/Family Planning* 17 (January).

Easterlin, Richard. 1975. "An Economic Framework for Fertility Analysis." *Studies in Family Planning* 6, no. 3 (March): 54–63.

Enke, Stephen. 1966. "The Economic Aspects of Slowing Population Growth." *Economic Journal* 75 (March): 44–56.

Evenson, Robert, Mark Rosenzweig, and Kenneth Wolpin. 1980. "Economic Determinants of Fertility and Child Health in Philippine and Indian Rural Households," mimeo. New Haven, Connecticut. AID/otr-g-1723.

Family Health Care. 1979. "Planning for Health and Development: A Strategic Perspective for Technical Cooperation." AID/afr-C-1138. Washington, D.C.

Feldstein, Martin, M. A. Piot, and T. K. Sunderesan. 1973. "Resource Allocation Model for Public Health Planning: A Case Study of Tuberculosis Control." Supplement to *Bulletin of the World Health Organization,* vol. 48. Geneva: World Health Organization.

Fenwick, A. 1972. "Costs and Cost Benefit Analysis of an S. Mansoni Control Program on a Sugar Estate in Tanzania," mimeo. Geneva: World Health Organization.

Findley, Sally. 1977. "Planning for Internal Migration: A Review of Issues and Policies in Developing Countries." Bureau of the Census. Washington, D.C.: U.S. Government Printing Office.

Findley, Sally, and Ann Orr. 1978. "Patterns of Urban-Rural Fertility Differentials in Developing Countries: A Suggested Framework." AID/UD monograph. Washington, D.C.

Fisher, Joseph L., and Neal Polter. 1971. "The Effects of Population Growth on Resources Adequacy and Quality." In *Rapid Population Growth,* vol. 2, pp. 222–244. Baltimore: The Johns Hopkins Press.

Fleuret, Patrick. 1979. "Nutrition, Consumption and Agricultural Change," mimeo. Washington, D.C.: AID.

Florencio, Cecilia, and Victor Smith. 1969. "Efficiency of Food Purchasing among Working Class Families in Colombia." *Journal of the American Dietician Association* 55, no. 3 (September): 239–245.

Food and Agriculture Organization Yearbook. 1977. *Production Yearbook.* Rome.

Freeman, Howard, Robert Klein, Jerome Kagan, and Charles Yarbrough. 1977. "Relations between Nutrition and Cognition in Rural Guatemala." *American Journal of Public Health* 67, no. 3 (March): 233–239.

Freedman, Ronald, and Bernard Berelson. 1976. "The Record of Family Planning Programs." *Studies in Family Planning* 7, no. 1 (January): 1–40.

Germaine, Adrienne. 1975. "Status and Roles of Women as Factors in Fertility Behavior: A Policy Analysis." *Studies in Family Planning* 6, no. 7 (July): 192–201.

Graham, G. G. 1967. "Effects of Infantile Malnutrition on Growth." *Federation Proceedings* 26, no. 1: 139–143.

———. 1979. "Draft Proposal," mimeo. Baltimore, Maryland: Johns Hopkins University (July).

Grosse, Robert N., and Barbara Perry. 1979. "Correlates of Life Expectancy in Less Developed Countries," mimeo. Ann Arbor, Michigan: University of Michigan.

Grosse, Robert, Jan L. DeVries, Robert Tilden, Anne Dievler, and Suzanne Rie Day. 1979. "A Health Development Model Application to Rural Java," mimeo. AID Grant No. AID/otr-G-1651 (October). Ann Arbor, Michigan.

Gwatkin, D., J. R. Wilcox, and J. D. Wray. 1979. "Can Interventions Make a Difference? The Policy Implications of Field Experiment Experience," mimeo. A Report to the World Bank. Washington, D.C. March.

Head, J. G. 1974. *Public Goods and Public Welfare.* Durham, N.C.: Duke University Press.

Heller, Peter. 1975. "Issues in the Costing of Public Sector Outputs: The Public Medical Services of Malaysia." Washington, D.C.: World Bank Staff Working Paper No. 207. June.

———. 1976. "A Model of the Demand for Medical and Health Services in West Malaysia." Discussion Paper No. 62 (October). Ann Arbor, Michigan: Center for Research on Economic Development.

Heller, Peter S., and William D. Drake. 1976. "Malnutrition, Child Morbidity and the Family Decision Process." Discussion Paper No. 58. Ann Arbor, Michigan: Center for Research on Economic Development.

Hertzig, M., H. Birch, S. Richardson, and J. Tizard. 1972. "Intellectual Levels of School Children Severely Malnourished During the First Two Years of Life." *Pediatrics* 49, no. 6 (June): 814–824.

Hicks, Norman L. 1979. "Sector Priorities in Meeting Basic Needs: Some Statistical Evidence," mimeo. Washington, D.C. April.

Hill, E. L., and B. S. Sanders. 1960. "Murine Typhus Control in the U.S.: A Success Story of Public Health Practices," mimeo. Washington, D.C.: U.S. Public Health Service.

Intergovernmental Coordinating Committee. 1976. "Report on Regional Workshop Reducing Fertility through Beyond Family Planning Measures," mimeo. Penang, Malaysia. January.

IBRD. 1975. *Health Sector Policy Paper.* Washington, D.C.: World Bank, May.

———. 1976. *Village Water Supply.* Washington, D.C.: World Bank.

———. 1977. *World Atlas.* Washington, D.C.

———. 1977–1979. *World Bank Annual Report.* Washington, D.C.

———. 1978. *World Development Report.* Washington, D.C.

———. 1979. *World Atlas.* Washington, D.C.

———. 1979. *World Development Report.* Washington, D.C.

———. 1980. *World Development Report.* Washington, D.C.

International Food Policy Research Institute. 1977. *Food Needs of Developing Countries: Projections of Production and Consumption to 1990.* Washington, D.C.

International Labor Organization. 1976. *Employment, Growth and Basic Needs.* Geneva.

International Monetary Fund. 1978a. *International Financial Statistics.* Washington, D.C.

———. 1978b. *Government Finance Statistics Yearbook.* Washington, D.C.

Isenman, Paul. 1980. "Basic Needs: The Case of Sri Lanka." *World Development* 8 (June): 237–258.

Jain, S. 1975. *Size Distribution of Income: A Compilation of Data.* Washington, D.C.

Jelliffe, Derrick B. 1957. "Social Culture and Nutrition: Cultural Block and Protein Malnutrition in Early Childhood in Rural West Bengal." *Pediatrics* 20: 128–138.

———. 1966. *The Assessment of the Nutritional Status of the Community.* Geneva: World Health Organization.

———. 1968. "Infant Nutrition in the Tropics and Subtropics." Monograph Series No. 29. Geneva: World Health Organization.

Jelliffe, D. B., and E. F. P. Jelliffe. 1978. "The Volume and Composition of Human Milk in Poorly Nourished Communities: A Review." *American Journal of Clinical Nutrition* 31: 492.

Keeley, Michael, ed. 1976. *Population, Public Policy and Economic Development.* New York: Praeger.

Kocher, James E. 1976. "Socio-economic Development and Fertility Change in Rural Africa." Harvard Institute for International Development. Discussion Paper No. 16. Cambridge, Massachusetts.

Kocher, James, and Richard Cash. 1979. "Achieving Health and Nutritional Objectives within a Basic Needs Framework." HIID Discussion Paper No. 55. Cambridge, Massachusetts.

Lechtig, A. 1975. "Effect of Food Supplementation During Pregnancy on Birthweight." *Journal of Pediatrics* 56, no. 4 (October): 508–520.

Leff, Nathaniel. 1969. "Dependency Rates and Savings Rates." *American Economic Review* 59, no. 5 (December): 886–896.

Leibenstein, Harvey. 1974. "An Interpretation of the Economic Theory of Fertility: Promising Path or Blind Alley?" *Journal of Economic Literature* 12 (June): 457–479.

Leipziger, Danny, and Maureen Lewis. 1977. "A Basic Human Needs Approach to Development," mimeo. Washington, D.C.: AID.

————. 1980. "Social Indicators, Growth and Distribution." *World Development* 8 (July): 299–302.

Lockheed, Marlaine, Dean Jamison, and Lawrence Lau. 1980. "Farmer Education and Farm Efficiency: A Survey." In *Economic Development and Cultural Change* (forthcoming).

Mason, Karen O., and Abraham David, eds. 1971. *Social and Economic Correlates of Family Fertility: A Survey of the Evidence.* Research Triangle Park, N.C.: Research Triangle Institute.

Mauldin, Parker, and Bernard Berelson. 1978. "Conditions of Fertility Decline in Developing Countries, 1965–75." *Studies in Family Planning* 9, no. 5 (May): 1–147.

McGreevey, William P., and Nancy Birdsall. 1974. *The Policy Relevance of Recent Research of Fertility.* Washington, D.C.: The Smithsonian Institution.

McKay, H. E., A. McKay, and L. Sinisterra. 1973. "Behavioral Intervention Studies with Malnourished Children: A Review of Experiences." In D. Kallen, ed., *Nutrition, Development and Social Behavior,* pp. 121–145. DHEW Publication No. (NIH) 73–242. Washington, D.C.: U.S. Government Printing Office.

Meadows, Donella H., et al. 1972. *The Limits to Growth.* New York: Signet.

Monckeberg, F. 1975. "The Effect of Malnutrition on Physical Growth and Brain Development." In J. W. Prescott, M. S. Read, and D. B. Coursin, eds., *Brain Function and Malnutrition.* New York: Wiley.

Morawetz, David. 1978. "Basic Needs Policies and Population Growth." *World Development* 6, no. 11/12: 1251–1259.

Mueller, Eva. 1976. "The Economic Value of Children in Peasant Agriculture." In *Population and Development: The Search for Selective Interventions.* Baltimore: Johns Hopkins University Press.

Muscat, Robert J., and Ronald G. Ridker. 1973. "Incentives for Family Welfare and Fertility Reduction: An Illustration for Malaysia." *Studies in Family Planning* 4, no. 1 (January): 1–11.

Musgrave, Richard, and Peggy Musgrave. 1976. *Public Finance in Theory and Practice.* New York: McGraw-Hill.

Mushkin, Selma J. 1962. "Health as an Investment." *Journal of Political Economy Supplement, Investments in Human Beings* 70, no. 5 (October): 129–157.

Pan American Health Organization. 1971. "Inter-American Investigation of Mortality in Childhood, First Year of Investigation, Provisional Report." Washington, D.C.

Parker, Robert L., et al. 1978. "The Narangwal Experiment on Interactions of Nutrition and Infections: III. Measurement of Services and Costs and Their Relation to Outcome." *Indian Medical Journal.*

Pinstrup-Anderson, P., et al. 1976. "The Impact of Increasing Food Supply on Human Nutrition: Implications for Commodity Priorities in Agricultural Research and Policy." *American Journal of Agricultural Economics* (May).

Pinstrup-Anderson, P., and E. Caicedo. 1978. "The Potential Impact of Changes in Income Distribution on Food Demand and Nutrition." *American Journal of Agricultural Economies* (March).

Preston, Samuel. 1980. "Causes and Consequences of Mortality Declines in Less Developed Countries during the Twentieth Century." In Richard Easterlin, ed., *Population and Economic Change in Developing Countries*. Chicago: University of Chicago Press.

Pryor, G. 1975. "Malnutrition and the Critical Period Hypothesis." In J. W. Prescott, M. S. Read, and D. B. Coursin, eds., *Brain Function and Malnutrition*. New York: Wiley.

Puffer, Ruth, and Carlos Serrano. 1971. *Patterns of Mortality in Childhood*. Washington, D.C.: Pan American Health Organization.

———. 1973. "Patterns of Mortality in Childhood." Scientific Publication No. 262. Washington, D.C.: Pan American Health Organization.

———. 1975. *Birth Weight, Maternal Age and Birth Order: Those Important Determinants of Infant Mortality*. Washington, D.C.: Pan American Health Organization.

Ram, Rati, and Theodore Shultz. 1979. "Life Span, Health, Savings, and Productivity." *Economic Development and Cultural Change* 27, no. 3 (April): 399–421.

Repetto, Robert. 1974. "The Interaction of Fertility and Size Distribution of Income," mimeo. Cambridge, Mass.

Reutlinger, Shlomo. 1977. "Malnutrition: A Poverty or a Food Problem?" *World Development* 5, no. 8 (May): 715–724.

Reutlinger, Shlomo, and Marcelo Selowsky. 1978. *Malnutrition and Poverty: Magnitude and Policy Options*. Baltimore: Johns Hopkins University Press.

Rhoda, Richard. 1979. "Development Activities and Rural-Urban Migration," mimeo. AID/UD Monograph. Washington, D.C.

Rich, William. 1973. *Smaller Families through Social and Economic Progress*. Washington, D.C. Overseas Development Council.

Ridker, Ronald G., ed. 1976. *Population and Development—The Search for Selective Interventions*. Baltimore: Johns Hopkins University Press.

Robinson, Warren. 1979. "The Cost per Unit of Family Planning Services." *Journal of Biosocial Science* 11: 93–103.

Rubey, Jane. 1976. "Malnutrition, Learning and Behavior—Selected Annotated Bibliography," mimeo. Berkeley, Calif.

Scrimshaw, N. S., C. E. Taylor, and J. E. Gordon. 1968. *Interactions of Nutrition and Infection*. Monograph Series No. 57. Geneva: World Health Organization.

Selowsky, Marcelo, and Lance Taylor. 1973. "The Economics of Malnourished Children: An Example of Disinvestment in Human Capital." *Economic Development and Cultural Change* 22, no. 1 (October): 18–30.

Sharpston, Michael. 1976. "A Health Policy for Developing Countries." In *Leading Issues in Economic Development*. Oxford: Oxford University Press.

Shields, Nwanganga. 1980. "Female Labor Force Participation and Fertility: Review of Empirical Evidence." World Bank Staff Paper. Washington, D.C.

Shryock, Henry S., and Jacob Siegel. 1975. *The Methods and Materials of Demography*. Washington, D.C.: Bureau of the Census.

Shultz, T. Paul. 1976. "Interrelationship Between Mortality and Fertility." In Ronald Ridker, ed., *Population and Development: The Search for Selective Interventions*. Baltimore: Johns Hopkins University Press.

Shultz, Theodore W. 1980. "Investment in Population Quality throughout Low-Income Countries." In Philip Hansen, ed., *World Population and Development*. Syracuse, N.Y.: Syracuse University Press.

Sinha, Jai N. 1976. "Demographic Aspects of Employment in the Third World." In Leon Tabah, ed., *Population Growth and Economic Development in the Third World,* vol. 2, pp. 707–740. Liege, Belgium: Ordina Editions.

Singer, H. W., and S. Maxwell. 1978. "Food Aid and Supplementary Feeding." Report for the World Food Program. Sussex, England: Institute of Development Studies.

Sirageldin, Ismail, ed. 1979. *Research in Human Capital and Development*. Greenwich, Connecticut: Jai Press, Inc.

Smithsonian Institution Interdisciplinary Communications Programs. 1976. "The Dynamics of Migration: Internal Migration and Migration and Fertility." Monograph No. 5, Volume 1. Washington, D.C.: Smithsonian Institution. December.

Sorkin, Alan L. 1976. *Health Economics in Developing Countries*. Lexington, Mass.: D.C. Heath and Company.

Standing, Guy. 1978. *Labour Force Participation and Development*. Geneva: ILO.

Streeten, Paul. 1977. "The Distinctive Features of a Basic Needs Approach to Development," mimeo. Washington, D.C.: IBRD.

Taylor, Carl E., and Marie-Françoise Hall. 1967. "Health, Population and Economic Development." *Science* (August): 651–657.

Taylor, C. E., J. S. Newman, and N. U. Kelly. 1976. "Interactions Between Health and Population." *Studies in Family Planning* 7, no. 4 (April): 94–100.

Todaro, Michael. 1969. "A Model of Labour Migration and Urban Unemployment in Less Developed Countries." *American Economic Review* 59, no. 1 (March): 138–148.

Tsui, Ann, and Donald Bogue. 1978. "Declining World Fertility: Trends, Causes, Implications." In *Population Bulletin,* vol. 33, no. 4. Washington, D.C.: Population Reference Bureau, Inc.

United Nations. 1977. *U.N. Demographic Yearbook*. New York.

United Nations Fund for Population Activities. 1977–1979. *Annual Report*. New York.

U.S. Bureau of the Census. 1980. "Infant Mortality Rates by Urban-Rural and Sex Breakdown for Selected LDCs," mimeo. Washington, D.C.

U.S. Congress. 1976. "A Discursive Dictionary of Health Care." Report by Subcommittee on Health and Environment of the House of Representatives Committee on Interstate and Foreign Commerce. Washington, D.C.: U.S. Government Printing Office, February.

Van Zijl, W. J. 1966. "Studies on Diarrheal Disease in Seven Countries." *Bulletin of the World Health Organization* 35:249–261.

Williams, Anne D. 1976. "Review and Evaluation of the Literature." In Michael Keeley, ed., *Population, Public Policy and Economic Development.* New York: Praeger.

Winick, M. 1970. "Nutrition and Mental Development." *Medical Clinics of North America* 54, no. 6: 1413–1429.

Winikoff, Beverly. 1978. "Nutrition, Population, and Health: Some Implications for Policy." *Science* 200 (May): 895–902.

World Health Organization (WHO) Expert Committee. 1965. "Nutrition in Pregnancy and Lactation." Geneva.

World Health Organization. 1974–1978. *Proposed Programme Budget.* Geneva.

Wray, Joe D. 1971. "Population Pressure on Families: Family Size and Child Spacing." *Rapid Population Growth,* Volume 2: 403–461. Baltimore: The Johns Hopkins University Press.

Wrigley, E. A. 1971. *Population and History.* New York: McGraw-Hill.

Zeitlin, Marian, Nina Schlossman, Michael Meurer, Joe Wray, and John Stanbury. 1980. "Nutrition-Fertility Interactions in Developing Countries: Implications for Program Design," mimeo. AID/otr-147-79-32. Cambridge, Mass.

*Chapter 3*

# Policy Issues and the Basic
# Human Needs Approach

*Danny M. Leipziger*

## INTRODUCTION

The development community, faced with inadequate economic progress by many developing countries, has expressed extensive interest in a new approach to development, the so-called basic human needs (BHN) approach. First formally developed by the International Labor Organization (ILO), this approach aims at increasing the access of the world's poor to vital goods and services in order to improve their well-being (International Labor Organization 1976). Thus, the ultimate objective of domestic and international development policies would no longer be aggregate growth per se, nor simply growth with a concern for equity (income distribution), but rather the attainment on a sustainable basis of a minimum standard of living defined in terms of goods and services that meet basic needs.

Although the specification of what are basic needs is normative, food

This chapter is in part based on a paper presented to the Conference on the New International Economic Order sponsored by The City College of New York, April 26, 1979. The views expressed are personal and do not necessarily reflect those of the Department of State or the U.S. government. Helpful insights were gained from discussions with Michael Crosswell and Maureen Lewis. These are gratefully acknowledged; however, they are of course not implicated by the views expressed. Expert statistical assistance was rendered by Karen Peake and Daniel Smaller.

and safe water, health care, shelter, clothing, and education are normally included as vital elements—or in Paul Streeten's (1977) terminology as "core needs." Recent statistical evidence on indicators of progress shows most of the low-income developing countries lagging far behind average levels of BHN-related indicators. The group of low-income LDCs—those with (1975) per capita GNP levels below $250 and including most of those countries designated as "least developed" by the United Nations—have registered virtually no progress between 1960 and 1975 in increasing per capita production of goods and services; and in many of them, per capita food production has actually fallen in the course of the last decade. While there has been some significant progress in reducing infant mortality rates; increasing life expectancies, literacy, and access to primary education; and improving nutrition and access to health care, it is estimated that one billion people in the developing countries are lacking one or more of the basic needs of human existence (ul Haq 1977): about 80 percent of them are in rural areas, and more than 75 percent of them are in the low-income countries of South and East Asia and in sub-Saharan Africa (IBRD sources).

Statistical evidence shows that a child born in a low-income LDC has only one-third as good a chance of survival to age one as in a middle-income country (MIC), and if he or she reaches that age, life expectancy will on average be fourteen years less than in an MIC (IBRD: 1978). When compared to the industrialized countries, these disparities are magnified even further. While indexes of economic and social progress do vary significantly by income group—that is, the average levels for low-income LDCs are well below those for middle-income LDCs—more rigorous statistical tests by Morawetz (1977) and Hicks and Streeten (1978) do not reveal statistically significant correlations between those indexes and GNP levels. Work by Morris (1978) and Grant (1978) on physical quality of life indexes (PQLI) also reveals wide disparities between those indexes and GNP levels. Thus, improvements in aggregate performance will not ensure improvements in standards of living.

What makes the BHN approach of considerable current importance is that it has moved from an abstract concept to an explicit policy objective endorsed by major donors such as the United States and by multilateral institutions such as the Development Assistance Committee of the OECD.[1] Yet the BHN approach requires further conceptualization before it can be embraced either by donor countries and institutions or by the developing countries. (These issues have been explored recently by Streeten 1977; Srinivasan 1977; Crosswell 1978; and Leipziger and Lewis 1977, among others.) Therefore, it is the purpose of this chapter to explore some of the issues involved in the basic needs discussion, focusing primarily on policy implications.

We proceed to pose a number of questions, including: (1) What is the BHN approach, and what is it not? (2) What are some of the policy issues involved in implementing a BHN approach? (3) How does it relate to other development approaches? (4) What are the implications for donors? (5) How does BHN fit into the overall north-south dialogue? It should be noted that our purpose is to raise issues rather than to offer firm solutions.

## WHAT IS THE BHN APPROACH . . . AND WHAT IS IT NOT?

The basic human needs approach was first formalized by the ILO in the World Employment Conference of 1976 as a means of improving living standards of the poor in developing countries. It was a response to the perceived shortcomings of previous development efforts that have left approximately one billion people lacking the basics of subsistence. In many indicators of well-being, improvements have been noticeable over time (see Morawetz 1977; IBRD *World Development Report* 1980); however, the lowest income segments of society have tended to share very little in what progress has occurred.

The BHN approach represents an explicit attempt to single out the needs of the poor in developing countries and to specify a bundle of goods and services that are needed if they are to reach at least minimal subsistence. It focuses on both the demand and supply sides—on the income side because sufficient purchasing power must be generated within low-income groups to sustain demand for goods and services and on the production side because the relevant goods and services must be supplied either by the market or by the government. The basic needs approach is thus a strategy of growth, employment, and income generation. However, it aims at a pattern of growth that provides purchasing power to the poor, while at the same time influencing the composition of output and supplementing earnings with appropriate public expenditure.

Initial reactions to the BHN approach have included the views that (1) the basic needs approach is a welfare approach, (2) it is nothing new, and (3) it is a political ploy by the developed countries to justify inadequate donor performance in the transfer of official development assistance. A coherent strategy to improve standards of living on a sustainable basis cannot be based on a welfare approach: it must create employment and income among the poor to be effective. Transfers can be a part of such a strategy, but for transfers to be sustainable, they must be supported by income and product generation. The BHN approach adds a new dimension even to enlightened development strategies such as "growth with equity" because it focuses on ultimate objectives of policy and forces planners to specify the linkages between resources, policies, and those ultimate objectives. It also focuses more explicitly on absolute poverty alleviation rather than solely on distribution. (The third view deals with motives rather than the concept per se and will be addressed later in the chapter.)

The distinction between BHN elements that can be supplied by the private sector and those elements that are provided by government directly is a crucial one. In any discussion of BHN elements, food, shelter, and clothing are seen as goods that are at least conceptually supplied by the private market, and health care, safe water, education, and, some would add, family planning as services that probably need to be supplied by the public sector.[2] These needs focus exclusively on tangible goods and services and do not include other needs such as local participation in decisionmaking and other social and political goals that have equal merit.

Even though consumption studies have indicated that the poor spend the bulk of their income for food, shelter, and clothing[3]—goods that conceptually are private goods—the private market in LDCs may not operate efficiently. Therefore, there may well be a role for government in the supply of these goods, especially to rural areas. Streeten (1977) thus speaks of the need for "supply management." Crosswell (see Chapter 1) sees a role for government intervention if the market is inefficient or if self-sufficiency is a national goal. Other observers see governments intervening to provide for imports that may be needed, to relieve bottlenecks in marketing and transport, and to plan or coordinate overall production levels.

If the private market fails to produce basic needs elements when demand exists—because of indivisibilities or nonexcludability—then the government can intervene to supply public goods.[4] Even in cases where some private sector supply is possible—such as education—its distribution may well be uneven, and social benefit accruing to the nation (in excess of those captured by the private market) can justify further government intervention. Leipziger and Lewis (1977) point out that the theory of public goods is not well suited to developing countries with tremendous income disparities, since most principles assume an even distribution of income.

In the cases where the demand for specific goods or services does not exist—and it is unlikely that demand would exist even if the market operated effectively and purchasing power existed—government can provide "merit goods"—goods that are produced because it is felt there are merits to encouraging their current consumption and future demand. Merit goods can be supplied in cases where government feels that inadequate knowledge on the part of consumers is distorting consumer preferences—for example, consumers prefer using contaminated river water rather than safe water or less rather than more nutritious foods.[5] (Concrete examples of merit goods are high nutrition foods such as triposha, distributed in Sri Lanka, and bienestaril, in Colombia.) No one would quarrel with the right of the individual to allocate his or her earned income freely—although governments do often tax goods that are considered socially undesirable. However, governments do encourage specific consumption patterns that implicitly impose preferences: often this takes the form of transfers to ensure that consumption favors certain types of goods.[6]

The role of government in providing social services is certainly crucial to the achievement of progress in health, family planning, nutrition, and education. Since there is widespread agreement concerning the objectives of government policy in these areas, the relevant policy issues concern the distribution and the financing of services. In the Malaysian context, for example, Meerman (1977) finds that the lowest 40 percent of the peninsular population by income had its real income increased by 40 percent through social services; the lowest two deciles of the population earned 14 percent of national income but consumed 18 percent of national goods and services, the transfer being financed by the top two deciles of the income distribution. In Sri Lanka, Alailima (1978) reports that the lowest 25 percent of the income distribution gained an additional 21 percent of income through services, transfers, and subsidies. Sri Lanka's record on redistribution is telling in the BHN context, since its policies have coincided with abnormally high social indicators.[7]

There are at least three major misconceptions concerning the BHN approach that should be explicitly addressed: first, it is not a unique *strategy* of development; second, it is not an international *welfare* program; and third, it is not a clearly *optimal* approach. All these caveats are important. The BHN approach is not in and of itself a strategy, to the exclusion of others, but rather a set of objectives by which to appraise alternative development strategies. Thus, to associate a BHN approach with autarkic development is no more valid than to associate it with an export-oriented trade strategy or a primarily agricultural strategy. Basic needs objectives are attainable through a number of strategies. What is of paramount importance is the calculation of effectiveness of alternative strategies in terms of achieving the stated objectives in a country-specific context. This effectiveness will be a function of the natural resources base, the political orientation of the system, and other social and economic factors. However, in all countries, the ability to raise living standards of the poor to levels sufficient to meet basic needs rests with the creation of purchasing power and access to basic social services.

Thus, the BHN approach is distinguishable from a welfare approach insofar as it is based on the generation of employment and earned income. With respect to public and merit goods, the BHN approach may involve a reorientation of public expenditure and a widened distribution of social servies favoring the poor. Aside from their direct effects on well-being, such investments in human capital—in upgrading the health, nutrition, and education of the population—yield significant economic benefits in the long run.[8] The real issues are the opportunity cost of capital invested in such a fashion, the budgetary implications of such a pattern of fiscal expenditure, and the effects on national savings of a pattern of income distribution that favors the poor.

This leads to the third point—namely, that the BHN approach is not clearly optimal if by optimal one means the maximization of growth in the near term. There are long-run benefits to a program involving broadened access to social services, human capital investments and improved income distribution through greater employment of the poor. There are also costs, primarily in the medium term, with respect to reduced investments elsewhere, increased budgeting expenditures (to finance increased—and recurrent—expenses), and potentially reduced levels of national savings associated with a widened distributed income. These tradeoffs need to be considered explicitly (we attempt this in a later section), and they require the attention of donors who can offset some of the opportunity costs of a strategy aimed at satisfying basic needs. The extent to which actual donor assistance efforts match up with the distribution of absolute parity is discussed by Crosswell (Chapter 5).

## IMPLEMENTATION OF A BASIC NEEDS APPROACH

The basis of implementation is the conceptual underpinning of a strategy and the policy framework needed to carry it out. The execution of those policies can lead to actual success or failure. Our purpose here should be to highlight important policy issues that are relevant in a multicountry context. In particular, we will focus on (1) the role of political commitment, (2) the role of planning, (3) aspects of public finance, and (4) tradeoffs between economic objectives.

A commitment to basic needs objectives requires concomitant economic and political decisions favoring the poor. Grant (1977) states that it is no coincidence that countries successfully improving the conditions of the poor—including China, Korea, Taiwan, and Sri Lanka—have all successfully redistributed economic power. Land reform, for example, tends to be a prerequisite for economic progress in the rural sector. We have also noted that the distribution of social services can be a major redistributive device (see Alailima 1978; and Meerman 1977, 1978). Decisions on redistribution require the political will to transfer resources to the disenfranchised and deprived.

Since the costs of redistribution must be borne by the upper-income groups, there are major political implications for governments undertaking redistributive policies. Traditional "elites" are reluctant to surrender economic and political power. Such shifts can presumably be accommodated more easily in a dynamic economic context—people tend to part more easily with portions of incremental wealth than with existing stocks of wealth.

Stewart and Streeten (1976) draw distinctions between strategies of radical redistribution, incremental redistribution, and redistribution through growth. A prime example of the theory of radical redistribution is Adelman (1975, 1978), who argues that the most successful sequence for effective development is radical redistribution of assets, followed by massive investments in human capital and labor-intensive growth. Using the Korea-Taiwan paradigm, Adelman argues for large-scale land reform, investments in education far in excess of current needs, and export-led growth. The results, she claims, can be seen in cases like Korea where the income share of the poorest 40 percent exceeds that of Sweden (Adelman 1978: 11). One argument for redistribution before growth is that investments and growth increase the value of the asset to be redistributed, thereby making the task more difficult. This approach can be effective in raising the incomes, productivity, and living standards of the poor, but it requires major inflows of external capital to substitute for reduced domestic savings and redirected domestic investments and a strong political regime that is capable of redistributing economic power.

Incremental redistribution would rely on the fiscal system of taxes and trasfers to increase the incomes of the poor. Taken to an extreme, this course could be taken to correspond to the pure transfer policy to enhance consumption by the poor, as simulated in the Ahluwalia and Chenery (1974) classic model of growth and distribution. This approach in and of itself is not sustainable in the long run. The major missing element is employment generation.

A third strategy could involve diversion of increments to growth toward increased investments in physical, financial, and human capital among the low-income groups. This redistribution through growth would entail some short-term costs; however, as Ahluwalia and Chenery

(1974) point out, it would result in long-term accelerated growth in incomes of the poor.

The basic needs approach implies an integration of aspects of all three strategies; it would redistribute assets; it would involve some transfers for the very poor, but also would broaden access to public services; and it would create employment and emphasize human capital investments. The method for integrating these strategies, for adding specificity to ultimate outputs and the distribution of those outputs, is the planning process. BHN as a planning approach would not only focus on ultimate income levels and distribution shares, but also on the composition of output (see Chapter 1). The ILO (1976) stresses the fact that increased employment and incomes for the poor will alter demand for basic consumer goods and public services, shifting the composition of demand toward more labor-intensive goods.

Employment generation is the key policy objective to achieve BHN targets. Policy measures can include (1) appropriate factor prices, (2) labor-using technologies, (3) access to productive assets, (4) investments in human capital, and (5) labor-intensive exports. Planning exercises can sharpen the linkages among policies and target levels and identify combinations of target levels that are feasible.

The planning process is particularly sensitive when the objectives are socioeconomic improvements in nutrition, health, longevity, and education. The interrelationships are complex: improved nutrition affects health; increased education affects fertility and longevity; and longevity and health affect population growth rates. (See Chapter 2.) To plan and implement effectively and to allocate resources efficiently, the linkages need to be well established in a country-specific context. It should be stressed that there will, of necessity, be considerable national differences concerning the level of BHN targets, the time period for meeting them, and the relevant national policies needed to attain them. Crosswell (1978b) would add the importance of the BHN framework in relating intermediate targets (e.g., employment, distribution of health care expenditure) to ultimate objectives (e.g., longevity).

The planning process under a BHN approach may lead to a greater emphasis on integrated programs—for example, those that deliver such services as health care, nutrition and family planning information, personal hygiene practices, nutritious food production, and safe water use to rural areas. Increased community participation is a vital element of this approach. Although integrated programming has not always been successful, there may be significant efficiency gains to providing such package services, each of which exhibits positive externalities for other objectives.

The ILO (1976) suspects that a basic needs approach will involve some shifts in production—toward greater self-sufficiency in food production and toward a greater emphasis on nontraded goods such as sanitation, housing, irrigation, and transport. Greater "self-reliance" need not imply autarky; still, one can imagine some shift in production by food-importing LDCs from cash crops to food production as being fully consistent with long-run national interest. Often it is inappropriate domestic agricultural price policies that limit domestic food production, or it is an agricultural pattern left over from colonial days that does not reflect trends in terms of trade. In any case, the number of food-deficit LDCs is increasing because of increases in population growth, declines in the stock of arable land, and other policies affecting production (see the report of the International Food Policy Research Institute 1976).

A basic needs plan must also stress human capital investments in broad-based and relevant education and training. Just as investments in improved sanitation improve health status and ultimately productivity, so too does education. Balassa (1977) has produced some interesting results concerning the relationship between export performance and the level of physical and human capital.[9] He uses this to support the view that comparative advantage changes in relation to changes in the accumulation of human and physical capital. It is no accident that countries investing to upgrade the productivity of the labor force are dominating LDC exports of labor-intensive manufactured products.

A specific issue that has not received sufficient attention in the basic needs discussion is the issue of recurrent costs. Rather than focus on investment expenditures to achieve BHN target levels for the target population, which is adequately addressed in Burki and Voorhoeve (1977),[10] we should stress the fact that annual recurrent expenditure for investments in basic needs sectors may constitute a significant percentage of those total investment levels. Recurrent costs for education projects often run at the rate of 20 cents annually per dollar of investment. Recurrent costs are also high for health care and food production, while they are lower for housing and for water and sewage. (See Heller [1978] on the problems of recurrent costs.) The implication of high recurrent costs is that resources will be needed to continue investments and, since economic returns on these investments may be slow to materialize, these public expenditures must be supported by dynamic sectors of the economy and by foreign concessional assistance. It should be recalled that LDCs like Korea and Taiwan, which have invested heavily in human capital, also received massive amounts of foreign assistance.

Consider, for example, that the cost estimates for eradicating prevalent tropical diseases—onchocerciasis (river blindness), trypanosomiasis (sleeping sickness), schistosomiasis, and malaria—may be $20 billion (1975 prices) in capital outlays over the next twenty years; however, the recurrent costs may be $22 billion over the same period (Burki and Voorhoeve 1977: 43).[11] When considering the absorptive capacity of a country, financial absorptive capacity is very relevant. Thus, the ability of a BHN approach to be implemented successfully may well turn on a country's ability to finance public expenditures.

One of the most interesting—and controversial—aspects of implementing a basic needs approach is the relationship between BHN and growth. We have stressed that economic growth, employment, and income generation are necessary to achieve BHN objectives. Still, there are aspects of a basic needs plan that could reduce aggregate growth: (1) a shift in income distribution to favor lower income groups raising consumption (see Lluch, Powell, and Williams 1977) on savings patterns in LDCs; (2) a shift in public expenditure toward social services or capital investment with long gestation periods at the expense of investments in physical capital; and (3) the possible redistribution of assets such as land and water rights. The implications are that savings and investment levels would be reduced in the aggregate, thus lowering growth rates.

There are a number of possible offsetting factors, as noted by Crosswell (see Chapter 1), including (1) increased efficiency of production, especially fuller utilization of labor and increased long-run productivity; (2) higher levels of savings and investment, even though rates may actually have declined; (3) technological progress that improves productivity, especially in agriculture; and (4) high returns to BHN-related investments that may be far more income-generating than financial investments undertaken by upper income classes (including capital that leaves the country). The feasible tradeoffs between growth and other objectives of policy can really be assessed only in a country-specific fashion. The selection of the optimal combination of economic objectives is normative, like selecting and weighting the arguments in a social welfare function and also doing so over successive time periods with an appropriately subjective rate of time preference. We turn to this issue in greater detail in the following section.

## GROWTH, EQUITY, AND BASIC NEEDS

The issue of tradeoffs between growth and other policy objectives merits further attention, both on a cross-country basis and on a selected case-by-case basis. (For pioneering work on growth tradeoffs, see Chenery et al. 1974.) Needless to say, the evidence is quite mixed concerning the relationship between growth, equity, and improvements in social indicators (which can be taken to reflect basic needs). The issues relate only secondarily to the selection of indicators per se, since there is some broad agreement concerning relevant indicators,[12] but rather concern primarily the lack of significant relationships found between GNP levels and those indicators. Neither Hicks and Streeten (1978) nor Morawetz (1977) find satisfactory correlations between aggregate income levels and social indicators. While this could perhaps be due to the failure to adjust GNP levels to reflect purchasing power or to technical constraints such as nonlinearities, more probably it reflects disparate performance by individual LDCs.

On a case-by-case basis, counterintuitive examples are given by Fields (1977b) and Grant (1978) to show that neither growth nor improved equity alone are sufficient to ensure absolute poverty alleviation or reductions in disparities among social indicators.[13] No examples have been suggested for countries experiencing both growth and improved distribution which have not improved social indicators. Thus the growth with equity approach of Chenery and his associates has proved to be successful in a few LDCs—Korea, Taiwan, and Costa Rica—which have sustained high rates of growth, high shares of income accruing to the lowest 40 percent of the income distribution, and high social indicators of progress in the achievement of basic needs. Still, attention is too often focussed on the same few countries for whom the strategy has worked. For the majority, it has not.

Following the work of Ahluwalia (1976), who tests the Kuznets' "U-shaped hypothesis" that income distribution worsens at early stages of growth only to improve later,[14] Leipziger and Lewis (1977) have tested the notion that at lower levels of income per capita, it is growth that matters most in improving social indicators, while at higher levels of income, it is distribution that is more relevant to improve BHN-related indexes. A caveat should be added that social indicators are averages and say little about the distribution of those measures of well-being.[15]

What was found in examining seven social indicators—life expectancy, infant mortality, literacy, per capita protein consumption, per capita number of medical personnel, first level enrollment, and percentage of starch in diet—was that for nineteen LDCs with per capita GNP levels below (1975) $550, indexes were significantly correlated with income per capita (with the correct sign) in five out of seven cases, whereas the correlations with measures of income distribution were insignificant. For the sample of LDCs with per capita GNP levels above (1975) $550, the reverse was found; six of the seven indicators of basic needs were significantly correlated with the Gini coefficient, and none were significant with respect to per capita GNP. The results are reproduced in Table 3–1.

While these simple correlations are by no means conclusive, they do support an interesting point: in countries that are too poor to sustain

**Table 3–1. Basic Human Needs Indicators: Correlation Analysis**

| | Life Expectancy (years) | Infant Mortality (per 1000) | Protein Consumption (grams/person) | Doctors and Dentists (per 10,000) | Literacy Rate (population above 15 years) | Starch Percent of Diet (percent of calories) | First Level Enrollment (5–14 Years) |
|---|---|---|---|---|---|---|---|
| **LDCs with per capita GNP above $ (1975) 550 N = 19** | | | | | | | |
| Gini coefficient | .084 (.732) | .457 (.047)[a] | −.638 (.004)[a] | −.489 (.032)[a] | −.564 (.012)[a] | .465 (.043)[a] | −.423 (.068)[a] |
| Per capita income | .121 (.625) | −.100 (.685) | −.253 (.297) | −.166 (.504) | −.019 (.938) | .197 (.575) | −.129 (.603) |
| **LDCs with per capita GNP below $ (1975) 550 N = 19** | | | | | | | |
| Gini coefficient | .042 (.857) | −.214 (.618) | .165 (.505) | −.003 (.988) | .019 (.936) | −.354 (.134) | −.037 (.875) |
| Per capita income | .557 (.013)[a] | −.676 (.002)[a] | .323 (.175) | .343 (.147) | .450 (.051)[a] | −.598 (.007)[a] | .492 (.031)[a] |

Source: Leipziger and Lewis (1977, 1980). Significance levels in parentheses.
[a] Significant correlations at 5 percent or better.

Table 3–2. Correlation Matrix (per capita GNP $1977)

|  | < 580 (N = 13) | > 580 (N = 9) |
|---|---|---|
| Income Share of the Lowest Forty Percent (1975) | − .589[a] | + .602[a] |

[a] Statistically significant at .05 or better.

the basic needs of their populace, a redistribution of existing, inadequate income will not be helpful—that is, there must be something to redistribute. This simple fact is consistent with the finding of Ahluwalia (1977) that the elasticity of income accruing to the lowest 20 percent of the population rises from .18 at GNP per capita levels of $100 to .65 at GNP per capita levels of $500 in 1965–1971 dollars unadjusted for purchasing power equivalents. In a separate test, albeit with a small sample, we have correlated the income accruing to the lowest 40 percent of the populace—using income measures that have been adjusted for purchasing power equivalents[16]—in 1975 with per capita income in 1977, bifurcating the sample as before. The results, reported in Table 3–2, support the findings of Kuznets (1955, 1963) and Ahluwalia (1977) on the U-shaped relationship between income and distribution.

Is an improving income distribution a prerequisite for improvements in basic needs indicators? Our response would be not necessarily, since income distribution is a relative concept and BHN an absolute one. If I am starving, whether you eat two or three meals a day is of academic interest unless we consider your ability to give up a meal on my behalf. Fields (1977a) reports that Brazil's considerable growth in recent years has reduced the actual number of absolute poor while at the same time further worsening the distribution of income. Morley (1978) delves into the measure of income inequality, the Gini coefficient, and follows the recent literature on disaggregation of the Gini (see Paglin 1975; Danziger, Haveman, and Smolensky 1977; and Pyatt 1976). He criticizes Fields for not differentiating among the base period population and the current population. Morley finds that changing income distribution is due to an increasing population and a change in profile of lifetime income rather than relatively low rates of income growth among the poor. His conclusion that considerable upward mobility and rising inequality coexist is consistent with the view that it is people close to the poverty line that move out of the absolute poverty rubric at the same time that new entrants enter the lowest end of the distribution (see Leipziger and Lewis 1977).

Is rapid growth a prerequisite for improvements in basic need indica-

Table 3–3.  Per Capita Impact of Subsidies, Taxes, and Transfers in Sri Lanka, 1973 Income Group by Spending Unit (annual Rs.)

| Per Capita | Less than 600 (.3% of I.D.) | 600–1200 (2.4% of I.D.) | 1200–2400 (21.7% of I.D.) | 2400–4800 (49.5% of I.D.) |
|---|---|---|---|---|
| Food subsidy | 12.5 | 21 | 41 | 59 |
| Health care | ............28............ | | 24 | 19 |
| Education | ............37............ | | 43 | 53 |
| Social welfare | 101 | 89 | – | – |
| Total subsidy | 200 | 170 | 128 | 153 |
| Total income[a] | 444 | 654 | 664 | 902 |
| Percentage of income | 45 | 30 | 19 | 17 |
| Total tax[b] | 67 | 64 | 83 | 139 |
| Percentage of income | 15 | 10 | 12 | 15 |
| Net subsidy as $ of income | 30 | 15 | 7 | 2 |

Source: Alailima (1978:34–36, 71–75) and Sri Lanka (1978).

[a] Personal disposable income.

[b] Much of the taxation is export duties on rural poor.

tors? Here again, the answer is not necessarily, but the answer is a more ambiguous one. The obvious case that comes to mind is Sri Lanka, a country whose populace enjoys a life expectancy equal to that of most industrialized countries although its per capita income level places it in the low-income LDC group. Sri Lanka is an anomaly with respect to other social indicators, including literacy, infant mortality, fertility, and income distribution. Much of this is due to redistributive policies, including a food subsidy program that has averaged 20 percent of current government expenditures over the past fifteen years, and to an educational system that is quite advanced.[17] It is estimated that the food "ration" in Sri Lanka provides 20 percent of total caloric intake for families with household incomes below Rp. 400 per month (corresponding to approximately the seven lowest deciles of the distribution). This demonstrates how pervasive the food ration actually is. Table 3–3 provides some details of Sri Lankan fiscal incidence.

It is important to note that Sri Lanka's per capita growth has been rather low during the period from 1960 to 1976, averaging 2 percent per capita. During roughly the same period, the adult literacy rate increased from 61 to 78 percent, infant mortality dropped from 57 to 45 per 1000, the birth rate fell from 38 to 27 per 1000, and life expectancy increased from sixty-one to sixty-eight years (IBRD 1978). Sri Lanka has had some growth, and it has stretched those resources to achieve very respectable indicators of well-being. However, the consensus is that the excessive reliance on transfers (often transfers to the bulk of the population) and in education per se (rather than on relevant education cum jobs) has created an unsustainable situation.

The Sri Lankan experience demonstrates that a pattern of growth that can improve income distribution is feasible. Sri Lanka's growth during the 1960s was 2.4 percent per capita (which ranks ninth in the category of LDCs below [1975] $265); during approximately the same period (1963–1973), the Gini coefficient improved 22 percent, from .45 to .35, and the income share of the poorest 20 percent increased by almost two-thirds, from 4.4 to 7.2 percent of income (Sri Lanka 1978). It also demonstrates that the provision of subsidized food and free health care and education must be balanced with the creation of employment and income. In that connection, it should be noted that Sri Lanka has recently moved to restructure the economy to reduce price subsidies and to open the economy to imports in light of a stagnant economy, rising prices, and declining real incomes among broad segments of the population.

What can we conclude about the relationship between growth, equity, and poverty—perhaps the most tantalizing current development policy issue? Since the rate of population growth is increasing the number of people in absolute poverty at an alarming rate, progress in the alleviation of poverty requires major increases in national output. There must be growth. Growth can create employment, can allow for an easier redistribution of assets, and can finance public expenditures. The question is what the pattern of growth will be. Although historically growth has been accompanied by a more uneven distribution of income—according to Adelman and Morris (1973), Ahluwalia (1977), and others—we have found that growth can be the most important element in raising indicators of well-being in low-income developing countries. This is probably especially true for the Indian subcontinent, where the bulk of the "absolute poor" are to be found, because income distribution is fairly equal—income happens to be equally too low.

Furthermore, history need not always be a guide; alternative patterns of growth are possible. The Sri Lankan emphasis on equity and social services is noteworthy. So is the emphasis by Korea and Taiwan on land reform and education and labor-intensive exports. Also relevant is the emphasis on social services in Costa Rica. (Workman's compensation began in 1924. Sickness, maternity, disability, retirement, and death funds were established in 1941. A family assistance scheme, aimed at raising the standard of living of the low-income groups, especially in rural areas, was begun in 1975. Our statistical evidence shows that in middle-income LDCs in particular, where a minimum growth process has begun, redistributive policies can be very effective in improving indicators associated with basic needs objectives. Some indicators of well-being are indirect, such as physicians per 1000 inhabitants, and therefore require more information on access before firmer conclusions can be drawn; other indicators, which more directly measure well-being, such as caloric intake, are still averages and can therefore hide significant disparities. Nevertheless, a basic, supportable finding for middle-income countries is that redistributive policies with respect to income, access to education, land reform, and basic social services can meaningfully improve the lives of the poor.[18]

Chenery, Ahluwalia, and Carter (1978) simulate a number of alternative patterns of growth for LDCs until the year 2000. They find that redistributive policies (i.e., the poorest 60 percent of the population receive 45 percent of incremental income until the year 2000) will reduce the number in absolute poverty (defined as the lowest 40 percent of India's population applied to all LDCs with country purchasing power equivalents) by more than 50 percent compared to the base case. They report that growth rates would be lower with this scenario (although the rationale for the growth versus equity tradeoffs remaining immutable for twenty years is not given). Still, a "reasonable" social welfare function might well consider this outcome preferable. A second alternative shows that 1 percent higher growth in the low-income LDCs reduces poverty by one-quarter. Additional growth and redistribution reduces the number of absolute poor by over three-quarters.

These simulations are really based on static behavioral assumptions. The importance of the basic needs discussion may well be in altering those static assumptions and stimulating patterns of growth that provide more favorable combinations of growth, equity, and improvement in well-being of the poor. Let us summarize some of the important issues raised by the basic needs approach:

1. The approach stresses not only the creation of income among the poor, but also the production of vital goods and services; thus it deals with employment generation and supply management.
2. The role of government is vital, not only for planning purposes, which are important if the linkages to the poor and complementarities among programs are to be sharpened, but also because market interventions will be required.[19]
3. The government must broaden the distribution of assets and the distribution of services and will often provide merit goods.
4. There is a role for transfers to the poorest of the poor, but welfare measures are a relatively small part of a basic needs approach.
5. Nontangible aspects such as social and political participation are relevant, especially for local implementation.
6. The social objective function can be expanded to include other as-

pects of well-being than growth and equity and policies can be directed at changing the implicit tradeoff by creating more employment, investing in human capital, and taking account of the externalities of public expenditure programs.

## IMPLICATIONS FOR DONORS

The endorsement of the BHN approach can provide an opportunity for donors to identify more closely with ultimate development objectives, and it can provide developing countries with a framework with which to appraise their own development strategies. The key is planning, which serves to highlight linkages between resource allocation, policies, and objectives within a country-specific context. For some bilateral donors, like the United States, a BHN approach is perceived to be more clearly humanitarian and perhaps is more readily supported by a domestic constituency that does not generally view foreign assistance as a major priority. While it has been argued by Sewell (1978) and others that assistance should be based on economic self-interest, the countries with the bulk of the world's poor tend not to be those with whom the United States has major commercial interests. Indeed, since 1973, the U.S. development assistance program has focused on what might be termed "direct impact sectors" [20] and is currently experimenting with "indicative allocation formulas for" aid recipients based on per capita income, population or population below subsistence, and commitment of the recipient government to development strategies that will benefit a broad spectrum of the population.[21]

Care must be taken, however, that a basic needs approach to foreign assistance does not result in an artificial dichotomy of projects into "BHN projects" and "others," with the result that many worthy projects will go unfunded. While it is true that some development projects—for example, the provision of safe water, subsidized enriched foods, and agricultural extension services—can impact more directly on the poor, the long-run attainment of BHN objectives requires not only employable individuals but also the creation of employment. BHN is not an antigrowth strategy.

BHN objectives do not imply that "small is beautiful," that only feeder roads be built or only cottage industries be supported. It is not an exclusively agrarian concept, although it is true that most of the poor are in rural areas. What it is, however, is a recognition of the distributive impact of policies and projects on the poor, not only in a relative sense (of income distribution) but also in an absolute sense (of alleviating poverty).

The *Economist* (1978:26) states that "the basic needs approach is not incompatible with other models of development." It goes on to say that the BHN approach requires basic infrastructure as well but involves the posing of the fundamental question of who benefits from policies and programs. The question of who benefits has been and continues to be a central issue of development policy. What the BHN discussion adds to the "incidence assessment" is specificity with respect to ultimate objectives of policy.

The perception is increasingly widespread that if the basic needs approach is to be useful to donors and recipients, it must be viewed within the context of strategies to increase output, income and employment of the poor. Recent U.S. policy papers on the subject emphasize that:

> insofar as the basic needs approach is concerned with sustainable improvements in living standards, it follows that the impact on the poor of some programs and projects can be longer-term rather than immediate, direct rather than indirect, and non-exclusive rather than exclusive. So long as this impact is verifiable, timely, and ultimately significant, foreign assistance efforts need not focus only on direct impact activities. (U.S. Special Topic Paper 1978:10)

Developing countries, which have been highly skeptical of the approach because of its perceived anti-industry bias or its perceived rigid egalitarianism, may find it a more workable concept as it evolves. If a country can lay out economic objectives that enfranchise the poor and a strategy demonstrates the linkages to other economic activities, then "no sector should be excluded *a priori* as a legitimate target for economic assistance under a BHN strategy" (USAID 1978:12).

The position of the U.K.'s Overseas Development Ministry (1978) is worth a brief examination. While the U.K.'s assistance program makes clear that the focus is on the poorest countries and the poorest people, it emphatically rejects a "welfare approach" that would limit support to particular sectors:

> We recognise the dangers of too narrow an approach to helping the poor. Improvements in the production and productivity of the rural poor can be brought about not only by rural development or by projects such as small-scale irrigation or rural electrification schemes, but also by major infrastructure projects such as dams and power stations which will make the small scale rural projects possible, and by processing plants for agricultural products. [p. 5]

The U.K. also advocates financing alternative sound economic projects, given the difficulties of finding and implementing projects that help the poor to meet their basic needs. The U.K. mandate is thus quite a bit wider than that of USAID and probably closer to the wishes of the developing countries.

The basic needs framework presents new challenges to both donors and recipients of foreign assistance. The task falls on recipients to articulate final objectives or targets, to devise a consistent set of policies to achieve them, and to marshall the needed domestic and external resources. If external transfers are to be effective, domestic redistribution of assets may be required. For donors, the resource requirements needed by developing countries will not fall, especially if there is to be a more specific commitment to the alleviation of absolute poverty.[22] Already the evidence is developing that the more specific project orientation of donors is slowing disbursements. (This has been true for USAID. See Gayoso 1978.) Not only are the infrastructure needs as pronounced as ever, but the human capital investments that are to be encouraged involve high recurrent fiscal expenditures and economic returns that are apparent only in the longer run. Donors cannot be insensitive to the full implications of the basic needs approach.

If greater proportions of fiscal budgets are to be earmarked for health, nutrition, education, and family planning, then greater demands for public expenditure may, at least in the short to medium term, outstrip domestic resources. Even with increased employment generation (which takes time to implement) and more effective taxation, fiscal crises will develop, and the macroeconomic consequences will be increased domestic money creation, inflation, and balance of payments crises. Although increased concessional assistance and lengthened maturities for private capital flows are needed, somewhat altered procedures for handling payments crises may also be required.

I have argued elsewhere (Leipziger 1978) that greater coordination between the IMF and IBRD would be desirable and that increased IBRD resources for program lending—recently totaling only 2 percent of total lending—is called for. Countries committed to social development may need additional resources and/or additional time to bring their external accounts into balance in order not to jeopardize their development plans too drastically and in order to buffer the effects of adjustment programs on the lower income segments of society. With increasing recurrent expenditures on the fiscal side accompanying BHN-oriented development strategies, donors may wish to increase foreign exchange assistance while at the same time earmarking the domestic currency equivalents for specific purposes.

## INTERNATIONAL IMPLICATIONS

There is a pronounced tendency to place the basic needs discussion squarely in the middle of the North-South dialogue. It would be in our view rather unfortunate to use BHN objectives as a counterweight to the demands by LDCs for a new international economic order. They should not be presented as demands for internal policy changes in LDCs to substitute for changes in the international economic structure.

The challenge to the developed countries—and to those rapidly advancing developing countries—is to demonstrate that the current economic system is capable of directing increased resources to LDCs in support of basic needs objectives. Part of that challenge is to show that the open economic system, which has fostered unprecedented postwar growth, can accommodate new entrants capable of obtaining an increasing share of world output. In order to compete successfully for larger shares of incremental world income and in order to contribute to the long-term growth in world income, LDCs need to satisfy the basic needs of their people.

Thus, we would argue that reforms in the international economy that enable a larger number of developing countries to effectively participate in the world's trade and investment flows can be complementary to domestic and donor efforts to foster more equitable growth in developing countries. Observers have noted a tendency, at least in the United States, not to integrate development policies with overall economic policies.[23]

Now that the first phase of euphoria about a "new development strategy" has been surpassed by realism, it is clear that very poor countries in the Indian subcontinent and in sub-Saharan Africa cannot create employment and income for the poor without substantial new inflows of resources, sustained economic growth, and a major political commitment to rural development. At the recent Colombo Plan Annual Meeting in Washington, developing countries had little difficulty in accepting BHN objectives as part of an overall development strategy (see Colombo Plan 1978:ch. IV).

The Colombo Plan Consultative Committee, consisting of eighteen LDCs of South and East Asia and six major donors (including the United States, the United Kingdom, Canada, Japan, New Zealand, and Australia) agreed to a common report concerning basic needs. Inter alia, they report that "the emphasis on basic human needs is not a rejection of the need for economic growth, but rather a sharper focus on achieving patterns of growth that increase the capacity of people to provide for their own basic needs." It was further agreed, therefore, that "the basic needs concept is a useful approach to organize enhanced domestic and international efforts for greater economic cooperation among [Colombo Plan] members in order to achieve accelerated growth and distributive justice" and that "there is no single development strategy for meeting basic needs which is appropriate for all countries and members recognize and respect this diversity" (Colombo Plan 1978:ch. IV). This type of consensus document may be significant in reopening the dialogue on development issues, perhaps in the context of the International Development Strategy (IDS) for the third development decade (1980–1990) to be negotiated in the United Nations.

The IDS serves to highlight the potential positive linkage between a new international economic order that developing countries see as the sine qua non for their own progress and approaches such as basic needs that aim at substantial improvements in living standards. While I would argue that the BHN approach has relevance primarily in a country context, there are international policies that reflect the nature of the system that can improve the chances of success of a humanistic and sustainable growth strategy. The first link is trade, and the second is the flow of capital.

With respect to trade we have stressed the importance of employment generation. An employment-generating industrialization strategy will be likely to concentrate on labor-intensive products. Increasingly, we are witnessing the "product cycle theory" in action as newly industrializing LDCs enter new areas of production, and quite a few of them have done remarkably well.[24] Although rates of employment generation have not in general kept pace with individual output increases—due in part to inappropriate technologies by LDCs[25]—lower labor-cost products have made significant inroads in selected industries. In the United States, for example, Anne Krueger (1979) documents those inroads to be a small fraction of the market in most industries.[26] Keesing (1978) estimates total employment displacement in 1975 in the OECD countries attributable to the slowdown in demand that was twenty times larger than displacement caused by increased imports from LDCs.[27] At the same time, protectionist pressures are increasing, OECD countries' commitments to "positive adjustment" to changes in dynamic comparative advantage are mostly rhetoric, and the results of the multilateral trade negotiations (MTN) are reported by GATT do involve smaller tariff cuts for LDCs than for DCs. In addition, much of the current protectionism is in the form of nontariff barriers (see Perez 1978).

The main conceptual difficulties to be overcome in the trade area are reciprocity and graduation. It is unrealistic for LDCs to think that protectionism can be unilateral. Often, LDC tariffs are not imposed for infant industry arguments, but rather to dampen imports or raise revenue. Some LDCs—notably Chile of late—are drastically reducing tariff levels, partly to eliminate inefficient import substitution industries and partly to reduce inflation. The DCs, for their part, do not have plans to phase out inefficient and antiquated industries and thus often buckle to domestic pressures to grant protection. In agriculture, this is especially true in the EEC, where the "common agricultural policy" limits free trade. With the LDC labor force growing at 2–3 percent a year and unemployment and underemployment rates running at 30 percent, LDCs cannot hope to cope with the estimated 700 million new entrants by the year 2000 without massive new employment opportunities (ILO 1976:47). Massive employment generation needed to create income in LDCs cannot progress in the long run unless a really open trading system exists.

Graduation may be a method of directing trade preferences to those LDCs whose needs are greatest and whose ability to compete internationally is weakest. Special and differential treatment for LDCs, such as that granted through generalized special preferences (GSP), has tended to benefit the more industrialized LDCs.[28] Many of these successful exporters no longer require special measures and in fact are now strong enough competitors internationally that they can open their own markets to increased competition.

On the capital side, there is no doubt that increases in concessional resource transfers are needed. While the exact quantification of external resource needs to achieve certain growth targets—such as those proposed by the United Nations to achieve IDS growth targets (see UNCTAD 1976; UNESCO 1979)[29]—are not practical, it is clear that savings rates in the low-income LDCs have been far too low to sustain acceptable growth rates. In 1976, the low-income LDCs (GNP per capita below $250) had average savings rates of 8 percent of GDP (IBRD 1978:84). And of total official development assistance (ODA) in 1976 of almost $14 billion (0.33 percent of donor countries' GNP), perhaps 55 percent, or $7.7 billion, went to those low-income LDCs, which would amount to less than an additional 4 percent of their GDP.[30]

Increases in concessional assistance are extremely difficult to eke out of national legislatures. It is argued by some that greater appropriations can be justified to legislatures only if assistance actually helps the lowest income segments of the Third World. Others, including Sewell (1978), the Swedish government, and international secretariats, argue that increasing the transfer of resources to LDCs is in the best interests of the developed countries, since it will prompt additional demand for exports and stimulate growth in the OECD countries.[31] While one can argue about the size of the relevant multipliers of any scheme and assess the costs and benefits accruing to any nation and group of nations, the real question remains: Are the developed countries willing to improve the economic system by placing greater emphasis on equity concerns; or must the system be revamped along the lines of the New International Economic Order, which would reduce its efficiency but enhance its potential for equity?

Two areas where fairly effortless transfers were possible and where the equity of the system could have been improved were the Law of the Sea Conference and the decisions concerning distribution of special drawing rights (SDRs). These are selected because in both cases the "resources" were not yet appropriated by nations—offshore drilling past 200 miles or below 200 meters was not yet commonplace; no commercial ventures are as yet mining the deep seabed for manganese nodules; and SDRs were first created in 1970, 1971, and 1972, only to be continued after a six-year hiatus by the International Monetary Fund this year. In both cases, however, the distribution of benefits from new resources has reinforced maldistributions of global income.[32]

## CONCLUDING REMARK

What does this have to do with the basic needs discussion? The answer to my mind is that the current economic system and the national policies of governments (which are dependent to some extent on the international system but retain independent elements as well) must deal with the problem of absolute impoverishment. The BHN framework provides a means for both developing countries and donors to organize their efforts to alleviate absolute poverty. Even with enlightened domestic policies, a commitment to upgrade peoples' standards of living and enhance access to basic goods and services will require additional external resources. An international economic order cannot tolerate conditions where one out of every four individuals on this earth lacks a vital element of subsistence. An economic system must strike a balance between efficiency and equity. The basic human needs thrust may well be the test for the viability of the current order.

## NOTES

1. A Basic Needs approach was endorsed by Secretary Vance at the OECD in June of 1977 and has since been an accepted policy of the U.S. government as reflected in the Foreign Assistance Act of 1978. For the DAC's views, see DAC (1977).
2. The ILO (1976) also included public transportation among core needs. Others have stressed the importance of family planning; see, for example, Leipziger and Lewis (1977).
3. See Musgrove (1978) for consumption studies in urban Latin America.
4. The classic case of a public good, of course, is national defense, which the private market cannot supply to individual consumers.

5. See Head (1974) and Musgrave and Musgrave (1976) for a discussion of merit goods in theory and Leipziger and Lewis (1977) for an application to the basic needs issue.
6. The food stamp analogy in the United States is a case in point, as are the food subsidies in Sri Lanka and Colombia.
7. Sri Lanka's life expectancy of sixty-eight years equals that of many developed countries and makes it an anomaly in the group of countries with similar per capita incomes.
8. See Selowsky and Taylor (1973) on the negative effects of malnutrition in children on lifetime earnings performance, and see Jamieson and Lau (1978) and Psacharapoulos and Hinchliffe (1973) on the returns to investments in education. With respect to human capital investments, Selowsky (1979) argues that those investments can be a redistributive tool if the focus is primary education or a regressive investment if the focus is higher education. A full blown cost-benefit assessment would of course have to deal with societal returns to investments in the long run as well as individual benefits.
9. The countries in which comparative advantage in labor-intensive goods is influenced most by the flow measure of human capital are Colombia, Hong Kong, India, Israel, Korea, Malaysia, Mexico, Morocco, Pakistan, Philippines, Singapore, Taiwan and Turkey (Balassa 1977:13).
10. They conclude that $19 billion of investment annually between 1980 and the year 2000 is needed in order to make available adequate diet, sewage and water, education and health to the target population. These estimates do not include recurrent costs, however.
11. These estimates should be viewed as illustrative of the problem rather than as accurate measures of the costs of preventive and curative health care.
12. There are differences perhaps concerning the aggregation (i.e., scaling and weighting) of selected indicators in the so-called "physical quality of life index" (PQLI), although most indicators are fairly highly correlated with one another. See Morris (1978) on PQLIs and Hicks and Streeten (1978) on indicators.
13. Fields (1977b) reports Brazil and the Philippines as cases of growth without equity. The number of people in absolute poverty is reported to have increased over time in the Philippines and to have been reduced in Brazil. He also reports India and Sri Lanka as cases of improved equity with poor growth performance. In Sri Lanka, absolute poverty was reduced, while in India it increased. Grant's (1978) "disparity reduction rates," which measure percentage improvements in the PQLI versus an absolute standard, tend to correspond to the alleviation of poverty measures and are similarly unrelated to GNP growth.
14. Ahluwalia (1976) finds that below a certain income level (say $400 in mid-sixties dollars per capita), higher income is associated with worsening distribution, but that this trend is reversed at higher income levels (above $400 per capita). These cross-section results tend to confirm the results of the original Adelman-Morris (1973) work that growth tends to worsen distribution, but it does not confirm their finding that growth produces greater absolute impoverishment of the poor. See also Kuznets (1955, 1963). Cline (1975b) surveys the income distribution literature.
15. As an example, Selowsky (1979) reports data on Turkish per capita consumption as a percentage of daily requirements. While the national average is 104 percent of requirements, 17.4 percent of the populace consumed less than 75 percent of requirements and another 23.6 percent of the populace consumes between 75 percent and 90 percent of requirements.
16. See Chenery et al. (1978). For a further discussion of growth, distribution, and social indicators, see Leipziger and Lewis (1980).
17. It is reported that literacy is a significant explanator of (lowered) infant mortality across countries and is also significantly related to life expectancy (see Isenman 1979).

18. Our view would be that the costs of this approach may well be absorbable. Selowsky (1979) demonstrates that the GNP losses associated with eliminating caloric deficits in individual LDCs, for example, are rather sustainable.
19. Srinivasan (1977) makes the excellent point that through selective government intervention, BHN objectives can be met at lower levels of national income than would otherwise occur. He also traces the origin of the BHN approach to the Fifth Indian Development Plan of 1972. See Srinivasan (1977:21, 31) and his review of the Bellagio Conference.
20. These sectors are health, education, population, and agricultural development.
21. The current thrust of the foreign assistance program is to concentrate aid on those countries committed to improving the basic needs of the poor majority (see U.S. Congress 1978).
22. Aggregate resource requirements to eliminate absolute poverty have been estimated for the next two decades by a number of sources. The ILO has developed cost estimates based on an income-generating approach—namely, how much would it cost to generate sufficient growth in income of the poor so that they could purchase a BHN bundle of goods and services. See Hopkins and Scolnik (1976) and Stern (1976). The IBRD has produced estimates concentrating on the supply side—namely, the investment costs (and recurrent costs) to supply BHN elements to the target population until the year 2000. See Burki and Voorhoeve (1977).

    Such aggregate estimates are fraught with peril; furthermore, the estimates are, each in their own way, distortions. The ILO estimates are based on a static trade model that does not include prices, so that no purchasing power equivalents for income are possible. They cannot deal adequately with nonpurchasable social services. The resulting resource requirements are therefore quite misleading. IBRD estimates of investment requirements are dependent on the particular technology chosen (e.g., for sewage, food production) and speculation on recurrent costs. They also ignore important aspects of distribution.

    Just as one approach ignores supply, the other ignores demand. If one were to estimate resource requirements, it would have to be part of a country-specific planning exercise. Khan (1976) has produced a rudimentary estimate of resource requirements for Bangladesh; however, to integrate the supply and demand sides, one would need to turn to an integrated, disaggregated general equilibrium model that includes income distribution and prices. This approach is followed by Adelman and Robinson (1977), and DeMelo and Robinson (1976), although it has yet to be applied in the basic needs context.
23. Michalopoulos (1979) points to the failure to integrate U.S. trade policy with our foreign assistance strategy, which is based on employment generation in labor-intensive industries.
24. In the aggregate, LDC exports of manufactures have increased fivefold between 1967 and 1977 and are projected by the IBRD to triple again by 1985. While total LDC-manufactured exports totaled $58 billion in 1977, production was highly concentrated in a dozen or so LDCs.
25. Often technology choice reflects the activities of multinationals (see Courtney and Leipziger 1975), or incorrect factor prices, or national considerations.
26. Krueger (1979:18) estimates that only 9 percent of incremental manufactured imports into DC markets during 1960–1976 originated in LDCs. She also estimates that the level of imports is only the major determinant of employment changes (compared with demand shifts and productivity changes) in one industry, leather goods, during 1970–1976 (ibid., p. 29) and that only in three industries would the elimination of the increased import share have reversed the declines in employment (ibid., p. 35).

27. Keesing (1978:21) also reports that for the 1962–1975 period in the Federal Republic of Germany the proportion of employment losses attributable to increased LDC imports were 2 percent of losses due to increased labor productivity.
28. In the U.S. case, five LDCs—Taiwan, Korea, Hong Kong, Brazil, and Mexico—accounted for two-thirds of the GSP benefits in 1979. Total duty-free GSP imports in 1979 were $6.3 billion.
29. Fixed relationships between external resource requirements and aggregate performance tend to ignore differential performance among LDCs, the importance of complementary domestic resources and policies, and the limits of models used to estimate those relationships.
30. Assuming that the 1975 bilateral ODA share to countries below $250 is 55 percent and that 1975 GNPs for low-income LDCs total approximately $220 billion. These are rough orders of magnitude, since we assume that 1975 and 1976 shares are equal and that bilateral ODA and multilateral ODA shares are equal (see OECD/DAC 1976: statistical annex).
31. A number of other proposals have surfaced recently to transfer massive resources to the Third World in a manner similar to the postwar Marshall Plan. A number of factors that are not considered are (1) the basic difference between constraints facing LDCs and war-ravaged Europe; (2) the source, method, terms, and recipients of such a flow of capital; and (3) the basic dichotomy between policies to stimulate OECD countries' growth, including inflation tradeoffs and linkages to a few major industrializing LDCs, and policies to reach the majority of the poor in LDCs through appropriate project assistance and employment generation.
32. Leipziger and Mudge (1977:213–16) show that offshore oil potential is positively correlated with income and that the Gini coefficient with respect to offshore hydrocarbons is significantly higher (the distribution is more uneven) than with respect to income. Therefore the geographic distribution of revenue—and the absence of any meaningful revenue sharing—will exacerbate international income inequalities.

    With respect to SDRs, distributions are according to IMF quota shares, so that more seigniorage accrues to larger, richer nations. Alternative methods of distribution are discussed by Howe (1972), Michalopoulos and Leipziger (1972) and Cline (1975a) as part of the debate on the "SDR-aid link."

## BIBLIOGRAPHY

Adelman, I. 1975. "Development Economics—A Reassessment of Goals." *American Economic Review* 65, no. 2:302–309.

———. 1978. "Redistribution Before Growth—A Strategy for Developing Countries." University of Maryland Department of Economics Working Paper 78-14. Mimeo.

Adelman, I., and C. Morris. 1973. *Social Equity and Economic Growth in Developing Countries*. Stanford, Calif.: Stanford University Press.

Adelman, I., and S. Robinson. 1977. *Income Distribution Policy in Developing Countries: A Case Study of Korea*. Stanford: Stanford University Press.

Ahluwalia, M. S. 1976. "Inequality, Poverty, and Development." *Journal of Development Economics* 3, no. 4:307–342.

Ahluwalia, M. S., and H. Chenery. 1974. "A Model of Distribution and Growth."

In H. Chenery et al., *Redistribution with Growth*. London: Oxford University Press.

Alailima, P. 1978. "Income Distribution and Employment Programme: Fiscal Incidence in Sri Lanka." Geneva: International Labor Office.

Balassa, B. 1977. "A *Stages* Approach to Comparative Advantage." World Bank Staff Working Paper No. 256. Washington, D.C.: IBRD.

Burki, S. J., and J. J. C. Voorhoeve. 1977. "Global Estimates for Meeting Basic Needs: Background Paper." Washington, D.C.: IBRD. Mimeo.

Chenery, H. B.; M. S. Ahluwalia; and N. Carter. 1978. "Growth and Poverty in Developing Countries." World Bank Staff Working Paper No. 309. Washington, D.C.: IBRD.

Chenery, H. B.; M. S. Ahluwalia; C. L. G. Bell; J. Duloy; and R. Jolly. 1974. *Redistribution with Growth*. Oxford: Oxford University Press.

Cline, W. 1975a. "Distribution and Development: A Survey of Literature." *Journal of Development Economics* 1, no. 4:359–400.

———. 1975b. *The Reform of the International Monetary System*. Washington, D.C.: Brookings Institution.

Colombo Plan. 1978. Twenty-Seventh Consultative Committee Meeting Annual Report. Washington, D.C., December.

Courtney, W., and D. Leipziger. 1975. "Multinational Corporations in Developing Countries: The Choice of Technology." *Oxford Bulletin of Economics and Statistics* 37, no. 4:297–304.

Crosswell, M. 1978a. "Basic Human Needs: A Development Planning Approach." AID Discussion Paper, No. 38. Washington, D.C.: Agency for International Development.

———. 1978b. "Basic Human Needs: Objectives, Policies, and Implications for Growth." Washington, D.C.: Agency for International Development. Mimeo.

Danziger, S.; R. Haveman; and E. Smolensky. 1977. "The Measurement and Trend of Inequality: Comment." *American Economic Review* 67, no. 2:507–12.

De Melo, J., and S. Robinson. 1976. "A Planning Model Featuring Trade, Intra-Sector Product Differentiation and Income Distribution." Discussion Paper No. 69, Woodrow Wilson School, Princeton University.

Development Assistance Committee (DAC). 1977. "Statement by DAC Members on Development Cooperation for Economic Growth and Meeting Basic Human Needs." Annex to the Communiqué of the DAC High-Level Meeting (October). Paris: OECD.

*The Economist*, April 22, 1978, p. 26 (survey).

Fields, G. 1977a. "Who Benefits from Economic Development: A Reexamination of Brazilian Growth in the 1960s." *American Economic Review* 67, no. 4:570–82.

———. 1977b. "Poverty, Inequality, and the Measurement of Development Performance." Washington, D.C.: Agency for International Development. Mimeo.

Gayoso, A. 1978. "Aid Instruments—A Review of Their Implications for Speed of Program Implementation." Washington, D.C.: Agency for International Development. Mimeo.

Grant, J. 1977. "The New International Economic Order and the World's Poorest Billion: A Fresh Appoach." Washington, D.C.: Overseas Development Council. Mimeo.

———. 1978. "Disparity Reduction Rates in Social Indicators: A Proposal for Measuring and Targeting Progress in Meeting Basic Needs." Monograph No. 11, Washington, D.C.: Overseas Development Council.

Head, J. 1974. *Public Goods and Public Welfare.* Durham, N.C.: Duke University Press.

Heller, P. 1978. The Under-financing of Recurrent Development Costs." *Finance and Development* (IMF/IBRD), Washington, D.C.) 16, no. 1, 38–41.

Hicks, N., and P. Streeten. 1978. "Indicators for Development: The Search for a Basic Needs Yardstick." Washington, D.C.: IBRD. Mimeo.

Hopkins, M., and H. Scolnik. 1976. "Basic Needs, Growth and Redistribution: A Quantitative Approach." In ILO, *Employment, Growth and Basic Needs.* Tripartite World Conference on Employment, Income Distribution and Social Progress and the International Division of Labor. Geneva.

Howe, J. 1972. "Let's Spread Them Around." *Foreign Policy* 8 (Fall): 110–12.

International Bank for Reconstruction and Development (IBRD). 1978. *World Development Report.* Washington, D.C.

International Food Policy Research Institute. 1976. "Meeting Food Needs in the Development World." Research Report No. 1. Washington, D.C.

International Labor Organization (ILO). 1976. *Employment, Growth and Basic Needs.* Tripartite World Conference on Employment, Income Distribution and Social Progress and the International Division of Labor. Geneva.

Isenman, P. 1979. "The Relationship of Basic Needs to Growth, Income Distribution and Employment: The Case of Sri Lanka." Washington, D.C.: IBRD. Mimeo.

Jamieson, D., and L. Lau. 1978. "Farmer Education, and Farm Efficiency." Washington, D.C.: World Bank. Mimeo.

Keesing, D. 1979. "World Trade and Output of Manufactures: Structural Trends and Development Countries' Exports." World Bank Staff Working Paper No. 316. Washington, D.C.: IBRD.

Khan, A. R. 1976. "Basic Needs: An Illustrative Exercise in Identification and Quantification with Reference to Bangladesh." Geneva: ILO. Mimeo.

Krueger, A. 1979. "LDC Manufacturing Production and Implications for OECD Comparative Advantage." in I. Leveson and J. Wheeler 1980. *Western Economies in Transition: Structural Change and Adjustment Policies in Industrial Countries.* Boulder, Col.: Westview Press, pp. 216–249.

Kuznets, S. 1955. "Economic Growth and Income Inequality." *American Economic Review* 45, no. 1: 1–28.

———. 1963. "Quantitative Aspects of Economic Growth of Nations: Distribution of Income by Size." *Economic Development and Cultural Change* 11, no. 2, pt, II.

Leipziger, D. M. 1978. "Short-Term Stabilization and Long-Term Development." Paper presented at the Southern Economics Association Meeting, Washington, D.C.

Leipziger, D. M., and M. Lewis. 1977. "A Basic Human Needs Approach to Development." Paper presented at the Western Economics Association Meetings, Honolulu, Hawaii.

————. 1980. "Social Indicators, Growth, and Distribution." *World Development* 8 (April):299–302.

Leipziger, D. M., and J. L. Mudge. 1977. *Seabed Mineral Resources and the Economic Interests of Developing Nations.* Cambridge, Mass.: Ballinger Publishing Company.

Lluch, C.; A. Powell; and R. Williams. 1977. *Patterns in Household Demand and Savings.* London: Oxford University Press.

Meerman, J. 1977. "Meeting Basic Needs in Malaysia: A Summary of Findings." World Bank Staff Working Paper No. 260. Washington, D.C.: IBRD.

————. 1978. *"Public Expenditure in Malaysia: Who Gets What and Why."* Washington, D.C.: IBRD. Mimeo.

Michalopoulos, C. 1979. "Policy Implementation Issues of Basic Needs Strategies." Paper presented to the Seminar on Moral and Political Implications of Policy Alternatives, Georgetown University, Washington, D.C.

Michalopoulos, C., and D. M. Leipziger. 1972. "The Nature of an SDR-Aid Link." Washington, D.C.: Agency for International Development. Mimeo.

Morawetz, D. 1977. "Twenty-Five Years of Economic Development." Washington, D.C.: IBRD. Mimeo.

Morley, S. 1978. "The Effect of Changes in the Population on Several Measures of Income Distribution." Nashville, Tenn.: Vanderbilt University. Mimeo.

Morris, M. D. 1978. "Measuring the Condition of the World's Poor: The Physical Quality of Life Index." Washington, D.C.: Overseas Development Council. Mimeo.

Musgrave, R., and P. Musgrave. 1976. *Public Finance in Theory and Practice.* New York: McGraw-Hill.

Musgrove, P. 1978. *Consumer Behavior in Latin America: Income and Spending of Families in Ten Andean Cities.* Washington, D.C.: Brookings Institute.

Organization for Economic Cooperation and Development–Development Assistance Committee. 1976. *Development Cooperation: 1976.* Paris.

Paglin, M. 1975. "The Measurement and Trend of Inequality: A Basic Revision." *American Economic Review* 65, no. 3: 598–609.

Perez, Lorenzo, ed. 1978. *Trade Policies Toward Developing Countries.* Washington, D.C.: Agency for International Development.

Psacharopoulos, G., and K. Hinchliffe. 1973. *Returns to Education: An International Comparison.* Amsterdam: Elsevier.

Pyatt, G. 1976. "On the Interpretation and Disaggregation of Gini Coefficients." *Economic Journal* 86, no. 2: 243–55.

Selowsky, M. 1979. "Balancing Trickle Down and Basic Needs Strategies: Income Distribution Issues in Large Middle-Income Countries with Special Reference to Latin America." World Bank Staff Working Paper No. 335. Washington, D.C.: IBRD.

Selowsky, M., and L. Taylor. 1973. "The Economics of Malnourished Children: An Example of Disinvestment in Human Capital." *Economic Development and Cultural Change* 22, no. 1: 17–30.

Sewell, J. 1978. "Can the Rich Prosper Without Progress by the Poor." Washington, D.C.: Overseas Development Council. Mimeo.

Sri Lanka, Government of. 1978. "Sri Lanka Development Programs and Strategies for Economic Cooperation for Meeting Basic Human Needs and Raising Incomes and Standards of Living with Emphasis on Rural Poor." Special Topic Paper. Twenty-Seventh Consultative Group Meeting of the Colombo Plan, Washington, D.C., November.

Srinivasan, T. N. 1977. "Development Policies and Levels of Living of the Poor: Some Issues." A Report on the Workshop on Analysis of Distributional Issues in Development Planning, Bellagio, April. Washington, D.C.: IBRD. Mimeo.

Stern, J. J. 1976. "Growth, Redistribution and Resource Use." in ILO, *Employment, Growth and Basic Needs*. Tripartite World Conference on Employment, Income Distribution and Social Progress and the International Division of Labor. Geneva.

Stewart, F., and P. Streeten. 1976. "New Strategies for Development: Poverty, Income Distribution and Growth." *Oxford Economic Papers* 28, no. 3: 381–405.

Streeten, P. 1977. "The Distinctive Features of a Basic Needs Approach to Development." Washington, D.C.: IBRD. Mimeo.

ul Haq, M. 1977. "Basic Needs: A Progress Report." Washington, D.C.: IBRD. Mimeo.

UNCTAD. 1976. "Trade Prospects and Capital Needs of Developing Countries: 1976–1980." Geneva: Trade and Development Board, Committee on Invisibles.

UNESCO. 1979. "Prospective Growth Rates and International Resource Transfer Implications." New York: Committee for Development Planning: Fifteenth Session.

United Kingdom, Ministry of Overseas Development. 1978. "Basic Needs: The British Position." Overseas Development Paper No. 11. London.

U.S. Special Topic Paper. 1978. "U.S. Development Programs and Strategies for Economic Cooperation for Meeting Basic Human Needs and Raising Incomes and Standards of Living With Emphasis on Rural Areas." Twenty-Seventh Consultative Group Meeting of the Colombo Plan, Washington, D.C.

U.S. Agency for International Development (USAID). 1978. "Evolution of the Basic Needs Concept." Report of the Development Coordinating Committee. Washington, D.C.

U.S. Congress. 1978. *The Foreign Assistance Act*. Washington, D.C.

*Chapter 4*

# Modeling the Effects of Alternative Approaches to Basic Human Needs: Case Study of Sri Lanka

*Martha de Melo*

## INTRODUCTION

One main, unresolved controversy surrounding basic needs approaches to development is the extent to which concentration on the satisfaction of basic needs is compatible with overall growth in per capita income and hence sustainable over time. Consider, for example, the frequently cited basic needs policy—food subsidies. Food subsidies are defended for their favorable impact on the standard of living of the poor, and yet they are criticized for imposing a severe burden on scarce government budgetary resources. Would a reallocation of government funds away from food subsidies and toward investment then be desirable? Would this reallocation increase the growth rate sufficiently to permit a broadening of the benefits of growth to the poor, thus raising their standard of living over and above the level it would have reached with food subsidies?

To answer such a question, one must assess quantitatively the chain of events that would take place under the two alternative policy regimes.

Any views expressed in this chapter are those of the author and should not be attributed to the World Bank. I would like to thank Jaime A. P. de Melo and Danny Leipziger for comments and Sherman Robinson for the use of his computer program for generating measures of income distribution.

This is a difficult task for several reasons. First, significant policy changes, such as those usually mentioned under a basic needs approach, cannot be considered in isolation; their repercussions are felt throughout the economy and over time as they affect consumption, production, and investment decisions. Conceptually, these repercussions can be captured by choosing an economywide model with intertemporal linkages. However, one then faces the difficulty inherent in that methodology—namely, the need to specify a large number of relationships based on behavior that is difficult to portray adequately. Moreover, many developing countries do not have enough data over sufficiently long periods of time to permit a statistical estimation of important relationships. Under these circumstances, one possibility is to use a simulation approach that stresses relationships based on economic theory (utility maximization, cost minimization, etc.) and believed to be robust, thus minimizing the need for statistical estimates based on fragmentary time series data. This is the approach used here, in an attempt to assess the likely quantitative impact of several policy measures that have been identified as potentially important in achieving improvements in basic needs (see International Labor Office [1976] and Chapter 1 for a categorization and full discussion of these alternative policy measures).

Abstracting from many tangible as well as intangible microlevel dimensions of basic needs, this chapter uses a model that captures the major interactions among economic sectors, factors of production, and institutions to investigate these policy measures. The satisfaction of basic needs is measured by household income, including imputed income from government social services, adjusted for its purchasing power. The analysis concentrates on the effects of policies on various socioeconomic groups, since knowledge of the composition as well as the extent of poverty is considered important in choosing among alternative policies. Thus it becomes possible to determine whether a strategy that alleviates overall poverty, as defined by some aggregate measure, worsens the plight of a specific socioeconomic group.

The case study for the analysis is Sri Lanka, a country that in recent years has been credited with a basic needs approach to development and that has itself been a source of controversy, with some praising the government's development program in the early and mid-1970s for its favorable effect on the quality of life of the average citizen and others criticizing it for its contribution to high unemployment and economic stagnation. The difficulty in clarifying this type of controversy lies partly in the impossibility of separating out, in retrospect, either the short- or long-term effects of individual policies within the program. These effects can, however, be distinguished with the help of the simulation approach used here.

The following section provides some general background information on Sri Lanka, followed by a description of the structural characteristics of the economy in 1970. Particular attention is given to the contribution of economic sectors to employment and income (value added), the sectoral trade orientation, and the income shares of socioeconomic groups, as these features form crucial links between policy measures and their ultimate effects. The section closes with a review of the government's apparent success in addressing basic needs concerns.

The section on methodology first discusses the social accounting matrix, which provides the data base for the economywide model used in the analysis of policy alternatives. Next, the model itself is described in general terms, with emphasis on the importance of endogenous determination of prices and model consistency. The adjustment of household incomes for changes in the real value of nonfood subsidies and for group-specific purchasing power is briefly explained, as is the method used to generate an overall income distribution from the group-specific household incomes produced by the model.

The fourth section explores the effects of selected economic policies that have been advocated for a basic needs approach, including supply management, redistribution of assets, and improvements in factor markets. In the analysis, emphasis is placed on the number of households falling below a given poverty line and the composition of these households by socioeconomic group. The final section draws some implications from the policy simulations and discusses their relevance for the recently increased emphasis in Sri Lanka on economic growth.

## SRI LANKA

### General Background

The island of Sri Lanka, formerly known as Ceylon, lies off the southeast tip of India. The proximity to India is reflected in the present-day Sri Lanka population, which has been determined largely by successive waves of settlers from the subcontinent. The Singhalese, who are mostly Buddhist and trace their origins to an early invasion from North India, constitute approximately 70 percent of the present-day population; the Tamils, who are primarily Hindu and from South India, form the most important minority group, with more than 20 percent of the population. Among Tamils, the "Ceylon Tamils" are distinguished from the "Indian Tamils," who are more recent immigrants, largely recruited in the late nineteenth and early twentieth centuries as workers on the agricultural estates. Other minority groups include Moslems of mixed Indian and Arab origins and Christians of mixed Indian and European origins.

In the late eighteenth century, the British claimed hegemony over Sri Lanka and eventually introduced the tea and rubber plantations that are an important and distinctive characteristic of the Sri Lanka economy today. As Donald Snodgrass (1966) has pointed out in his case study of Sri Lanka, the plantation system was an enclave economy, characteristic of dualistic development. The modern sector exported raw materials and imported consumer goods, while the traditional sector continued its subsistence activities relatively undisturbed. As with many examples of extractive industry during colonial times, the difference between the modern and traditional sectors lay more in the production scale and the external access to markets and capital than in the level of technology employed. This is still true in Sri Lanka today.

Snodgrass identifies the period of World War II with the switch from classical export growth to "transitional" growth in Sri Lanka. The latter is associated with political and economic constraints on further export-led growth and an attendant policy emphasis on protection and industrialization. In Sri Lanka, however, the "transition" was not accompanied by the required government stress on economic growth and diversification. Following the attainment of full independence in 1948, the new government's intentions to increase the level and effectiveness of public investment were largely overridden by desires to provide an immediate increase in social welfare. Thus, although total government financial resources grew in part through higher taxes on the estate sector and in part through government borrowing, they were largely spent on food subsidies, as well as on public health and education services.

To make matters more difficult, the period since the mid-1950s was marked by declining terms of trade for Sri Lanka vis-à-vis the rest of the world. This trend has put direct pressure on the balance of payments and on the ability and incentive to invest. The 1960s, therefore, saw two trends in government industrial policy: (1) a growing interest in state participation in industrial development to compensate for the low level of private sector activity, and (2) an effort to encourage industries that would alleviate balance of payments pressures by using domestic, rather than imported, materials or by producing nontraditional exports. In agriculture, the government made a major and rather successful push to increase domestic food production, especially rice, and hence to reduce reliance on food imports. Unfavorable weather conditions in the first half of the 1970s, however, contributed to stagnant overall production and reduced paddy harvests.

In July 1977, a new government was elected in Sri Lanka. During its first two years in office, it has instituted a number of reforms, including a major devaluation of the exchange rate, an elimination of domestic price and import controls, and the creation of an export processing zone to encourage both foreign and domestic investment. Although it is perhaps too early to assess the effects of the changing policy environment, it is clear that the government's intent is to promote faster economic growth while maintaining, if not augmenting, the existing standard of living for the lower income groups. The policy simulations presented in this chapter provide us with some insight into whether or not these two objectives are likely to be achieved simultaneously. Before considering this, however, let us review the structure of the Sri Lanka economy in 1970, the base year for the policy simulations, along with the government's efforts in the early and mid-1970s to address basic needs concerns.

## The Economy in 1970

In 1970, the gross domestic product (GDP) of Sri Lanka stood at an estimated 11.5 billion rupees.[1] With a population of 12.5 million, GDP per capita was 920 rupees. (At the 1970 official exchange rate of 5.95 rupees to the dollar, GDP approximated $1.9 billion total and $155 per capita.) GDP was growing at a rate slightly below 3 percent, and population was growing at a rate slightly below 2 percent, so that GDP per capita was growing at about 1 percent per annum. Both urban unemployment and rural underemployment were high. What follows is a discussion of the structural characteristic of the economy highlighting the features incorporated in the model described in the subsequent section.

Table 4–1 describes the structure of production, value added, and employment among the seven sectors distinguished in the policy simula-

**Table 4–1. Economic Structure in Sri Lanka, 1970 (percentage shares in total)**

| Sectors | Gross Sectoral Output | Value Added | Employment |
|---|---|---|---|
| Tea and rubber[a] | .101 | .089 | .239 |
| Rice[a] | .069 | .086 | .211 |
| Other agriculture | .142 | .184 | .099 |
| Light manufacturing | .133 | .059 | .100 |
| Modern industry, mining, and construction | .208 | .156 | .063 |
| Trade and transport | .166 | .202 | .128 |
| Services | .181 | .224 | .160 |
| | 1.000 | 1.000 | 1.000 |

*Source:* Pyatt, Roe, et al. (1978).

[a] Including processing.

tions reported later in the chapter. This level of disaggregation appears to be the minimal one necessary to capture the main variations in sectoral structure relevant for a quantitative assessment of alternative basic need approaches in the medium term. As can be seen from this table, there are substantial differences in structure across sectors. For example, tea and rubber, and rice, are among the smallest sectors in terms of gross sectoral output; yet these are precisely the sectors with the largest employment of labor. By contrast, modern industry, mining, and construction, with the largest share in gross output, has the smallest labor employment. Table 4–1 also indicates that there is a wide variation in value added per employee, which ranges from 1.3 thousand rupees in the former two sectors to 8.3 in the latter sector.

Table 4–2 describes the pattern of trade in Sri Lanka. Total demand generated by domestic markets is small, and international trade is relatively important. Thus imports accounted for 18 percent of GDP in 1970, while exports accounted for 19 percent. The structure of foreign trade is an important dimension of the analysis here, as foreign exchange receipts and expenditures are affected by alternative policy regimes and in turn affect real household incomes. Table 4–2 indicates the shares of intermediate and consumer imports by sector of destination (the two are about equal in value), along with export shares by sector of origin. Here, too, there is a great variation across sectors. Two-thirds of all exports come from tea and rubber, with the remaining one-third concentrated in light manufacturing and services. Forty-five percent of consumer imports are in light manufacturing, and another one-third are in rice. The overwhelming importance of rice both as a budgetary expenditure item for the poor and as an imported commodity suggests that it is important to capture the factors that account for its purchase cost. One important factor, for example, is the domestic currency price of imports as deter-

**Table 4–2. Trade Flows for Sri Lanka, 1970 (percentage shares in total c.i.f. and f.o.b. values)**

| Sectors | Intermediate Imports | Consumer Imports | Exports |
|---|---|---|---|
| Tea and rubber | .076 | ... | .664 |
| Rice | .027 | .324 | ... |
| Other agriculture | .054 | .128 | .045 |
| Light manufacturing | .287 | .449 | .102 |
| Modern industry, mining, and construction | .254 | .072 | .038 |
| Trade and transport | .060 | .010 | .031 |
| Services | .242 | .017 | .120 |
| | 1.000 | 1.000 | 1.000 |

Source: Pyatt, Roe, et al. (1978).

mined by the exchange rate. Note also that light manufacturing accounts for the largest amount of intermediate imports and thus, with the exception of tea and rubber, has the strongest trade orientation.

In addition to sectoral disaggregation and trade orientation, a quantitative assessment of basic needs approaches calls for a categorization of income recipients into socioeconomic groups along lines that are interesting for policy analysis. Needless to say, such a categorization reflects a certain arbitrariness in the selection of groups and is fraught with difficulties in obtaining reliable information about the sources of income for each group. This study distinguishes six socioeconomic groups—urban rich, urban poor, rural rich, small farmers, rural landless, and estate workers. The urban rich include urban capitalists and skilled labor, and the urban poor include unskilled labor and small-scale nonfarm activities. The number and incomes of small farmers are related to the number and incomes of small holdings in each of the agricultural sectors. Estate workers, who are primarily Indian rather than Ceylonese, are composed of unskilled labor on agricultural estates (mostly tea and rubber). They are treated as a separate socioeconomic group because they have very limited mobility in the economy.

Table 4–3 shows the gross income and net income shares in 1970 for the six socioeconomic groups defined above. It can be seen that the groups that constitute the smallest share of total population lie at the extremes of the socioeconomic income distribution spectrum. Thus, the estate workers, who make up approximately 11 percent of the total population, receive only 6 percent of gross incomes and have an average household income of less than 3000 rupees. The urban rich, who account for 6 percent of population, receive 19 percent of income, while the rural rich claim 18 percent of income. As observed in most countries, per household incomes of the urban poor—despite high unemployment—are higher than per household incomes of small farmers and landless rural workers.

A comparison of household net incomes—after direct taxes and transfers—with gross incomes in Table 4–3 shows that the fiscal impact is progressive. Net incomes of the urban and rural rich are less than gross incomes, but net incomes of all other groups are higher than gross incomes. The progressivity of direct taxes and transfers can also be seen by looking at the change in group shares in total income when measured on a net rather than a gross basis. Table 4–3 shows, for example, that the share of the urban and rural rich declines from 37 to 34 percent of the total while that of the lower income groups increases from 63 to 66 percent of the total. The discussion below shows that further reduction in income inequality is achieved through consumer subsidies and social services.

**Table 4–3. Population and Annual Household Incomes of Socioeconomic Groups in Sri Lanka, 1970**

| | Population | | Gross Income | | Net Income[c] | |
|---|---|---|---|---|---|---|
| | Number of households[a] | Percent of total | Per household[b] | Percent of total | Per household[b] | Percent of total |
| Urban rich | 123.8 | .059 | 16.58 | .192 | 14.43 | .171 |
| Urban poor | 251.5 | .121 | 5.29 | .125 | 5.47 | .131 |
| Rural rich | 154.7 | .074 | 12.17 | .176 | 11.49 | .170 |
| Small farmers | 515.6 | .247 | 3.89 | .188 | 3.98 | .196 |
| Landless | 817.8 | .392 | 3.38 | .258 | 3.46 | .270 |
| Estate workers | 222.2 | .107 | 2.92 | .061 | 2.94 | .062 |
| Total | 2,085.6 | 1.000 | 5.12 | 1.000 | 5.02 | 1.000 |

*Source:* Estimates based on Pyatt, Roe, et al. (1978) and Karunatilake (1975).
[a] Thousands of standardized (six person) households.
[b] In thousand rupees.
[c] Net of direct taxes and transfers.

## Satisfaction of Basic Needs

Sri Lanka gained considerable international attention by scoring higher
on the so-called physical quality of life index (PQLI) than any other
country in its income range (see Sewell [1977] for a discription of the
PQLI and Isenman [1980] for a discussion of basic needs in Sri Lanka).
Average life expectancy for the 1970–1975 period, for example, was sixty-
eight years, or only three years less than that for the United States, and
average literacy was 76 percent (Hansen 1976). Without entering the
argument over whether Sri Lanka's accomplishments in the area of basic
needs are attributable primarily to preindependence initial conditions or
to policies of the postindependence governments, it is perhaps sufficient
to point out that for a twenty-year period, starting in the mid-1950s, welfare expenditure ranged between 35 and 45 percent of government's current expenditures (see Pyatt, Roe, et al. [1978:26], citing Karunatilake).
Although there is some controversy surrounding the interpretation of
the change in the distribution of gross income between 1963 and 1973, it
appears that income inequality did decline during this period. A recent
cross-country study of thirty-six countries shows that Sri Lanka was the
only country for which the incremental income share of the lowest 60
percent of income recipients exceeded 40 percent (Chapter 11 in Chenery
1979:456–495).

The major components of welfare expenditure in Sri Lanka over the
years have been food subsidies and provision of free health and education
services. These expenditures have been estimated as a percent of personal disposable income in 1973 as follows—food subsidies, 5 percent;
education, 5 percent; health, 2 percent; agriculture producer subsidies, 1
percent; other (transport, social welfare), 1 percent—for an overall total
of 14 percent (see Alailima 1978:71–75, table 3.8). In 1970, food subsidies
were virtually confined to rice, with a free ration of 2 pounds of rice per
person per week and a further 2 pound ration at a subsidized price. Between 1970 and 1973, a subsidy on wheat flour was introduced, largely
benefiting the estate workers. Other subsidies remained largely the same.

The effect of government intervention through taxes and subsidies can
be seen through its effect on the Lorenz curve for household income
shown in Figure 4–1. The Lorenz curve shows the percent of total income
accruing to households ranked from poorest to richest along the horizontal axis. The degree of inequality in the income distribution is shown by
the ratio of the area between the 45° line and the Lorenz curve to the
total area beneath the 45° line. Thus, it can be seen that government
intervention, first through the tax system and subsequently through the
pattern of subsidies, produces progressively more income equality.

A controversial point with respect to government welfare expenditures

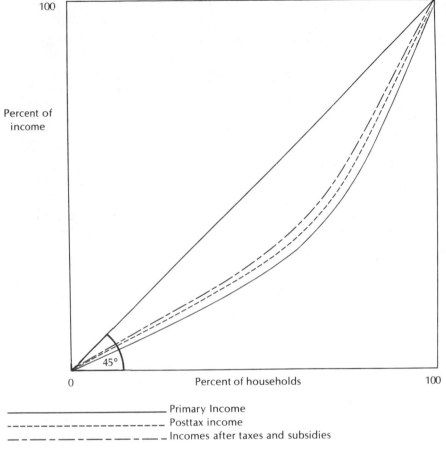

Primary Income
---------------- Posttax income
— — — — — — — Incomes after taxes and subsidies

*Source:* Alailima (1978: 89).

**Figure 4–1. Lorenz curves showing the effect of taxes and subsidies on income distribution in Sri Lanka, 1973.**

in Sri Lanka, however, is the extent to which these expenditures have contributed to lower investment, higher unemployment, and slower growth in overall income that might itself have contributed to the satisfaction of basic needs of the lower income groups. Unemployment, which is today perhaps the most serious social and economic problem that Sri Lanka faces, has been linked both to the failure of the economy to create more jobs and to the reluctance of the jobseeker to accept blue collar jobs, and the use of public funds for welfare expenditure is seen as inhibiting job creation and encouraging job selectivity. There are, of course, many other factors involved, and it will never be possible to adequately measure these links. Nevertheless, the model described below does attempt to simulate some of the major economywide interactions that contribute to this suspected tradeoff between equity and growth.

## METHODOLOGY

### A Social Accounting Matrix

The key feature of the model used in this study is that it determines the circular flow of income from producers to consumers and, through consumer expenditure, back again to producers by means of a set of mutually consistent accounting relationships. While such a consistency among production, expenditure, and accumulation accounts appears natural, it should be noted that, until recently, economywide models have not typically achieved consistency in all accounts. In fact, economic models usually only achieved consistency among production accounts, which is a reason why they are not well suited for an analysis of basic needs and income distribution issues. Achievement of what has often been referred to as a high degree of "closure" calls for a specification of the income and expenditure accounts for each sector in the economy. With an endogenous determination of the income and expenditure accounts, it becomes possible to conduct policy simulations to assess the impact of alternative policies on the distribution of income and more particularly on the attainment of basic needs by various socioeconomic groups.

Perhaps the best way to get an overview and gain an understanding of the scope and structure of the model is to look first at a social accounting matrix (SAM), which is in fact required as a data base. The SAM is in many ways the ideal format for an economywide model oriented toward income distribution and basic needs, since it provides a conceptual and informational framework for organizing data in a way that permits a balanced focus on both production and income distribution. It can be argued that this balanced focus is particularly important in a low-income country where fluctuations in real income seriously affect the ability of lower income groups to satisfy their basic needs.

Table 4–4 presents a SAM for Sri Lanka in 1970; it is a simplified and aggregated version of the Pyatt, Roe, et al. (1978) SAM that has served as a data base for this study.[2] As can be seen, the accounting framework is based on a matrix of receipts and expenditures, where the former are given by the rows and the latter by the columns in the matrix. Since receipts must equal expenditures, the row sums are equal to the corresponding column sums. Thus, the SAM presents a set of consistent data

## Table 4-4. A Social Accounting Matrix for Sri Lanka, 1970 (Rs million)

| | Factors | | Institutions | | | | Activities | | | ROW | Total |
|---|---|---|---|---|---|---|---|---|---|---|---|
| | Labor | Capital | Urban HH | Rural HH | Govt. | Capital Account | Ag. | Ind. | Serv. | | |
| **Factors** | | | | | | | | | | | |
| Labor | | | 38 | 62 | 1275 | | 2122 | 715 | 1356 | | 5568 |
| Capital | | | | | | | 1867 | 1766 | 2273 | −113 | 5793 |
| **Institutions[a]** | | | | | | | | | | | |
| Urban HH | 1673 | 2375 | 434 | 385 | | | | | | 6 | 4873 |
| Rural HH | 3895 | 3418 | 210 | 157 | | | | | | 12 | 7694 |
| Government | | | 744 | 199 | 104 | 313 | 75 | 575 | 206 | 130 | 2346 |
| Capital account | | | 1353 | 819 | 43 | | | | | 425 | 2640 |
| **Activities** | | | | | | | | | | | |
| Agriculture | | | 416 | 1425 | 22 | 48 | 177 | 1371 | 47 | 1288 | 4794 |
| Industry | | | 618 | 2226 | 184 | 1760 | 245 | 1244 | 308 | 335 | 6920 |
| Services | | | 837 | 2079 | 96 | 154 | 130 | 606 | 230 | 490 | 4622 |
| ROW | | | 223 | 884 | 79 | 364 | 179 | 642 | 202 | | 2573 |
| Total | 5568 | 5793 | 4873 | 7694 | 2346 | 2640 | 4794 | 6920 | 4622 | 2573 | |

Source: Pyatt, Roe, et al. (1978).

[a] Receipts and expenditures of firms are combined with urban households.

on transactions among production activities (agriculture, industry, and services), factors of production (labor and capital), and institutions (urban and rural households and government). Accounts are also kept for capital flows (in the capital account) and external trade (rest of world [ROW]).

The four heavily outlined rectangles in Table 4–4 highlight the circular flow of income that is captured by the SAM. The rectangle on the lower right-hand side of the SAM gives the familiar interindustry transactions matrix, or input-output table, which shows the flows of current purchases (and sales) among the three sectors. Until recently, this transactions matrix along with a set of production relations (represented by the rectangle on the upper right-hand side), which together impose consistency on commodity supplies, were the only major consistency checks in economywide models.[3] The SAM, however, imposes two additional data consistencies—one between factor income and institutional income and the other between institutional income and expenditure. Assuming for the moment that the government account, the capital account, and the ROW account all have zero entries, the former is accomplished in the upper left-hand rectangle, where factor income is distributed to urban and rural households according to their ownership of capital and labor. Urban household earnings from capital and labor are thus 4048 Rm. (rupees million)—that is, the horizontal sum of 1673 Rm. of labor earnings and 2375 Rm. of capital earnings. The lower left-hand rectangle shows that commodity demand as derived from the distribution of income among institutions must be equal to the residual commodity supplies after intermediate demands have been taken into account. In sum, a model that satisfies the accounting relationships embodied in a SAM imposes a full-fledged consistency between (1) commodity supply and available inputs; (2) factor payments and the distribution of income to institutions; (3) the distribution of income among institutions and commodity demand; and (4) commodity demand and supply. To take an example, if there is a drop in the export demand for Sri Lanka's tea, the repercussions of this event can be traced through to production, employment, incomes, household demand, taxes, and imports, as well as to production in other sectors (via the interindustry transactions matrix).

## Outline of the Model

In order to maintain the above-described accounting consistencies in the face of policy changes, a model featuring a high degree of flexibility is required. The model used in this study belongs to a new class of models, often referred to as computable general equilibrium (CGE) models, which provide for such flexibility. Subject to given factor endowments, these models determine endogenously factor prices, commodity prices, quantities of factors allocated to each sector, and commodities produced by each sector. The endogenous determination of prices and quantities leads to an endogenous determination of factor (and household) incomes—the feature that makes these models appropriate for a study of basic needs. It is also the endogenous determination of market-clearing prices that permits them to capture the effects of changes in policies on the real incomes of the different socioeconomic groups in the economy by measuring the impact of changes in relative prices on the consumption baskets (and hence on real incomes) of these various groups.

Based on general equilibrium theory, CGE models emphasize the suboptimizing behavior of various agents in the economy subject to their respective budget constraints. These models are normally called price-endogenous models because prices must adjust until the independently undertaken decisions in the productive sphere of the economy are made consistent with the independently undertaken decisions on the demand side by the various institutions. The behavior of government is modeled separately; and as such, the approach is well suited to planning and policy analysis in the mixed market economies of many developing countries. A CGE model is therefore useful when analyzing problems such as those associated with basic needs strategies directed toward income distribution, where it is important to take explicit account of general equilibrium interactions.

Without going into the detailed workings of the model, it is sufficient to note that a consistent set of product and factor market prices is obtained by deriving numerically a set of physical excess demands and adjusting prices until these excess demands are eliminated. By means of nonlinear specifications, the model incorporates continous substitution in both production and consumption, in response to relative price and income changes. The explicit consideration of the budget constraints facing each of the activities and institutions in the economy and the resulting feedback mechanisms between the demand and the supply side of the economy make it possible to fully "close" the model for any one time period by accounting for all income flows.[4] Because the set of excess demand functions is homogeneous of degree zero in prices and income, a normalization rule is added to the set of simultaneous equations describing the interaction of demand and supply to permit the determination of the price level.[5]

The within period solution to the CGE model described above is updated over time through a series of "dynamic linkage" equations that provide for population growth, investment allocation, and technical change. In addition, the model incorporates socioeconomic mobility, both geographically and socially. The former depends on the urban-rural differential in expected wages, and the latter depends on the growth in demand for skilled labor, which is provided by the "rich" socioeconomic groups described above. The Appendix to this chapter provides the full equation system for the within period, or static, model as well as the key dynamic linkage equations.

## Application of the Model to Study BHN Approaches

In the application of the model, seven production activities (or sectors), six factors of production, and six socioeconomic groups have been distinguished. The factors of production are land, labor, urban skilled labor, urban unskilled labor, rural skilled labor, and rural unskilled labor. The production activities and socioeconomic groups were given above. From the description of the model, it should be clear that it concentrates on macroeconomic and intersectoral interactions. It does not pretend to address the political, administrative, technical, and social issues related to basic needs or even the economic issues at the microlevel. Nor does the model provide any insight into how the various policies can best be implemented. Rather, it is used to gain insight into the effects of a policy once it has taken hold by tracing through the economywide interactions and observing the cumulative impact through time. Thus, the effects of different basic needs approaches are analyzed by comparing real incomes of the six socioeconomic groups after a period of ten years with and without a given policy. The model traces through the changes both in factor incomes and in the purchasing power of these incomes for each socioeconomic group, by taking into account cost variations in each group's consumption basket.

Two steps are required, however, to generate income distribution statistics that permit a detailed analysis of the composition of poverty. The first step is to adjust each socioeconomic group's real income in 1970 for the imputed income from public expenditure on social services. The value of these social services—namely, health and education—is estimated on the basis of information for 1973 in Alailima (1978),[6] and distribution among socioeconomic groups is assumed to remain the same under all simulations. Expenditure on social services is assumed to expand at the same rate as total government consumption, but the real value depends on the relative price of services. Thus, the real value is determined endogenously and affected by the policy choice.

The second step is to generate information on the overall income distribution in order to derive statistics on the number of households falling below a given poverty line and the incidence of poverty among socioeconomic groups. Robinson (1976) has developed a method to do this, given knowledge of average incomes and an assumption of constant log variances for each subgroup.[7] For Sri Lanka, the average incomes under various policies are estimated with the model described above; an estimate of the log-variance for each socioeconomic group can be obtained directly from the group-specific Gini coefficient, a more familiar statistic ranging from 0 to 1, with lower values representing less inequality in the distribution of income.[8]

| Socioeconomic Group | Gini Coefficient |
|---|---|
| Urban rich | .33 |
| Urban poor | .25 |
| Rural rich | 30 |
| Small farmers | .25 |
| Rural landless | .20 |
| Estate workers | .10 |

Using Robinson's method, the statistics on income distribution and poverty given in the next section are derived from these estimates, as are the Lorenz curves for each of the socioeconomic groups shown in Figure 4–2.

The following section provides a quantitative evaluation of three alternative approaches to basic needs development—namely, increasing domestic food supplies, redistributing assets, and improving the functioning of markets for capital and labor. These alternatives are concrete examples of the prototypes of supply management, redistribution, and improved access that have been identified as potentially beneficial. Each approach is evaluated, in comparison to a base case, in terms of its effect on the extent and composition of poverty. They are not comparable in terms of either their budgetary effects, although these are incorporated in the model, or their political feasibility. Of interest is the association of each approach with changes in absolute and relative incomes, particularly of the lower income groups, and the increased insight into the economic mechanisms that lie behind this association. For the most part, policies are only evaluated after a ten year period, since we are primarily interested in the satisfaction of basic needs on a sustainable basis. Also, some policies, such as stimulation of technical change or increased mobility of new capital investment, require time to take effect. The removal of food subsidies, however, is one policy that can have an immediate effect that may differ substantially from its longer term effect. The impact of this policy is therefore compared to the base case in year 1 as well as in year 10.

The income level required to meet the basic needs of a household for food, clothing, shelter, education, and other requirements has been esti-

Percent of income

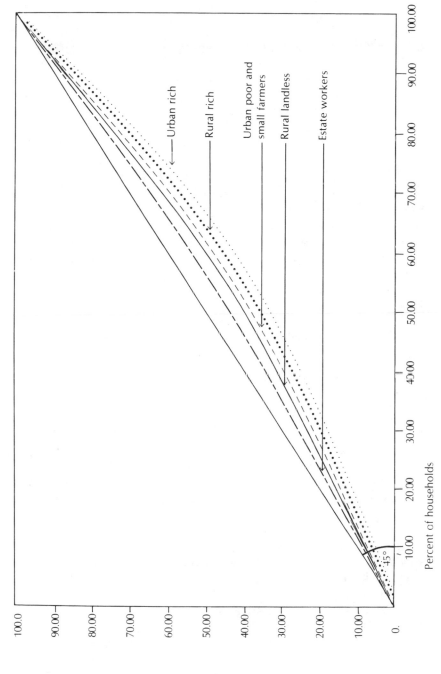

Percent of households

Urban rich

Rural rich

Urban poor and
small farmers

Rural landless

Estate workers

45°

**Figure 4–2. Lorenz curves for socioeconomic groups in Sri Lanka, 1970.**

mated as 480 rupees per month, or 5760 rupees per year, in 1970.[9] Defining households not able to satisfy their basic needs as falling below a "poverty line," 74 percent of the population would be in poverty at this income level. Such an estimate might be overly pessimistic. Moreover, a more restrictive definition of basic needs is desirable—if for no other reason than to provide some hope that these needs can be met—and might be arrived at by identifying an income level leaving about 40 percent of households in poverty.[10]

In 1970, this income level was 300 Rs. per month, or 3600 Rs. a year, and it will be used as the poverty line here. Thus, each policy simulation will be evaluated by the percent of total population and the share of each of the lower income groups (urban poor, small farmers, rural landless, and estate workers) falling below it. Although the discussion focuses primarily on ultimate effects—that is, poverty elimination and hence the satisfaction of basic needs—the underlying interplay between production and consumption decisions, as well as the dynamic interactions, should be kept in mind.

## THREE BASIC NEEDS APPROACHES TO DEVELOPMENT

### Increase in Food Supplies

One approach to satisfying basic needs is to operate on the supply side to increase the domestic availability of particular items. In Sri Lanka, the government has followed this approach for food by using government revenues to subsidize the domestic consumer price of rice (as well as several other food items), thereby fostering somewhat higher consumption levels. The higher consumption is met by both domestic production and imported rice. Under the assumption that the share of imported rice is dependent on relative producer prices (with the share of imported rice declining as the relative producer price of domestic rice declines), the model can be used to investigate the effects of totally removing the rice subsidy. It is assumed that the funds formerly spent on the subsidy are available for public savings and investment.

The upper panel of Figure 4–3 shows the immediate effect of removing the rice subsidy in year 1 compared to the base case (with subsidy).[11] In the base case, 43 percent of the population is in poverty according to the chosen household poverty line of 3600 rupees a year. Without subsidy, the consumer price of rice increases by about one-third, or approximately 85 percent of the former subsidy, and the proportion of the population in poverty rises to 47 percent. The average real income of households declines in response to the increase in the consumer price; however,

## Comparison for Year 1

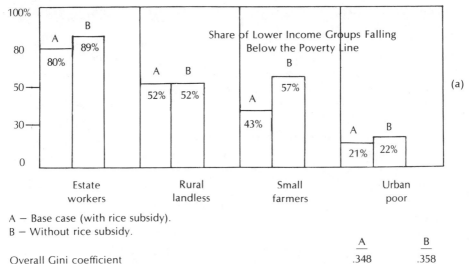

A — Base case (with rice subsidy).
B — Without rice subsidy.

| | A | B |
|---|---|---|
| Overall Gini coefficient | .348 | .358 |
| Percent of population below poverty line | .43 | .47 |
| Household mean (real) income in rupees | 5306 | 5105 |

(a)

## Comparison for Year 10

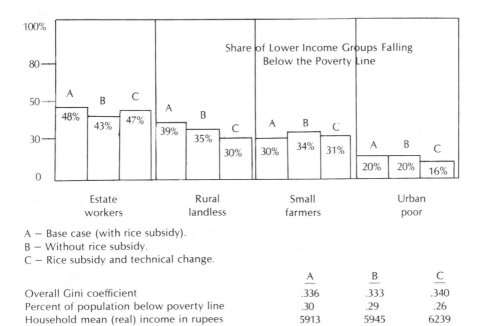

A — Base case (with rice subsidy).
B — Without rice subsidy.
C — Rice subsidy and technical change.

| | A | B | C |
|---|---|---|---|
| Overall Gini coefficient | .336 | .333 | .340 |
| Percent of population below poverty line | .30 | .29 | .26 |
| Household mean (real) income in rupees | 5913 | 5945 | 6239 |

**Figure 4–3. Increase in food supplies.**

the cost of living effect is considerably greater for the poor, as rice purchases constitute a larger share of total household expenditures than for the rich.

The initial drop in real incomes of the poor causes a subsequent decline in wages and employment resulting from the lower demand for rice and other labor-intensive products. The percent of small farmers with incomes below the poverty line increases from 43 to 57 percent as the decline in the producer price of rice reflects the drop in overall demand, and estate workers in poverty increase from 80 to 89 percent. The nationwide average real household income drops by almost 4 percent, but this masks substantial variation by income group. For the rural landless, wages drop slightly in all sectors, but the reallocation of labor from agricultural to nonagricultural activities, in accordance with the relative increase in demand for the latter, results in maintenance of the same average real incomes.

By year 10, a decline of population in poverty from 43 percent to 30 percent takes place in the base case (with subsidy), due both to the overall increase in real incomes and to the increase in the equality of income distribution, as illustrated by the decline in the calculated Gini coefficient from .35 to .34. The increased income equality results from (1) a slight rise in the agricultural terms of trade, which benefits rural versus urban households; (2) a small devaluation in the exchange rate, which benefits small farmers and estate workers; and (3) a demand for skilled labor, which is slightly higher than the growth rate of the labor force and hence expands the middle class while lowering the number of jobseekers among unskilled workers.

Looking at the no subsidy case, its implication for basic needs changes dramatically. As shown in the lower panel of Figure 4–3, reinvestment of public savings from the rice subsidy, which amounted to more than 20 percent of total budgetary expenditures in 1970, has generated average real incomes slightly higher than they would otherwise have been, despite the initial depressing effect shown in the figure's upper panel.[12] Estate workers and the rural landless both benefit from the increased economic activity, although there is still a larger proportion of small farmers (34 percent versus 30 percent) in poverty because of the overall drop in the demand for rice following the substantial rise in the consumer price. A more micro-oriented investigation than this one would be needed to determine to what extent the higher price of rice might inhibit adequate nutritional intake for the lowest income groups, despite the marginally higher levels of real income. The simulation shows, however, that by year 10, total rice consumption is 8 percent lower than in the base case, suggesting that nutritional standards might be expected to drop.

An alternative option for increasing the supply, and hence the consumption of food, is to promote technical change in agriculture. Let us assume that neutral technical change of 1 percent per annum can be introduced by increasing annual budgetary expenditures on research and extension and decreasing public savings accordingly. To simplify the analysis, identical adoption rates of improved technology will be assumed for small and large farmers. As shown in Figure 4–4, even technical change at this rather modest rate has a significant impact on real household incomes and on the extent of poverty, especially among the rural landless and the urban poor, who are heavily dependent on food purchases and who benefit from both the income and consumption effects of a declining agricultural terms of trade. It is not the purpose of this study to examine the feasibility of factor-neutral technical change, but its favorable effects on poverty reduction are appealing.[13] Small farmers are only marginally hurt at the rates assumed, as their income from increased quantities supplied offsets the overall decline in the purchase price.

The lot of both small farmers and estate workers fails to improve because of the revaluation in the exchange rate, resulting from increasing agricultural exports. Were additional foreign exchange to become available, however, the government would most likely choose not to revalue but rather to reduce tariffs or remove some of its quantitative trade restrictions, as it did in 1977 and 1978, allowing additional industrial and consumer imports. With domestic prices of agricultural exports remaining steady, the share of estate workers and small farmers in poverty might fall rather than rise. If increased imports are used to enhance industrial or agricultural productivity, the entire economy could benefit. If consumer imports rise, the increased competition with domestic production might depress incomes of the urban poor or the rural landless. Thus, the incidence would depend on the government's choice of import liberalization measures.

In sum, policies to increase food supplies and food consumption levels can have significant effects on both the level and composition of the poor. In regard to food subsidies, where the alternative use of funds is public savings, there is clearly a tradeoff between benefits in the short and the long term. There are, of course, intermediary positions to the subsidy–no subsidy choice, and these provide perhaps the most appealing alternatives to the policymaker interested in basic needs. The intermediary choices include (1) the reduction of the budgetary costs of subsidy by income policy aimed at the poorest households and (2) specification of the subsidy in nominal terms so that the real value is reduced over time, as real incomes hopefully are raised. Where the alternative use of funds is not savings, but rather some other consumption expenditure, benefits from the alternative uses should be compared. It is likely, however, that the marginal benefits from food subsidies to the upper half or even two-thirds of household can be shown to be low. In recent years, the Sri Lanka government has itself narrowed the household eligibility for rice subsidies and tried to convert other subsidies from a real to a nominal basis. Finally, the encouragement of food consumption by the introduction of cost-reducing technical change in domestic agriculture is a promising alternative to food subsidies in addressing basic needs concerns, especially if technical change is factor neutral. The higher average incomes and lower incidence of poverty associated with this approach (see lower panel of Figure 4–3) create a situation whereby the basic needs of an individual group, such as the estate workers, could be more easily addressed on a selective basis.

## Redistribution of Assets

During the early 1970s the government of Sri Lanka carried out a program of land redistribution and nationalization of private businesses.[14] This program appears to have been poorly executed, with efficiency levels dropping on the agricultural estates and capacity utilization falling in industry. The redistribution of assets is, nevertheless, an appealing means of promoting greater equality in the distribution of income and is frequently mentioned as a potentially effective approach to satisfying basic needs.[15]

Abstracting from arguments for more or less efficiency following redistribution, simulations here assume constant efficiency levels and trace through the effects on poverty and incomes under these conditions. No supplementary budget costs are introduced, although a more detailed study would have to account for these. The magnitude of the programs is greater than that of those the government actually carried out. The simulated land reform, for example, involves twice the area actually affected, or almost 25 percent of the cultivated area, with three-quarters of the associated capital transferred from large farmers and estates to small farmers. The nationalization of firms applies to all firms but is simulated simply by reallocating dividends from households, where they were used for both consumption and investment, to government, where they are used for investment only.

Figure 4–4 shows the effects of these two programs on incomes and poverty compared to the base case. Under the assumption of constant efficiency levels, average real household incomes in year 10 are slightly lower than those in the base case, although the average incomes of households in the lowest decile are 4 percent higher under nationalization. There is an increase in income equality under both redistribution

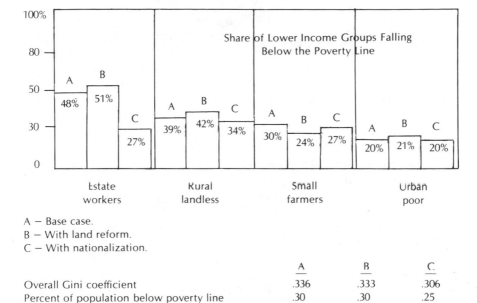

A — Base case.
B — With land reform.
C — With nationalization.

|  | A | B | C |
|---|---|---|---|
| Overall Gini coefficient | .336 | .333 | .306 |
| Percent of population below poverty line | .30 | .30 | .25 |
| Household mean (real) income in rupees | 5913 | 5892 | 5874 |

**Figure 4–4. Redistribution of assets (comparison for year 10).**

programs, although the increase under land reform is very small.

Looking at the contribution of land reform to the overall achievement of basic needs, it is perhaps surprising that the percent of the population falling below the poverty line has not declined relative to the base case. The percent of small farmers in poverty has of course declined, from 30 to 24 percent; but the percent of all other groups has risen. Given an assumption of higher average (and marginal) savings rates among the rich, the redistribution of productive assets to lower income groups results in a lower aggregate rate of savings and investment. The lower investment, in turn, results in lower GDP and income growth and hence higher urban unemployment and lower rural wages. Also, as the demand for domestic and imported capital goods falls off, as does the derived industrial demand for imported intermediate goods, there is a tendency toward a revaluation of the exchange rate and hence a countervailing effect on small farmer incomes. If the government chose to liberalize imports rather than to revalue, the share of estate workers and small farmers falling below the poverty line might be reduced, with additional effects dependent on the government's choice of import liberalization measures.

In sum, the policy simulation on land reform suggests that unless efficiency levels can be improved with land redistribution or unless external capital assistance is forthcoming in the early years so that the previous rate of investment can be maintained, a tradeoff between growth and equity may occur, with the result that by year 10 the improvement in the incomes of the poor has, on the average, been entirely eroded. In reality, the success of land reform may well depend on the availability of complementary factors. In the case of Taiwan and Korea, for example, land reform was instituted under authoritarian rule and was accompanied by complementary inputs and services as well as substantial foreign assistance. Growth with equity resulted. In Sri Lanka, where land reform appears to have been accompanied not only by an initial drop in efficiency levels but also by a deterioration in the investment climate, a negative impact on basic needs may have occurred.

Continuing under the assumption of constant efficiency levels, nationalization of firms, the second redistributive approach to satisfying basic needs, causes an initial decline in average household incomes and in employment of virtually all socioeconomic groups. This is due both directly to the decline in household dividend income and indirectly to the switch in demand from labor-intensive consumption goods by the household sector to capital-intensive investment goods by the government sector. By year 10, however, Figure 4–4 shows that real household income is similar to what it would have otherwise been, and poverty is considerably less. Not only has the percent of the population below the poverty line dropped from 30 to 25 percent, but poverty reduction is widespread. The greatest decline in poverty occurs among estate workers, who benefit from the significant devaluation (and hence increase in the domestic price of tea and rubber) that is provoked by the requirement for more imported investment goods.

With the faster growth rate caused by higher investment, even the urban poor, whose share in poverty is the only one not reduced, will eventually benefit; although the level of urban employment drops following nationalization, employment growth is higher than in the base case. The greater income equality produced through nationalization is reinforced by the equalizing effect of faster growth in skilled labor employment, which is assumed proportional to growth in the capital stock. As skilled labor employment in both urban and rural areas absorbs some of the unskilled labor force, a slight upward pressure is exerted on the wage rate for unskilled workers. Thus, unlike the case of land reform, where the chain of dynamic interactions set up erodes the initial equity gains, the dynamic interactions set off by nationalization appear to reinforce the equity gains.

However, as appealing as the nationalization policy may be under the constant efficiency assumptions, it is unfortunately the case that neither

Sri Lanka nor many other developing countries that have undertaken substantial nationalizations have been able to live up to this assumption. Previously profitable private businesses have become a drain on the government budget, claiming increasing subsidies over time. In addition, as with land reform, the nationalization and, frequently, associated policies cause a deterioration in the investment climate by increasing uncertainty and decreasing profits. This worsening of the investment climate may in fact be more serious for industry (e.g., as compared to tree crop agriculture), where the capital stock has a shorter lifetime and where technical change may be more rapid.

## Improvements in Factor Markets

Improvements in factor markets have also been mentioned as a means of spreading the benefits of development and of hastening the satisfaction of basic needs. In the market for unskilled labor, especially urban labor, a high institutional wage perpetuates unemployment by discouraging employers from hiring additional labor. In the base case, which incorporates a high institutional wage for urban unskilled labor, urban unemployment is 16 percent in year 1 and almost 30 percent by year 10. Case B in Figure 4–5 shows the effects of a drop in the urban wage for unskilled labor to a level that permits full employment—that is, a drop to the "equilibrium" wage. This equilibrium wage, which is 83 percent of the institutional wage in year 1, drops to about 73 percent of the institutional wage, which is assumed to increase by 1.5 percent a year in real terms, by year 10. This is because the need to absorb a moderately fast growing labor force, which reflects both rural-urban migration and population growth, prevents the equilibrium real wage from rising much beyond its initial level. In fact, the dynamic adjustment path during the intervening years shows a decline, followed by a subsequent rise in the real wage.

The principal effect of instituting a flexible wage for urban unskilled labor is to increase both the initial level and the subsequent growth rate of urban employment. This in turn stimulates GDP growth, leading to an increase in the demand for imported intermediate goods and hence to a small effective devaluation. The effective devaluation increases the domestic price of agricultural exports, and the increased consumption demand resulting from increased employment of unskilled labor bids up the prices of rice and other agriculture. Together, these pressures cause an increase in the agricultural terms of trade and hence an increase in the incomes of the rural poor. Real incomes of the urban poor, which benefit from increased employment, are nevertheless hurt by the chang-

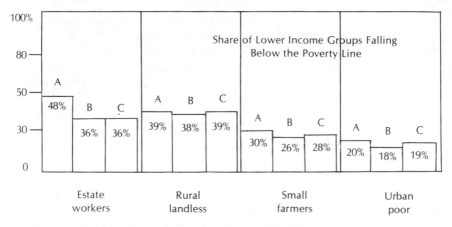

A — Base case (with institutional wage for urban unskilled labor).
B — Equilibrium wage for urban unskilled labor.
C — Increased capital mobility.

|  | A | B | C |
|---|---|---|---|
| Overall Gini coefficient | .336 | .334 | .334 |
| Percent of population below poverty line | .30 | .27 | .28 |
| Household mean (real) income in rupees | 5913 | 6067 | 5967 |

**Figure 4–5. Improvements in factor markets (comparison for year 10).**

ing agricultural terms of trade. However, the net effect is favorable. Thus, as can be seen in Figure 4–5, there is a drop in the share of each of the lower income groups falling below the poverty line.

In capital markets there are imperfections in both the sectoral allocation of capital, as illustrated by the large differences in sectoral rates of return, and in access to capital by the lower income groups. Here, only the former problem will be addressed, as the latter problem requires a rather comprehensive treatment of the variations in technologies and prices faced by different socioeconomic groups. In the base case, only 15 percent of new investment is assumed to be responsive to the differential sectoral rates of return, with the remaining 85 percent determined by various institutional constraints and hence allocated proportionately to existing capital stock. Case C in Figure 4–5 shows the effects on the poor of increasing to 30 percent the responsiveness of investment to differential rates of return; in practice, this would be accomplished by improving the system of financial intermediation. The share of the total population falling below the poverty line in year 10 falls, and the shares of estate workers and small farmers in poverty also fall. The shares of rural landless and urban poor in poverty remain the same.

The economic interactions that lie behind these effects are of some interest. The improvement in real incomes of small farmers and estate workers is due primarily to a devaluation that is stimulated by the reduction in output of tea and rubber as capital shifts toward sectors with higher returns. The lack of change in the share of rural landless and urban poor in poverty is a result of offsetting effects. Incomes of these groups are depressed as capital shifts out of the relatively labor-intensive tea and rubber and services sectors and into other agriculture; modern industry, mining, and construction; and trade and transport. Their incomes are enhanced, however, by the increased demand for employment associated with higher GDP growth. The latter is caused by higher growth in physical capital permitted by a drop in the price of investment goods, which in turn results from the expansion of the investment goods sectors offering a higher rate of return to capital.

Interestingly enough, despite the faster growth in physical capital, the average rate of profit is no lower than under the base case. This is due to the allocation of more capital to sectors with higher rates of return. As a consequence of this reallocation, the disparity in sectoral profit rates, as measured by the ratio of the highest to the lowest, is 10 percent lower by year 10 with higher capital mobility, and the tendency toward equalization of profit rates has a small positive effect on reducing income inequality.

In sum, improvements in factor markets for both labor and capital do appear to have a favorable impact on satisfaction of basic needs, as the number of households falling below the poverty line is reduced by about 10 percent in each case. The improvement in the market for unskilled labor appears particularly desirable and is unique among the approaches explored here in that it results in a reduction by at least one percentage point in the proportion of each socioeconomic group falling below the poverty line.

## CONCLUSIONS

The above simulations investigate the effects of alternative policies for improving basic needs in an environment where all other conditions are held constant. Although the approach used ignores many disaggregated and qualitative dimensions of economic behavior, it highlights a number of important repercussions of a given policy change. Analysis of the economic mechanisms that underlie these effects shows that both the rate and the pattern of growth are important determinants of poverty alleviation and that offsetting effects are at least as frequently generated as reinforcing effects.[16] Thus, the existence and extent of tradeoffs or complementarities among alternative goals becomes an empirical issue for the country in question.

Under assumptions of standard neoclassical behavior and constant efficiency levels, the simulations carried out here show that policies that minimize the number of households falling below the poverty line in the short run may not be those that minimize the number falling below the poverty line in the longer run. Thus, the suggestion made by some that a consumption-oriented approach to development is more important for a low-income developing country than for a middle-income developing country is questionable, although obviously a certain minimal standard of living needs to be provided on humanitarian grounds. Among alternatives considered, the policy of increasing the availability of basic needs through a production-oriented approach, which concentrates on increasing domestic supply through technical change or other productivity-raising measures, is particularly promising. To the extent possible, this approach should be supplemented by appropriate measures on the demand side to ensure that purchasing power is available to low-income groups.

Not only the number but also the distribution of households falling below a given poverty line is sensitive to the policy choice. Among the alternatives explored here for Sri Lanka, increased food production does the most to satisfy the real income needs of the urban poor and the rural landless. Small farmers gain the most from land reform, which involves a major transfer of resources to them, although other low income groups may suffer from any accompanying reduction in aggregate savings and investment. Estate workers benefit primarily from approaches that generate higher prices for tea and rubber; hence, they benefit indirectly from nationalization and improvements in factor markets, as these stimulate an exchange rate devaluation. Thus, who you want to help, or perhaps who is in greatest need of help, might have a strong influence on the policy choice.

Whether or not the new growth-oriented policies in Sri Lanka will have an adverse effect on the satisfaction of basic needs remains to be seen. The policy simulations conducted here on the basis of economic structure in 1970 and economic trends in the early 1970s suggest that there are strong complementarities over the medium to long run between growth and basic needs. However, strong ceteris paribus assumptions are involved. Moreover, an economic model provides only one of several different perspectives on the consequences of alternative policy choices and must therefore be supplemented by independent judgments on the likely effects of changes in its basic tenants. Nevertheless, with a moderately fast growing population, it is fairly clear that Sri Lanka cannot sustain the massive subsidies and transfers it has favored in the past without growth. And it is also clear that growth will not occur without increased investment and economic efficiency. The most sensible solution is for the government to run a tighter ship, with emphasis on well-designed incentives and investment policies together with a reduction of subsidies through improved income policies. Although these goals are complicated by problems of managerial expertise and political acceptability, they are currently espoused by the new regime.

## APPENDIX

## The Static Model

## 1. Production

*P-1: Sectoral aggregate fixed factor*

$$H_i^F = [\sum_q a_q \overline{F}_{qi}^{\ -\nu}]^{-1/\nu}; \ \sum_q a_q = 1 \qquad q = 1, \ldots, r_1$$

*P-2: Sectoral aggregate variable factor*

$$H_i^V = A_i' \ [\sum_q a_q F_{qi}^{-\sigma}]^{-1/\sigma}; \ \sum_q a_q = 1 \qquad q = r_1 + 1, \ldots, r$$

*P-3: Sectoral output*

$$X_i = A_i [\beta H_i^{F-\rho} + (1 - \beta) H_i^{V-\rho}]^{-1/\rho}$$

*P-4: Sectoral net price*

$$P_i^* = [1 - \overline{t}_i^E (X_i^E / X_i) - \overline{t}_i^P] P_i - \sum_j \overline{a}_{ji} P_j - (1 + \tau_i^M) \overline{a}_i' P^M$$

*P-5: Sectoral wages of fixed factors*

$$w_{qi}^F = P_i^* \beta a_q A_i^{-\rho} (X_i / H_i^F)^{1+\rho} (H_i^F / F_{qi})^{1+\nu} \qquad q = 1, \ldots, r_1$$

*P-6: Sectoral demand for variable factors*

$$F_{qi} = \left[ \frac{P_i^* (1 - \beta) a_q}{w_{qi}^V A_i^{\ \rho} A_i'^{\ \sigma}} \ X_i^{1+\rho} \ H_i^{V\sigma - \rho} \right]^{1/(1+\sigma)} \qquad q = r_1 + 1, \ldots, r$$

*P-7: Unemployment*

$$U_q = F_q - \sum_i F_{qi} \qquad q = r_1 + 1, \ldots, r$$

*P-7': Equilibrium wage for variable factor*

$$w_q^V = f(F_q, \sum_i F_{qi}^D); \quad w_{qi}^V = \lambda_{qi} w_q^V \qquad q = r_1 + 1, \ldots, r$$

*P-8: Labor supply*

$$F_q = e_q \left[ \frac{w_q^V}{\bar{w}_q^V I_q} \right]^{\eta_q} \sum_k \bar{c}_{kq} N_k \qquad \begin{array}{l} q = r_1 + 1, \ldots, r \\ k = 1, \ldots, m - 1 \end{array}$$

*P-9: Labor effort*

$$e_q = 1 + \iota [\sum_k (\bar{c}_{kq} / \sum_k \bar{c}_{kq}) ((y_k^* - \tilde{s}_k^*) / \tilde{s}_k^*)] ; \max (\tilde{y}_k^* - \tilde{s}_k^*) = 0$$

## 2. Income

*Y-1: Firm income*

$$\tilde{Y}_m = \sum_q \sum_i \phi_{mqi} w_{qi} F_{qi}$$

*Y-2: Household income*

$$\tilde{Y}_k = \sum_q \sum_i \phi_{kqi} w_{qi} F_{qi} + \bar{q}_k \tilde{Y}_m^* ; \sum_k \phi_{kqi} = 1 ; \sum_k \bar{q}_k = 1$$

$$k = 1, \ldots, m - 1$$

*Y-3: After tax income*

$$\tilde{Y}_k = (1 - \theta_k) \tilde{Y}_k$$

*Y-4: Household and firm total expenditure*

$$\tilde{Y}_k^* = \tilde{Y}_k' - \tilde{S}_k$$

*Y-5: Per household expenditure*

$$\tilde{y}_k^* = \tilde{Y}_k^* / N_k \qquad k = 1, \ldots, m - 1$$

*Y-6: Total household real expenditure*

$$\tilde{Y}^{**}_k = \tilde{Y}^*_k / I_k \qquad k = 1, \ldots, m - 1$$

*Y-7: Per household real expenditure*

$$\tilde{y}^{**}_k = \tilde{Y}^{**}_k / N_k \qquad k = 1, \ldots, m - 1$$

## 3. Government

*G-1: Total government revenue*

$$\tilde{G} = \sum_k \theta_k \tilde{Y}_k + \sum_i [\bar{t}^P_i + \bar{t}^E_i (X^E_i / X_i)] P_i X_i + \tau^Z \tilde{Z}^M$$

$$+ \sum_i \tau^M_i P^M X^M_i + \sum_i \tau^C_i C^M_i \pi_i R$$

$$+ \sum_i \bar{t}^C_i [P_i C^D_i + (1 + \tau^C_i) C^M_i \pi_i R]$$

*G-2: Government savings*

$$\tilde{S}' = \tilde{G} - \bar{\tilde{G}}'$$

*G-3: Government sectoral expenditure*

$$\tilde{G}_i = \bar{g}_i \bar{\tilde{G}}'; \ \sum_i \bar{g}_i = 1$$

## 4. Savings and Investment

*S-1: Savings of households and firms*

$$\tilde{S}_k = \bar{s}_k \tilde{Y}'_k$$

*S-2: Investment good imports*

$$\tilde{Z}^M = \bar{m}' K P^M$$

*S-3: Sectoral investment demand*

$$Z_i = \bar{z}_i Z; \ \sum_i \bar{z}_i = 1$$

*S-4: Total physical domestic investment*

$$Z = \tilde{Z}/P^Z \;;\; P^Z = \sum_i \bar{z}_i P_i$$

## 5. Trade

*T-1: Price of noncompetitive imports*

$$P^M = \pi^M R$$

*T-2: Import share of sectoral consumption*

$$m_i = \mu_i [P_i/(\pi_i R(1 + \tau_i^C))]^{\xi_i}$$

*T-3: Consumer imports*

$$C_i^M = m_i C_i$$

*T-4: Sectoral exports*

$$X_i^E = X_i - \sum_i X_{ij} - Z_i - C_i^D - G_i \qquad i = 1, \ldots, n_1$$

*T-5: World price of exports*

$$\pi_i = \mu_i^E/(X_i^E)^{1/\xi_i^E} \qquad i = 1, \ldots, n_1$$

*T-6: Domestic price of exports*

$$P_i = \pi_i R \qquad i = 1, \ldots, n_1$$

*T-7: Capital outflow*

$$\Lambda' = \omega \sum_i w_{qi}^F F_{qi}^F \qquad q = 1$$

## 6. Consumption

### C-1: *Demand by households with above subsistence expenditure*

$$c_{ki} = \delta_{ki} + (\epsilon_{ki}/P_i^C)\,(\tilde{y}_k^* - \sum_i P_i^C \delta_{ki}); \; c_{ki} > \delta_{ki} \qquad k = 1, \ldots, m - 1$$

### C-1': *Demand by households with below subsistence expenditure*

$$c_{ki} = \delta'_{ki} + (\epsilon'_{ki}/P_i^C)\,(\tilde{y}_k^* - \sum_i P_i^C \delta'_{ki}); \; c_{ki} \leq \delta'_{ki} \qquad k = 1, \ldots, m - 1$$

### C-2: *Consumer prices*

$$P_i^C = (1 + \bar{t}_i^C)\,[(1 - m_i)P_i + (1 + \tau_i^C)\,m_i \pi_i R]$$

### C-3: *Total sectoral consumer demand*

$$C_i = \sum_k c_{ki} N_k \qquad k = 1, \ldots, m - 1$$

### C-4: *Domestic sectoral consumer demand*

$$C_i^D = C_i - C_i^M$$

### C-5: *Sectoral reservation demand by farmers*

$$\ln \delta_{ki} = \gamma_{ki} - (\gamma'_{ki}\,\tilde{y}_k^{* *-1}) \qquad \text{e.g., for } 2k \text{ and } 2i$$

## 7. Normalization Rule

### N-1: *Price level*

$$\Upsilon = \sum_i (X_{i1}/\sum_i X_{i1})P_i$$

*N-2: Normalization of prices*

$$P'_i = (\Upsilon_1/\Upsilon)P_i; P^{M'} = (\Upsilon_1/\Upsilon)P^M; R' = (\Upsilon_1/\Upsilon)R$$

## 8. Closing the Accounts

*Z-1: Exchange rate*

$$\sum_i \pi_i X_i^E - \sum_i \pi_i C_i^M - \pi^M(\sum_i X_i^M + Z^M) + \Lambda - (\Lambda'/R) = \Delta$$

*Z-2: Aggregate investment*

$$\tilde{Z} = \sum_i P_i Z_i = \sum_k \tilde{S}_k + \tilde{S}' + R\Lambda - R\Delta - (1 + \tau^Z)Z^M$$

*Z-3: Material balances*

$$P_i X_i = P_i C_i^D + P_i Z_i + \tilde{G}_i + P_i \sum_j X_{ij} \qquad l = n_1 + 1, \ldots, n$$

## Dynamic Linkages

### Factor Stock Adjustments

*D-1: Population growth*

$$N_{k,t+1} = (1 + \bar{n}_k)N_{k,t} \qquad k = 1, \ldots, m - 1$$

*D-2: Sectoral capital accumulation*

$$F_{qi,t+1} = (1 - \bar{d}_i)F_{qi,t} + r_i(\tilde{Z}_t/P_t^{Z'}) \qquad q = 1$$

$$\text{where} \qquad \rho_i = \frac{w_{qi}}{P_{t-1}^Z} + \frac{P_t^Z - (1 - \bar{d}_i)P_{t-1}^Z}{P_{t-1}^Z}$$

$$\tilde{\rho} = \sum_i (F_{qi}/K)\rho_i; r_i = \frac{F_{qi}}{K} + v\frac{F_{qi}}{K}\left(\frac{\rho_i - \tilde{\rho}}{\tilde{\rho}}\right)$$

*D-3: Price of total investment*

$$P^{Z'} = (Z/Z')P^Z + (Z^M/Z')P^M(1 + \tau^Z)$$

*D-4: Rural-urban migration*

$$N_k' = \bar{u}_k \left[ \frac{F_q - U_q}{F_q} \left( \frac{w_q/I_q}{\varsigma w_{q'}/I_{q'}} \right) \right]^{\eta_k^u} N_k$$

## Notation for the Static Model[a]

### Subscripts

| | |
|---|---|
| Sectors | $i, j = 1, \ldots, n$ |
|   Export | $i, j = 1, \ldots, n_1$ |
|   Nonexport | $i, j = n_1 + 1, \ldots, n$ |
| Factors | $q = 1, \ldots, r$ |
|   Fixed | $q = 1, \ldots, r_1$ |
|   Variable | $q = r_1 + 1, \ldots, r$ |
| Institutions | $k = 1, \ldots, m$ |
|   Households | $k = 1, \ldots, m - 1$ |
|   Firms | $k = m$ |

### Superscripts

| | |
|---|---|
| Factors | |
|   Fixed | $F$ |
|   Variable | $V$ |
| Demand for goods and services | |
|   Domestic | $D$ |
|   Imported | $M$ |
|   Exported | $E$ |
| Prices, taxes | |
|   Consumer | $C$ |
|   Producer | $P$ |
|   Import | $M$ |
|   Export | $E$ |
|   Investment | $Z$ |

[a]Parameters are represented by lower-case Roman letters with a bar and Greek letters. Variables expressed in units of money are topped by a tilde ($\sim$). Primes (') and asterisks (*) are used to distinguish different but related variables and parameters.

**Variables and Parameters**

*Factors of production*

| | | |
|---|---|---|
| Sectoral aggregate fixed factor | $H_i^F$ | |
| Sectoral fixed factors | $\bar{F}_{qi}$ | $q = 1, \ldots, r_1$ |
| Sectoral aggregate variable factor | $H_i^V$ | |
| Sectoral variable factors | $F_{qi}$ | $q = r_1 + 1, \ldots r$ |
| Variable factor supply | $F_q$ | |
| Unemployment of variable factors | $U_q$ | $q = r_1 + 1, \ldots, r$ |
| Population by consumer groups (expressed by standardized households (HH): 1 HH = 6 persons) | $N_k$ | |
| Labor effort coefficient | $e_q$ | |
| Labor effort response rate | $\iota$ | |
| Labor supply elasticity | $\eta_q$ | |
| Labor participation rate | $\bar{c}_{kq}$ | |
| Labor cost of living index | $I_q$ | |
| Cost of subsistence by consumer group | $\tilde{s}_k^*$ | |
| Total capital stock | $K$ | |

*Physical goods and services*

| | | |
|---|---|---|
| Gross sectoral production | $X_i$ | |
| Shift parameter for sectoral production function | $A_i$ | |
| Shift parameter for unskilled labor aggregation | $A_i'$ | |
| Production function distribution parameters | | |
|    Aggregate factors (1st level) | $a$ | |
|    Sectoral (2nd level) | $\beta$ | |
| CES exponents | | |
|    Fixed factor | $\upsilon$ | |

| | |
|---|---|
| Variable factor | $\sigma$ |
| Sectoral | $\rho$ |
| Intermediate goods | $X_{ij}$ |
| Input/output coefficients | $\bar{a}_{ij}$ |

*Prices, wages, and income*

| | |
|---|---|
| Producer prices | $P_i$ |
| Net prices | $P_i^*$ |
| Consumer prices | $P_i^C$ |
| Constant producer price level | $\Upsilon_1$ |
| Producer price level in period $t$ with base year weights | $\Upsilon$ |
| Normalized prices and exchange rates | $P_i', P^{M'}, R'$ |
| Average wages for variable factors | $w_q \qquad q = r_1 + 1, \ldots, r$ |
| Wage differentials for variable factors | $\lambda_{qi}$ |
| Sectoral wages for variable factors | $w_{qi}^V$ |
| Wages for fixed factors | $w_{qi}^F$ |
| Household shares in total dividends | $\bar{q}_k$ |
| Consumer price index | $I_k$ |
| Institutional income | $\tilde{Y}_k$ |
| Factor ownership matrix | $\phi_{kqi}$ |
| Income after taxes | $\tilde{Y}_k'$ |
| Expenditure | $\tilde{Y}_k^*$ |
| Expenditure per household | $\tilde{y}_k^*$ |
| Real expenditure | $\tilde{Y}^{**}$ |
| Real expenditure per household | $\tilde{y}_k^{**}$ |

*Government*

| | |
|---|---|
| Total government revenue | $\tilde{G}$ |

| | |
|---|---|
| Government consumption expenditure | $\bar{\tilde{G}}'$ |
| Sectoral government consumption | $G_i'$ |
| Sectoral government consumption shares | $\bar{g}_i$ |
| Government saving | $\tilde{S}'$ |
| Government saving coefficient | $\tilde{s}'$ |
| Direct taxes $n$ subsidies | $\theta_k$ |
| Indirect taxes $n$ subsidies | |
|     Producer | $\bar{t}_i^P$ |
|     Export | $\bar{t}_i^E$ |
|     Consumer | $\bar{t}_i^C$ |
| Tariffs | |
|     Imported intermediate | $\tau_i^M$ |
|     Imported consumer | $\tau_i^C$ |
|     Imported investment | $\tau^Z$ |

*Saving and investment*

| | |
|---|---|
| Institutional savings | $\tilde{S}_k$ |
| Institutional saving shares | $\bar{s}_k$ |
| Domestic physical investment | $Z$ |
| Price of domestic investment | $P^Z$ |
| Investment demand | $Z_i$ |
| Investment demand coefficients | $\bar{z}_i$ |
| Investment good imports | $Z^M$ |
| Investment import ratio | $\bar{m}'$ |

*Trade*

| | |
|---|---|
| International prices | $\pi_i , \pi^M$ |
| Domestic price of noncompetitive imports | $P^M$ |
| Rate of foreign exchange | $R$ |
| Noncompetitive intermediate import coefficients | $\bar{a}_i'$ |

Noncompetitive intermediate
imports $X_i^M$

Proportion of total consumption imported $m_i$

Consumer import coefficient $\mu_i$

Consumer import price
elasticity $\xi_i$

Exports $X_i^E$ $\quad i = 1, \ldots, n_1$

Export demand coefficient $\mu_i^E$ $\quad i = 1, \ldots, n_1$

Export demand price
elasticity $\xi_i^E$ $\quad i = 1, \ldots, n_1$

Capital inflow in world prices $\Lambda$

Private capital outflow
coefficient $\omega$

Private capital outflow $\Lambda'$

Balance of payments surplus
(in foreign currency) $\Delta$

*Consumption*

Sectoral consumption $C_i$

Consumption of domestic
goods $C_i^D$

Consumption of imported
goods $C_i^M$

Sectoral consumption per
household $c_{ki}$

Subsistence minima of spliced
linear expenditure system $\delta_{ki}$

Marginal budget shares for
above subsistence consumption $\epsilon_{ki}$

Marginal budget shares for below
subsistence consumption $\epsilon'_{ki}$

Sectoral reservation demand
parameters $\gamma_{ki}, \gamma'_{ki}$

**Additional Notation for the
Dynamic Linkages**

**Subscript**

Time $\qquad t = 1, \ldots, T$

**Variables and Parameters**

*Factor stock adjustments*

Growth rate of households $\qquad \bar{n}_k$

Sectoral depreciation rates $\qquad d_i$

Investment allocation
   parameters $\qquad r_i$

Sectoral profit rate $\qquad \rho_i$

Average profit rate $\qquad \tilde{\rho}$

Investment mobility parameter $\qquad v$

Price of total investment $\qquad P^{Z'}$

Total physical investment $\qquad Z'$

*Rural-urban migration*

Constant migration differential $\qquad \zeta$

Migration elasticity $\qquad \eta_k^u$

Number of migrating households $\qquad N_k'$

Adjustment parameter $\qquad \bar{u}_k$

## NOTES

1. Trade and national accounts data referred to here are taken from the social accounting matrix for Sri Lanka presented in Pyatt, Roe, et al. (1978). The structure and incidence of taxes, income transfers, and food subsidies are also obtained from Pyatt, Roe, et al., but with adjustments for socioeconomic groups based on additional information provided by Karunatilake (1975). For a detailed discussion of these basic data, see de Melo (1978). In this study, household incomes have been further adjusted to reflect social services expenditures estimated by Alailima (1978). The primary data sources for these secondary sources were the *1969/70 Socioeconomic Survey of Ceylon* and the *1973 Survey of Consumer Finances*.
2. See note 1 on the data base. A good introduction to the use of SAMs in development planning can be found in Pyatt and Thorbecke (1976). The aggregations used for the simulations are those discussed above and summarized again below.
3. Linear programming models also include an overall budget constraint on demand; but, as explained in Taylor (1975), the prices used in the budget constraint are often not the same as those produced in the programming solutions. Thus, no real consistency in income flows is achieved.
4. See Dervis, de Melo, and Robinson (forthcoming) and Adelman and Robinson (1978: ch. 3) for a more thorough description of the basic CGE model. See de Melo (1978) for a complete description of the model used here and de Melo (1979) for a summary description of the model and a more general discussion of some agricultural policy experiments.
5. The government is implicitly assumed to be following a policy of maintaining a constant overall price level.
6. Assuming that the value of social services relative to GNP was the same in 1970 as in 1973, the imputed average 1970 household income from these services by socioeconomic group is as follows:

| | |
|---|---|
| Urban rich | 376 rupees per annum |
| Urban poor | 321 rupees per annum |
| Rural rich | 334 rupees per annum |
| Small farmers | 334 rupees per annum |
| Rural landless | 325 rupees per annum |
| Estate workers | 211 rupees per annum |

7. Justification for the use of the log normal function to describe the distribution of income is based on the consistency of this distribution function with (1) models of generation of income distribution and (2) empirical data (see Aitchison and Brown 1957: ch. 11). The log normal function basically takes into account the skewness of the original distribution, which results from the right-hand tail (of upper incomes) extending far out from the mean. There is little alternative to the assumption of constant income variance within subgroups.
8. These Gini coefficients are roughly consistent with information in the 1969–1970 socioeconomic survey.
9. This estimate is cited in Alailima (1978: 100) as derived from a background paper of the Ceylon Federation of University Women on "Estimated Monthly Expenditure" (mimeograph, July 1972).
10. A poverty line is in many respects arbitrary. The worldwide poverty line chosen by Chenery (1979) showed 14 percent of the Sri Lanka population in poverty in 1975.
11. The rice subsidy in 1970 is modeled here as an average effective subsidy of 39 percent rather than a graduated subsidy.

12. In the model, both public and private investment serve to increase sectoral capital stocks, which form part of the sectoral production functions. As indicated below, the allocation of investment across sectors is partially responsive to differential sectoral rates of return.
13. See de Melo (1979) for a discussion of the alternative effects of factor-neutral and capital-using technical change in agriculture on multiple goals.
14. This program was carried out under the Land Reform Act of 1972 and the Business Acquisition Act of 1970, respectively.
15. See Adelman (1977) for a strong defense of the need for redistribution prior to growth.
16. The importance of both the rate and pattern of growth is consistent, for example, with the conclusion of Fields (1979), who found in a study of six countries that a high aggregate growth rate is neither necessary nor sufficient for reducing poverty.

## BIBLIOGRAPHY

Adelman, I. 1977. "A Theory of Development Strategy for Equitable Growth in Developing Countries." The Cleveringa Lecture, 1977/78, University of Leiden. Mimeo.

Adelman, I., and S. Robinson. 1978. *Income Distribution Policy in Developing Countries: A Case Study of Korea*. London: Oxford University Press.

Aitchison, J., and J. A. C. Brown. 1957. *The Lognormal Distribution, with Special Reference to Its Use in Economics*. London: Cambridge University Press.

Alailima, P. J. 1978. "Fiscal Incidence in Sri Lanka." Provisional draft WEP 2-23/WP 69. Geneva: International Labour Organization.

Central Bank of Ceylon. 1974. *Survey of Consumer Finances 1973*. Colombo.

Chenery, H. 1979. *Structural Change and Development Policy*. New York: Oxford University Press.

Department of Census and Statistics, Government of Sri Lanka. 1973. *Socioeconomic Survey of Sri Lanka 1969–70*. Colombo.

Dervis, K.; J. A. P. de Melo; and S. Robinson. Forthcoming. *Planning Models and Development Policy*. Cambridge: Cambridge University Press.

Fields, G. S. 1979. "Poverty, Inequality and Development." Ithaca, N.Y.: Cornell University. Mimeo.

Hansen, R. D. 1976. *The U.S. and World Development: Agenda for Action, 1976*. Washington, D.C.: Overseas Development Council.

International Labor Office. 1976. *Employment, Growth, and Basic Needs: A One World Problem*. Geneva.

Isenman, Paul. 1980. "Basic Needs: The Case of Sri Lanka." *World Development* 8 (March): 237–258.

Karunatilake, H. N. S. 1975. "Changes in Income Distribution in Sri Lanka." In *Income Distribution, Employment, and Economic Development in Southeast and East Asia*. Papers and proceedings of a seminar sponsored jointly by the Japan Economic Research Center and the Council of Asian Manpower Studies. Tokyo.

de Melo, M. H. 1978. "A General Equilibrium Investigation of Agricultural Policies and Development Strategies: A Case Study of Sri Lanka." Ph.D. thesis, University of Maryland.

————. 1979. "Agricultural Policies and Development: A Socioeconomic Investigation Applied to Sri Lanka." *Journal of Policy Modeling* 1, no. 2: 217–234.

Pyatt, G., A. Roe, et al. 1978. *Social Accounting for Development Planning with Special Reference to Sri Lanka.* Cambridge: Cambridge University Press.

Pyatt, G., and E. Thorbecke. 1976. *Planning Techniques for a Better Future.* Geneva: International Labor Organization.

Robinson, S. 1976. "Income Distribution Within Groups, Among Groups, and Overall: A Technique of Analysis." Princeton University Research Program in Development Studies, Discussion Paper No. 65.

Sewell, J. W., et al. 1977. *The United States and World Development: Agenda, 1977.* New York: Praeger.

Snodgrass, D. M. 1966. *Ceylon: An Export Economy in Transition.* Homewood, Ill.: Irwin.

Taylor, L. 1975. "Theoretical Foundations and Technical Implications." In C. Blitzer, P. Clark, and L. Taylor, eds., *Economy Wide Models and Development Planning.* Oxford: Oxford University Press.

Chapter 5

# Growth, Poverty Alleviation, and Foreign Assistance

*Michael J. Crosswell*

## INTRODUCTION AND PRÉCIS

Most of the literature on basic human needs is motivated by the observation that rapid growth in less developed countries (LDCs) has failed to make a substantial impact in terms of alleviation of poverty and enhanced satisfaction of basic needs.[1] This failure of growth has typically been attributed to patterns of growth within countries, which allegedly have generated a worsened distribution of income, little or no increase in absolute incomes of the poor, and a pattern of production and supply ill suited to the task of meeting basic needs. The basic needs literature has placed great emphasis on achieving patterns of development that provide for "equitable growth" (through increased and more productive employment, asset redistribution, and other measures leading to a more equitable distribution of earned income) and enhanced development of human resources (through more effective direct intervention to address health, education and nutritional needs.)[2]

The main thesis of this chapter is that the persistence of widespread absolute poverty despite rapid growth of GNP in LDCs as a group results not so much from inadequate patterns of growth within countries as from the uneven patterns of growth among countries. Most of the world's poor are in low-income countries, and these countries have by and large experienced very slow rates of growth. Further, what data exist on trends in income distribution over time reveal no predominant tendency for income distribution to worsen with growth. Where rapid growth has occurred, it has almost always resulted in reduced incidence of poverty.

This certainly does not mean that the current emphasis on basic human needs is misplaced. No more urgent priority faces the development community than the pressing need to alleviate world poverty. Nor does it imply that intracountry patterns of growth are unimportant. The sorts of measures highlighted by the basic needs approach vitally affect the extent of poverty associated with a given level of per capita income, and arguably contribute to steady growth in income over time through investment in human resources, better utilization of existing resources, and so on.[3]

It does point to a dimension of the basic needs problem that has been relatively neglected, particularly by donors. For it turns out that while most of the developing world's poverty problem is heavily concentrated in low-income countries, the bulk of concessional foreign assistance (not to mention nonconcessional foreign assistance) is directed primarily toward middle-income countries.

The first section of this chapter takes as a point of departure the estimates of incidence of poverty for thirty-six developing countries derived by Ahluwalia, Carter, and Chenery (1979) and uses these as a basis for estimating the percentages of population in absolute poverty for sixty-eight other developing countries. This facilitates an analysis of the distribution of poverty among groups of countries, classified according to per capita income. The main findings are that over 80 percent of the world's poor are in low-income countries—those with per capita incomes in 1977 at or below $300 (1977 prices). About half of the population in this group is poor. Countries with per capita incomes above $450 account for less than 10 percent of LDC poor, and the incidence of poverty in this group is fairly low, about 14 percent.

The next section of the chapter critically examines the proposition that rapid growth has failed to make a substantial impact on absolute poverty because of adverse trends in income distribution as growth proceeds. While cross-section data lend some support to this latter proposition, time-series data do not. Further, simulations that incorporate an assumption of worsening income distribution for low-income countries nonetheless show a substantial impact of growth in terms of reduced incidence of poverty. Finally, empirical studies of a number of developing countries suggest that rapid growth has typically been associated with reductions in absolute poverty.

The third section of the chapter draws implications for donors of concessional foreign assistance. An examination of the distribution of Official Development Assistance (ODA) among groups of countries, using data on commitments over the 1976–1978 period, reveals that the low-income countries—with over 80 percent of LDC poor and over 60 percent of the total LDC population—received less than 45 percent of ODA commitments. In contrast, the group of countries with per capita incomes above $450—which account for less than 10 percent of the poor and about one-quarter of the total population—received over 35 percent of ODA commitments. Thus the distribution of concessional foreign assistance does not reflect the distribution of LDC poverty very well. The ensuing discussion reviews the literature on determinants of allocation patterns, pointing to biases in aid allocations in favor of small countries (as opposed to populous countries) and in favor of middle-income countries (as opposed to low-income countries). Econometric analysis of the recent commitments data under investigation here confirms a very sharp bias in favor of small countries but does not indicate a bias toward middle-income countries. These results lead to a discussion of allocation models that donors might use to effect a redistribution of ODA that would be more consistent with the objective of achieving substantial reductions in LDC poverty by the end of the century. The common features of these models include a softening or elimination of the bias against large countries; an explicit bias in favor of low-income countries; and inclusion of performance criteria as one determinant of allocations.

What are the prospects that increased ODA flows to low-income countries would result in accelerated growth? The final section of the chapter reviews some of the evidence on the relationship between foreign assistance and growth. Although this evidence is mixed, it suggests that shortfalls in foreign assistance played a significant role in the poor growth performance of the low-income group in the past, and that increased foreign assistance to low-income countries could make a substantial contribution to more rapid growth over the next ten to twenty years. Finally, an "illustrative scenario" of a substantial shift in allocations of ODA toward low-income countries is discussed.

## THE DISTRIBUTION OF POVERTY AMONG COUNTRIES

### Established Estimates for Thirty-Six Developing Countries

The methodology used here for determining the distribution of poverty among countries is based on, and extends, the work of Ahluwalia, Carter, and Chenery. They in turn used as a point of departure estimates of real GDP per capita published by Kravis, Heston, and Summers (KHS).[4] A brief review of this work will indicate the basis for the estimates of poverty contained in this paper.

The KHS paper is motivated by the observation that the purchasing power of a dollar (the "real" value of a dollar) varies considerably from country to country at any given point in time. Accordingly, a comparison between two countries in terms of per capita income measured in dollars using conventional exchange rates ("nominal" per capita income) does not give an accurate picture of one country's average real income relative to another's.

The KHS estimates of real GDP per capita represent an effort to measure disparities in real income with greater accuracy, by estimating a factor (called an *exchange rate deviation index* by KHS, and referred to elsewhere as a Kravis factor) that measures the extent to which nominal comparisons with income in the United States misstate real comparisons. For instance, the observed Kravis factor for India is 3.34, indicating (roughly) that a dollar in India in 1970 could purchase the equivalent of $3.34 in the United States in the same year.

The Kravis estimates were derived by (1) establishing detailed series of price comparisons for sixteen countries including the United States; (2) using these price comparisons to establish real levels of per capita income (i.e., per capita income in dollars of uniform purchasing power); (3) deriving the associated Kravis factors, measured as the ratio of real to nominal per capita income; and (4) finally seeking readily observable variables that would explain the real income levels and thus could be used to estimate real incomes and Kravis factors for other countries.

To give some flavor for the results of the KHS price comparisons, Table 5–1 lists nominal GDP per capita, real GDP per capita, and the ratio of the two in 1970 for the sixteen countries for which detailed price comparisons were made. (Real and nominal GDP per capita are expressed in index form relative to a base of $4790 = 100.0 for the U.S.).

The KHS results indicate that the comparisons of nominal GDP relative to the United States (contained in the first column) consistently understate comparisons of real GDP (the second column). The extent of the divergence between real and nominal GNP is measured by the Kravis factor. The values in the third column indicate that the Kravis factor tends to decline as nominal per capita income rises.

The remainder of the KHS analysis aims at finding variables for which data are readily available, which can explain the estimates of real GDP. This would provide a convenient basis for estimates of real GDP for other countries, as an alternative to the more costly procedure of making detailed price comparisons for each country. The authors use three such

**Table 5–1.  Nominal and Real GDP Per Capita and Kravis Factors, 1970** (*U.S.* = *100.0*)

|  | *Nominal GDP* (*n*) | *Real GDP* (*r*) | *Kravis Factor* (*r/n*) |
|---|---|---|---|
| India | 2.07 | 6.92 | 3.34 |
| Kenya | 2.99 | 6.33 | 2.12 |
| Philippines | 3.86 | 12.00 | 3.11 |
| Korea | 5.39 | 12.10 | 2.24 |
| Colombia | 7.24 | 18.10 | 2.50 |
| Malaysia | 8.10 | 19.10 | 2.36 |
| Iran | 8.37 | 20.30 | 2.42 |
| Hungary | 21.60 | 42.70 | 1.98 |
| Italy | 36.00 | 49.20 | 1.37 |
| Japan | 39.80 | 59.20 | 1.49 |
| United Kingdom | 45.70 | 63.50 | 1.39 |
| Netherlands | 50.80 | 68.70 | 1.35 |
| Belgium | 55.10 | 72.00 | 1.31 |
| France | 58.20 | 73.20 | 1.26 |
| Germany | 64.10 | 78.20 | 1.22 |
| United States | 100.00 | 100.00 | 1.00 |

*Source:* Kravis, Heston, and Summers (1978), Table 1 (p. 216).

variables: (1) nominal GDP; (2) an openness variable, measured by the ratio of exports plus imports to GDP; and (3) a price isolation variable measured by the extent to which movements in a country's GDP deflator deviate from a world average GDP deflator. Using regression analysis, these variables explain 98.9 percent of the observed variation in real GDP per capita among the sample countries. KHS then use these variables and the estimated coefficients to obtain estimates of real GDP per capita for some 139 other countries.[5]

Ahluwalia, Carter, and Chenery (ACC) used these results in estimating percentages of population in absolute poverty for thirty-six developing countries. They started with 1970 per capita GDP figures in nominal terms (i.e., measured in 1970 dollars on the basis of conventional foreign exchange rates) and converted these to dollars of uniform purchasing power (ICP dollars) using the Kravis factors estimated by KHS. Thus, for Indonesia, real per capita GDP (in ICP dollars) was roughly three times the level of nominal GDP per capita, corresponding to the econometrically estimated Kravis factor for Indonesia of 3.10.

ACC then posit a poverty line of 200 ICP dollars, which is about the income level of the forty-sixth percentile of income recipients in India. This income level would be approximately adequate to ensure a daily supply of 2250 calories in India. Thus, as ACC point out, the poverty line used for their estimates is essentially a South Asian standard, which is conservative in the sense of yielding estimates that understate the extent of the poverty problem by standards appropriate for more affluent developing countries. The poverty line also underestimates the per capita expenditure required to meet basic needs, including those for health and education. At the same time, it has the virtue of indicating the most acute poverty, which arguably is of greatest concern.

Given this poverty line and the estimates of real per capita income (in ICP dollars), ACC use information on income distribution to estimate the percentage of population in absolute poverty for the other thirty-five developing countries. Their sample size was limited by availability of income distribution data; indeed in eleven cases they had to estimate income distribution based on cross-country comparisons.[6] However, the sample is fairly comprehensive in that it accounts for about 80 percent of developing country populations (excluding China). The ACC estimates of poverty incidence using purchasing power adjustments are given in the fifth column of Table 5–2, along with their estimates based on official exchange rates.

## Estimates for Other Developing Countries

The task here is to estimate the incidence of poverty for some sixty-eight other countries. Since one objective is to consider the scope for reallocation of ODA (Official Development Assistance), the sample excludes countries that received less than $25 million in ODA commitments as an annual average over the 1976–1978 period.[7] The basis for the estimates is the following equation, which was estimated using the ACC results given in Table 5–2.[8]

$$PPK = 75.70 - .094 (PCIK) + .000030 (PCIK)^2 \qquad (1)$$
$$(18.58) \quad (-10.32) \qquad\qquad (7.33) \quad R^2 = .85$$

This equation indicates that most of the variation in percentages of population in absolute poverty (PPK) as estimated by ACC can be explained by levels of per capita income adjusted for purchasing power (PCIK). The missing information, of course, is the distribution of income. Surprisingly, including a single variable to represent income distribution—the estimated share of the lowest 40 percent of income recipients (YD) as reported by ACC—improves the explanatory power of the equation only slightly ($R^2 = .87$) and alters the value of each of the other coefficients by only about 8 percent.[9] In the absence of reliable in-

**Table 5–2. Estimates of Incidence of Poverty**

| Country | 1975 Per Capita Income | | Income Share of Lowest 40 Percent | Percentage of Population in Absolute Poverty | |
|---|---|---|---|---|---|
| | Official Exchange Rates, 1970 Prices (PCI) | ICP Dollars (PCIK) | | Official Exchange Rates (PP) | ICP Dollars (PPK) |
| Bangladesh | 72 | 200 | 20.1 | 60 | 64 |
| Ethiopia[a] | 81 | 213 | 16.8 | 62 | 68 |
| Burma[a] | 88 | 237 | 15.7 | 56 | 65 |
| Indonesia | 90 | 280 | 16.1 | 62 | 59 |
| India | 102 | 300 | 17.0 | 46 | 46 |
| Zaire[a] | 105 | 281 | 14.6 | 49 | 53 |
| Sudan[a] | 112 | 281 | 14.5 | 47 | 54 |
| Uganda[a] | 115 | 280 | 14.4 | 45 | 55 |
| Tanzania[a] | 118 | 297 | 14.3 | 46 | 51 |
| Pakistan | 121 | 299 | 16.5 | 34 | 43 |
| Kenya | 168 | 413 | 8.9 | 48 | 55 |
| Nigeria[a] | 176 | 433 | 13.0 | 27 | 35 |
| Philippines | 182 | 469 | 11.6 | 29 | 33 |
| Sri Lanka | 185 | 471 | 19.3 | 10 | 14 |
| Senegal | 227 | 550 | 9.6 | 29 | 35 |
| Thailand | 237 | 584 | 11.5 | 23 | 32 |
| Egypt | 238 | 561 | 13.9 | 14 | 20 |
| Ghana[a] | 255 | 628 | 11.2 | 19 | 25 |
| Morocco[a] | 266 | 643 | 13.3 | 16 | 26 |
| Ivory Coast | 325 | 695 | 10.4 | 14 | 25 |
| Korea | 325 | 797 | 16.9 | 6 | 8 |
| Colombia | 352 | 851 | 9.9 | 14 | 19 |
| Zambia | 363 | 798 | 13.0 | 7 | 10 |
| Turkey | 379 | 914 | 9.3 | 11 | 14 |
| Chile | 386 | 798 | 13.1 | 9 | 11 |
| Tunisia | 425 | 992 | 11.1 | 9 | 10 |
| Malaysia | 471 | 1006 | 11.1 | 8 | 12 |
| Guatemala[a] | 497 | 1128 | 11.3 | 9 | 10 |
| Taiwan | 499 | 1075 | 22.3 | 4 | 5 |
| Peru | 503 | 1183 | 7.3 | 15 | 18 |
| Brazil | 509 | 1136 | 9.1 | 8 | 15 |
| Iran[a] | 572 | 1257 | 8.2 | 8 | 13 |
| Mexico | 758 | 1429 | 8.2 | 10 | 14 |
| Yugoslavia | 828 | 1701 | 18.8 | 4 | 5 |
| Argentina | 1097 | 2094 | 15.1 | 3 | 5 |
| Venezuela | 1288 | 2286 | 8.5 | 5 | 9 |

*Source:* From data contained in Ahluwalia, Carter, and Chenery (1979), Table 1 (p. 303) and Table 2 (p. 312).

[a] Income distribution based on cross-country comparisons.

formation on income distribution for the sixty-eight countries under consideration, equation (1) was judged to provide a useful basis for estimating percentages of population in absolute poverty for those countries.

The inclusion of the squared term allows for the possibility that the effect of increases in real per capita income on the incidence of poverty becomes weaker as the percentage of the population in poverty declines. This is plausible considering that an increase of $100 in per capita income will tend to have a major effect on poverty in a country such as Ethiopia, where real income is low (213 ICP dollars) and over two-thirds of the people are poor. The same increase in a country like Taiwan (real income of 1075 ICP dollars and only 5 percent of the population in poverty) will have a much smaller absolute impact on the incidence of poverty, measured as a percentage of the total population. Indeed, the estimated coefficients call for the incidence of poverty to decline to a minimum of about 2 percent at a real income level of around 1567 ICP dollars (somewhat less than the figures for Cyprus or Portugal) and then to rise. (See Figure 5–1.) Since such a pattern of increasing incidence of absolute poverty at higher income levels does not appear plausible, a value of 5 percent was imposed on the estimates for countries with per capita income above 1250 ICP dollars. The figure of 5 percent represents the minimum value observed in the ACC sample (for Taiwan, Yugoslavia, and Argentina). This adjustment affected seventeen countries in the sample, with incomes at or above the level of Panama and Costa Rica. These countries had an aggregate population of only 30 million, about 1.5 percent of the total.

The figures for per capita income adjusted for purchasing power were those provided by KHS, updated to 1975 using trend growth rates of per capita GDP as reported in the *World Development Report 1979*.[10] The results of the estimates for individual countries are given in the Appendix Table. For the countries included in the ACC study, the estimates of incidence of poverty and real per capita income are those reported by ACC.

## The Distribution of Poverty among Countries

The estimates contained in the Appendix Table permit an analysis of the distribution of poverty among countries. Table 5–3 presents data on groups of countries determined by 1977 Per Capita GNP, the incidence of poverty within each income group, and the portion of total poverty accounted for by each group.

Perhaps the most striking result of this grouping of countries is the high concentration of total poverty in the low-income countries of the sample. About one-half of the countries in the sample have per capita

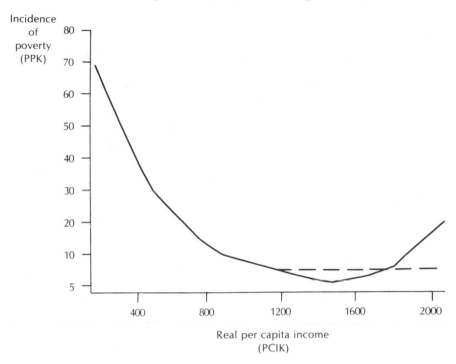

**Figure 5–1. The incidence of poverty.**

incomes at or below $450; collectively they account for 90 percent of total poverty in the sample. The bulk of this poverty is in countries with per capita income at or below $300, and a sizable portion is in India alone. This concentration of LDC poverty reflects not only low average levels of income, but also the concentration of *total* population in the low-income group. Countries with per capita incomes at or below $450 account for almost three-quarters of the total population under consideration, while countries at or below $300 comprise over 60 percent of the total.

A second important feature of the data is the fairly steady decline in incidence of poverty as per capita income increases. While this trend appears to decelerate sharply for countries in the highest income group, the results for this group are dominated by the estimates for Brazil and Iran. It can be argued that these countries have followed an unusually inequitable pattern of development and so are not representative.

Finally, it is worth noting that these estimates are in very close agreement with those reported in the *World Development Report 1978*, which was based on an earlier version of the ACC study.[11] For comparable

**Table 5–3. The Distribution of Poverty among Country Groups**

| Country Group (1977 Per Capita GNP) | 1977 Population (millions) | Percent Poor | Poor Population (millions) | Percent of Total Poor | Cumulative Percent of Total Poor |
|---|---|---|---|---|---|
| Less than $150 (14 countries) | 219.1 | 62 | 135.8 | 17.4 | 17.4 |
| India–$150 (24 countries) | 631.7 | 46 | 290.6 | 37.2 | 54.6 |
| $150–$300 | 401.3 | 51 | 203.6 | 26.1 | 80.7 |
| $301–$450 (13 countries) | 245.9 | 31 | 76.6 | 9.8 | 90.5 |
| $451–$1200 (28 countries) | 326.4 | 15 | 49.0 | 6.2 | 96.7 |
| $1201–$4800 (22 countries) | 208.5 | 12 | 24.9 | 3.2 | 99.9 |
| Total (102 countries) | 2032.9 | 38 | 780.6 | 99.9 | |

*Source:* Appendix Table. Country groupings are based on 1977 per capita GNP figures from the *World Development Report 1979*, or in a few cases from the *1979 World Bank Atlas*. Population figures are from the *1979 World Bank Atlas*.

**Table 5–4.  A Comparison of Estimates of Poverty**

|  | *Total Population* | *Poor Population* | *Incidence of Poverty* |
|---|---|---|---|
| Low-income group |  |  |  |
| *WDR 1978* | 1215 | 630 | 52 |
| Table 5–3 | 1252 | 630 | 50 |
| Middle-Income Group |  |  |  |
| *WDR 1978* | 895 | 140 | 16 |
| Table 5–3 | 781 | 151 | 19 |
| Total |  |  |  |
| *WDR 1978* | 2110 | 770 | 36.5 |
| Table 5–3 | 2033 | 781 | 38.4 |

groupings based on a 1977 per capita income cutoff of $300, the two sets of estimates are compared in Table 5–4.

## GROWTH AND POVERTY ALLEVIATION

Much of the discussion of basic needs has been motivated by a perception that growth has failed—that significant increases in GNP have not resulted in substantial reductions in world poverty. For instance, the introduction to the ILO volume, *Employment Growth and Basic Needs,* observed that ". . . policy has led to rapid and sustained growth in both developed and developing countries. However, it has become increasingly evident, particularly from the experience of the developing countries, that rapid growth at the national level does not automatically reduce poverty . . . ." The IBRD/Sussex volume, *Redistribution With Growth,* was introduced with the statement that "It is now clear that more than a decade of rapid growth in underdeveloped countries has been of little or no benefit to perhaps a third of their population." [12]

In part, this view stems from the aggregate data on LDC performance, which demonstrate rapid growth in LDCs as a group but only slow progress in reducing poverty. For instance, between 1960 and 1976, per capita GNP in developing countries grew at an average annual rate of 3.7 percent. [13]

At the same time there was little perceived progress in terms of poverty alleviation. The ILO estimates that between 1963 and 1972 the number of seriously poor in LDCs increased from 1.1 to 1.2 billion, and the incidence of poverty fell only slightly, from 73 percent of LDC population to 67 percent.[14]

The bulk of the analysis of the evident failure of LDC growth to alleviate LDC poverty has attributed this failure mainly to patterns of growth *within* countries. These patterns reveal a tendency for the distribution of income to worsen, so that the impact on the poor has been at best weakly positive.[15]

In the process of focusing on growth patterns *within* countries, there has been relative neglect until recently of the pattern of growth *among* countries as perhaps the key factor underlying the slow pace of poverty alleviation. Yet data on growth rates of per capita income for LDCs grouped by income level, in conjunction with the estimates of the distribution of LDC poverty presented earlier, suggest that arguments about the failure of rapid growth to alleviate poverty need to be carefully worded. Table 5–5 indicates that in the group of countries where most of the world's poor subsist—the low-income countries—growth has on average been very slow. In contrast, middle-income countries, where both the incidence and numbers of poor are relatively low, have been growing rapidly. If anything, these data point to the success rather than failure of rapid growth in alleviating poverty.[16]

Other evidence of the impact of growth on poverty alleviation can be adduced from the data on per capita income, the income share of the lowest 40 percent, and estimates of the incidence of poverty derived by Ahluwalia, Carter, and Chenery (1979) and presented earlier in Table 5–2. Recall that the preferred estimates of the incidence of poverty (PPK) are based on figures for per capita income measured in ICP dollars (PCIK) as well as income distribution estimates. The regression results reported earlier indicated that for the sample as a whole, most of the variation in poverty incidence could be explained by differences in

## Table 5–5. Growth and Poverty

| Country Group | Average per Capita Income Level ($) | Incidence of Poverty (%) | Share of LDC Poverty (%) | Average Annual per Capita GDP Growth (%) 1960–1970 | Average Annual per Capita GDP Growth (%) 1970–1977 |
|---|---|---|---|---|---|
| Low-income | 170 | 50 | 81 | 1.5 | 0.9 |
| Middle-income | 1,140 | 19 | 19 | 3.7 | 3.5 |

*Source:* Table 5–4 for data on poverty; *World Development Report 1979* for data on income levels and growth rates.

*Note:* "Low-income" refers to countries at or below $300 (1977 prices). Averages are weighted averages.

the level of real per capita income. However, this does not directly indicate the relation between reductions in the incidence of poverty and changes in GNP as conventionally measured.[17] Further, the estimated relationship pertains to the entire sample, whereas our concern is mainly with the effect of growth on poverty in low-income countries in particular. Therefore, the following equation was tested for the twenty-five lowest income countries of the ACC sample, using the data reported in Table 5–2 on 1975 per capita income (PCI) measured in 1970 prices and at official exchange rates, and on income shares of the lowest 40 percent of income recipients (YD).

$$\text{Log PPK} = 14.80 - 1.43 \text{ Log PCI} - 1.53 \text{ Log YD} \qquad (2)$$
$$\phantom{\text{Log PPK} = } (20.47) \quad (-20.30) \qquad (-9.05) \qquad R^2 = .95$$

As the variables are incorporated in logarithmic form, the coefficients are equivalent to elasticities, and we do not need to worry about which year's prices are used to measure per capita GNP. The equation suggests that an increase of 1 percent in per capita income will reduce the incidence of poverty by 1.43 percent (not percentage points) if income distribution remains unchanged. For instance, consider a country with a per capita income of $100 (1970 prices), in which 15 percent of income accrues to the lowest 40 percent of recipients. If per capita income increases at constant prices to $110, the incidence of poverty would tend to decline from 58.6 to 51.1 percent. With a doubling of per capita income, the incidence of poverty would fall below 22 percent, as long as the income share of the lower 40 percent remained unchanged.

The regression results also reveal the importance of variations in income distribution as represented by the share of the lowest 40 percent of income recipients. For instance, at a per capita income level of $100 the incidence of poverty will be about 58.6 percent with an income share of 15 percent, but it will rise to 73 percent if this share falls to 13 percent. The effect on the incidence of poverty of a doubling per capita income from $100 to $200 would be completely canceled out if the share of the lowest 40 percent fell from 15 to 7.8 percent.

What changes in income distribution can one reasonably expect to accompany growth? Ahluwalia's investigation of the "Kuznets Curve" suggests that the share of the lowest 40 percent tends to decline sharply as per capita income rises over the range of incomes that are of interest here.[18] However, as the author points out, the explanatory power of the estimated equation for his sample of forty developing countries is relatively limited; the equation explains only about a quarter of the observed variation in the share of the lowest 40 percent. This suggests substantial scope for other factors to influence this share, and to counteract or even reverse the tendency to decline. Indeed, much of the discussion of the basic needs approach is explicitly directed toward identifying patterns of growth that provide for an improved distribution of income.

Ahluwalia's estimates have been criticized for their exclusive reliance on cross-country observations. Emerging evidence on trends in income distribution over time (rather than across countries) casts doubt on the proposition that distribution tends to worsen with growth in per capita income up to a point, and then to improve. Gary Fields has investigated the experiences of thirteen countries for which data sources on changes in income distribution over time appear to be reliable. His findings indicate that inequality rose in seven countries (Argentina, Bangladesh, Brazil, El Salvador, Mexico, the Philippines, and Puerto Rico) but declined in five (Costa Rica, Pakistan, Singapore, Sri Lanka, and Taiwan) and probably declined in India as well. Based on this thirteen-country sample, Fields concludes that "No general relationship has thus far been encountered between changing inequality on the one hand and initial level of inequality, level of GNP or rate of growth of GNP on the other." [19]

The study by Ahluwalia, Chenery, and Carter also contains time series data on income distribution, for a group of twelve countries.[20] Their sample overlaps only partially with that of Fields. They present data on changes in the income share of the lowest 60 percent, whereas Fields relies mainly on the Gini coefficient for gauging the direction of change in income distribution. The ACC data indicate that in four countries there were substantial improvements in this share (Sri Lanka, Costa Rica, Colombia, and Turkey); in five countries the share changed very little (negligible changes in Yugoslavia, the Philippines, and Peru; a slight improvement in Taiwan; and a slight decline in Korea); and in three countries there was a significant decline (India, Mexico, and Brazil).

Table 5–6 combines the results of the two sets of data and facilitates a comparison with trends predicted by the Kuznets Curve. The turning point is assumed to be in the vicinity of $670 (1977 prices), the estimate contained in ACC.[21] Countries with incomes below the turning point over the period in question would be expected to experience increasing inequality with growth, while countries above the turning point should demonstrate decreasing inequality. The expectation for countries that pass from one side to the other is uncertain.

All the countries in the top group of the table experienced some degree of improvement in income distribution over the periods in question. For Colombia and Taiwan, the expected trend in inequality is uncertain. For Sri Lanka, Pakistan, and India (1960–1969) the actual trend in inequality runs counter to the expected decrease, although Fields reports that the evidence on India is not clear cut. For Costa Rica, Turkey, and Singapore, expectations are fulfilled.

**Table 5-6. Growth and Changes in Income Distribution over Time**

| Country | Period Covered | Per Capita Income[a] (1977 prices) Initial | Per Capita Income[a] (1977 prices) Final | Growth Rate | Expected Trend in Inequality from Kuznets Curve[c] | Actual Change in Inequality Fields | Actual Change in Inequality ACC |
|---|---|---|---|---|---|---|---|
| Sri Lanka | 1953–1973 | n.a. | 156 | 1.8[b] | increase | decrease | — |
| Sri Lanka | 1963–1973 | 124 | 156 | 2.3 | increase | — | decrease |
| Costa Rica | 1961–1971 | 827 | 1103 | 3.3 | decrease | decrease | decrease |
| Turkey | 1963–1973 | 652 | 942 | 3.8 | decrease | — | decrease |
| Colombia | 1964–1974 | 519 | 714 | 3.3 | uncertain | — | decrease |
| Taiwan | 1950s–1970s | n.a. | n.a. | 5.3[b] | uncertain | decrease | — |
| Taiwan | 1964–1974 | 524 | 1012 | 6.8 | uncertain | — | decrease |
| Pakistan | 1963/64–1969/70 | 145 | 188 | 4.5 | increase | decrease | — |
| Singapore | 1966–1975 | 1176 | 2514 | 8.8 | decrease | decrease | — |
| India | 1960/61–1968/69 | 125 | 137 | 1.2 | increase | decrease | — |
| Yugoslavia | 1963–1973 | 1024 | 1702 | 5.2 | decrease | — | unchanged |
| Peru | 1961–1971 | 483 | 676 | 3.4 | increase | — | unchanged |
| Philippines | 1961–1971 | 302 | 369 | 2.0 | increase | increase | unchanged |
| Korea | 1965–1976 | 399 | 901 | 7.7 | uncertain | — | increase |
| India | 1954–1964 | n.a. | 138 | 1.8[b] | increase | — | increase |
| Bangladesh | 1963/64–1973/74 | 82 | 72 | -1.5 | decrease | increase | — |
| Argentina | 1953–1961 | n.a. | 1305 | 1.4[b] | decrease | increase | — |
| Brazil | 1960–1970 | 667 | 903 | 3.1 | decrease | increase | increase |
| Mexico | 1963–1975 | 842 | 1216 | 3.1 | decrease | increase | increase |
| El Salvador | 1945–1961 | n.a. | 420 | 1.6[b] | increase | increase | — |
| Puerto Rico | 1953–1963 | n.a. | 1674 | n.a.[b] | decrease | increase | — |

[a] Figures for GNP per capita are from World Bank tables, December 1979. Growth rates are based on a comparison of initial and final year GNP per capita.

[b] Growth rate based on estimates for 1950–1960 and 1960–1970 contained in Morawetz (1977). The growth rate for Puerto Rico is assumed to be positive but less than 9.5 percent.

[c] Expected trend is based on a turning point in the vicinity of $570, at 1977 prices.

Of the countries in the middle group, Peru and Yugoslavia showed no change in the share of the lowest 60 percent, although the Kuznets Curve would have predicted a decline in inequality for Yugoslavia and an increase for Peru. Evidence on the Philippines is mixed. Fields finds that the Gini coefficient among families was unchanged but that the ratio of the income shares of the top quintile to the bottom quintile rose. On this basis, he judges distribution to have worsened. ACC find the share of the lowest 60 percent essentially unchanged, a result that is not inconsistent with Fields but does conflict with the decline predicted by the Kuznets Curve. Finally, Korea experienced a small decline in the share of the lowest 60 percent.

The final group includes seven cases for which inequality clearly increased. For El Salvador and India (1954–1964), the increase is in accord with the trend indicated by the Kuznets Curve. For Bangladesh, Argentina, Brazil, Mexico, and Puerto Rico, the increases in inequality are contrary to expectations. For Bangladesh, growth was negative, so that movement along the Kuznets Curve should have entailed decreasing inequality.

In sum, the experiences of only four countries (Costa Rica, Singapore, Turkey, and El Salvador) provide examples that clearly conform with the Kuznets Curve. Of these, inequality increased only in El Salvador. The Philippines and India provide mixed evidence. Seven countries (Sri Lanka, Pakistan, Bangladesh, Brazil, Mexico, Argentina, and Puerto Rico) provide strong counterexamples, and in two others (Yugoslavia and Peru) there was no change in inequality despite expectations. For Korea, Taiwan, and Colombia, expectations were uncertain.

More positively, these findings warrant cautious optimism about the effects of trends in income distribution on the scope for alleviation of poverty. LDC poverty is heavily concentrated in Asia and secondarily in Africa. Of the five countries in which experience has been clearly one of positive growth and significant increases in inequality, all are in Latin America and only one (El Salvador) would have fallen in the low-income group by 1977 standards. In contrast, the performance of the Asian countries is at worst ambiguous or fairly neutral (Bangladesh, India, the Philippines, and Korea) and in other cases positive (Sri Lanka, Pakistan, Taiwan, and Singapore). Further, for the low-income countries in this group (India, Pakistan, Sri Lanka, and Bangladesh) as well as for Indonesia, the estimated share of the lowest 40 percent is relatively high (Table 5–2). Unfortunately, the data for African countries are too scant to provide much information.

While evidence on the relationship between growth and income distribution is somewhat ambiguous, the evidence on growth and poverty alleviation is more clear cut. For virtually the same sample (with Thailand substituted for El Salvador), Fields finds ten cases in which the incidence of poverty fell and only three examples in which poverty increased— India, Argentina, and the Philippines.[22] Insofar as average annual growth rates of per capita income were fairly low for India and Argentina for the periods in question (1.2 percent and 1.4 percent, respectively), this hardly constitutes a failure of rapid growth.[23]

Furthermore, a number of simulation studies that incorporate the assumption that income distribution will follow the path described by the Kuznets Curve indicate that the incidence of poverty nonetheless declines substantially as per capita GNP increases. The preliminary results of a simulation study by Ahluwalia and Duloy (1977) indicate that for a country initially at an income level of $100 (1970 prices), the incidence of poverty would decline from 72 to 45 percent over a twenty-year period if an average annual growth rate for per capita income of 3 percent could be maintained, despite an assumed worsening of income distribution. Projections reported by Ahluwalia, Chenery, and Carter assume a 2.6 percent growth rate in real per capita GNP for low-income countries, and changes in income distribution that follow the Kuznets Curve. Over the 1975–2000 period, these assumptions would generate a decline in the incidence of poverty in low-income countries from 51 percent to 22 percent. Increasing the assumed growth rate to 3.6 percent would result in a greater decline in the incidence of poverty in low-income countries, to around 14 percent by the year 2000.[24]

The discussion so far has dealt with poverty alleviation, where poverty has been considered in terms of levels of income. The evidence points to a significant impact of growth on the incidence of poverty in low-income countries, even if income distribution worsens along the lines described by Ahluwalia's empirical estimates of the Kuznets Curve.[25] An important question is whether a similar relationship holds for indicators of basic needs satisfaction other than the incidence of poverty. Results of econometric work by Leipziger and Lewis indicate that for low-income countries, social indicators such as literacy, life expectancy, infant mortality, and first-level school enrollments are significantly correlated with per capita income levels, whereas the correlations of these indicators with Gini coefficients are statistically insignificant.[26] For middle-income countries (defined using the 1975 IDA eligibility criterion), the opposite set of results emerges: significant correlations of social indicators with Gini coefficients but not with per capita income levels. Their findings tend to support the proposition that growth in per capita income is of primary importance in achieving increased satisfaction of basic needs in low-income countries.

None of this is to deny the importance of the *pattern* of growth in terms of the distribution of increases in income and the composition of changes in output. The econometric results presented earlier indicate that for low-income countries variations in the share of the lowest 40 percent of income recipients can have powerful effects on the incidence of poverty associated with a given income level. The key point is that if rapid growth can be achieved in low-income countries, the effects in terms of poverty alleviation are likely to be substantial and positive, even with some worsening of the income distribution. If that worsening can be avoided—past experience suggests that it can—so much the better.

## THE DISTRIBUTION OF OFFICIAL DEVELOPMENT ASSISTANCE AMONG COUNTRIES

### The Current Distribution

This section of the paper examines the distribution of Official Development Assistance (ODA) among recipients. ODA is defined by the Development Assistance Committee of the OECD as grants or loans that are undertaken by the public sector (including multilateral agencies as well as bilateral donors), that have promotion of economic development and welfare as main objectives, and that are offered at concessional terms (if a loan, at least 25 percent grant element).[27]

This concessional assistance comprises only a portion of total resource flows to developing countries. For instance, in 1976 ODA accounted for about 30 percent of total disbursements of medium- and long-term capital to developing countries.[28] In particular, for the World Bank Group, lending by IDA ($2.86 billion in 1978) was counted as ODA, while IBRD lending ($6.55 billion) was not. Overall for multilateral agencies, grants amounted to $2.5 billion; concessional loans came to $4.8 billion, and nonconcessional lending totaled $9.88 billion in 1978.[29]

The data presented here represent average annual commitments of ODA during the 1976–1978 period from all sources except centrally planned economies.[30] More specifically, the data include commitments by multilateral institutions, members of the Development Assistance Committee, and countries belonging to OPEC. The data have been collected for 102 recipients, each of which received at least $75 million in ODA commitments over the three-year period. The countries collectively accounted on average for over $25 billion per year, nearly 90 percent of total ODA commitments reported by the DAC.

Figures for individual countries are reported in the Appendix Table. For the same groups of countries discussed earlier, Table 5–7 compares the distribution of poverty and the distribution of ODA.

**Table 5–7. The Distribution of Poverty and Official Development Assistance**

| Country Group (1977 per Capita GNP) | Percent of Total Poor | Cumulative Percentage of Poor | ODA Commitments ($ million) | Percent of Total ODA | Cumulative Percentage of Total |
|---|---|---|---|---|---|
| Less than $150 | 17.4 | 17.4 | 3,385 | 13.3 | 13.3 |
| India–$150 | 37.2 | 54.6 | 2,100 | 8.3 | 21.6 |
| $151–$300 | 26.1 | 80.7 | 5,793 | 22.8 | 44.4 |
| $301–$450 | 9.8 | 90.5 | 4,979 | 19.6 | 64.0 |
| $451–$1200 | 6.2 | 96.7 | 5,541 | 21.8 | 85.8 |
| $1201–$4800 | 3.2 | 99.9 | 3,605 | 14.2 | 100.0 |
| Total | 99.9 | | 25,403 | 100.0 | |

*Source:* Appendix Table; Table 5–3.

The data presented in Table 5–7 indicate that the distribution of concessional assistance among countries does not reflect the distribution of poverty. The group that accounts for 80 percent of the developing world's poor receives only 44 percent of concessional assistance, while countries accounting for less than 10 percent of the poor receive 36 percent of concessional assistance. India alone accounts for a great deal of the disparity between the distribution of poverty and the distribution of ODA.

## Explaining the Allocation Pattern

A number of studies in recent years have sought to explain allocation patterns of development assistance. Paul Isenman (1975, 1976) investigated flows of development assistance during the late 1960s and early 1970s from a variety of sources: USAID, DAC members as a group, the IBRD, the IDA, and the U.N. Development Programme. His results strongly confirmed two "biases" in aid allocations: a middle-income bias revealed in the tendency for per capita assistance to rise as per capita income increases to a level of $400 (1970 prices, equivalent to a per capita income of about $650 in 1977 prices) and then to fall; and a country-size bias reflected in the tendency for per capita assistance to fall, the larger the population size of the recipient. Edelman and Chenery (1977) used aggregate data on commitments of "Official Concessional Assistance" (i.e., ODA plus multilateral loan commitments that are not sufficiently concessional to qualify as ODA) from DAC bilateral sources, multilateral sources, and OPEC. They analyzed a considerably larger sample of countries (eighty-nine) than the samples investigated by Isenman, which for the most part ranged from twenty to forty-one countries. Their tests covered three successive time periods (1967–1969; 1970–1972; and 1973–

1974) and confirmed both the country-size and middle-income biases for each period, although the middle-income bias for the 1970–1972 period was not statistically significant. Dudley and Montmarquette (1976) tested 1970 commitments from various bilateral donors, according to a supply-side model of bilateral aid for each donor that included considerations of population, per capita income, political ties to the donor in question, economic ties to that donor, and bandwagon effects—the tendency for a donor to give more aid to countries receiving substantial amounts of aid from other sources. Their results indicated an insignificant role for population size in influencing aid allocations of most donors once political, economic, and bandwagon factors were taken into account. However, both the bandwagon variables (other donor assistance) and the economic ties variables (the previous years' exports from the donor in question to the recipient in question, divided by recipient population) may be proxies for the small-country bias rather than vice versa. If all donors have a small-country bias, the bandwagon variable will reflect and incorporate that bias. Similarly, insofar as most bilateral assistance has been tied to purchases in the donor country, the exports variable could simply represent the effects of country-size bias in allocations of previous years. Political variables surely help account for the small country bias. However, these were included in several of Isenman's tests, without negating the existence of a bias against large countries.

Are the middle-income and country-size biases reflected in more recent allocations of assistance? One might expect that the increasing concern of donors with poverty alleviation and basic needs, combined with the critical evaluation of allocation patterns contained in a number of papers including those cited here, would result in a reduction of these biases. To gain some perspective on this question, the following equation was tested for the entire sample of countries in the Appendix Table.

$$(3)$$

$$\text{Log PCA} = 10.38 - .73 \text{ Log Pop} - 1.89 \text{ Log PCY} + .147 \ (\text{Log PCY})^2$$
$$\quad\quad (3.2) \quad\quad (-13.0) \quad\quad\quad (-1.8) \quad\quad\quad\quad (1.8) \quad\quad R^2 = .69$$

The explanatory power of the equation is fairly high. The population coefficient is clearly significant and evidences a very strong bias against large countries; interpreting the coefficient as an elasticity, assistance in per capita terms tends to fall by 73 percent as population size doubles. The per capita income coefficients (based on 1977 GNP per capita) are each marginally significant. They indicate a *reversal* of the middle-income bias, that is, a tendency for per capita assistance to *fall* as per capita income *increases* to about \$620 and then to rise.

Before concluding that the behavior of donors has changed, several factors need to be mentioned that make it difficult to compare these results with those of Chenery and Edelman, and Isenman. The former included loans from multilateral banks that were not sufficiently concessional to qualify as ODA. At the same time, the authors emphasize that most of these funds go to middle-income countries and the scope for reallocation of such lending to low-income countries is extremely limited because of debt-servicing considerations. Including sources of funds directed primarily to middle-income countries would obviously alter the regression results. Since we are concerned with assistance that might hypothetically be reallocated to low-income countries, it seems sensible to exclude the harder loans of the multilateral banks. Second, our sample of countries excludes those that receive small amounts of ODA and includes a number of very small, high-income recipients of ODA not included in either of the other two studies. The argument for inclusion is that these countries receive significant amounts of ODA in absolute terms,[31] so that a discussion of the scope for reallocating ODA should take them into account. Again, it is clear that excluding these countries would affect the results. For instance, if a per capita income cutoff of $1900 is applied to the sample, then the per capita income coefficients are both statistically insignificant, and the elasticity that reflects the population bias falls to $-.65$. However, a regression that includes only population and per capita income yields a statistically significant negative coefficient for the latter variable, indicating that per capita assistance tends to decline as per capita income increases. Applying several different per capita income ceilings ($2825, $1900, $1500, and $1000), none of the results indicates a statistically significant bias in favor of middle-income countries.

While the equations tested omit political variables, it is obvious that these play an important role in the allocation pattern. For instance, the four largest deviations of actual from predicted allocation levels are accounted for by Egypt, Israel, Jordan, and Syria, which together claimed over $6 billion in annual ODA commitments, almost 25 percent of the total. The presence of other major political influences can be readily discerned from the per capita ODA figures contained in the Appendix Table.

## Mechanisms for Changing the Allocation Pattern

Positive questions about what factors determine or explain assistance allocations lead naturally to normative questions about what factors ought to determine allocation patterns and in what direction. Thus, both Isenman, and Chenery and Edelman argue that the country-size bias ought to be softened if not eliminated, and the bias toward middle-income countries ought to be converted to one toward low-income countries. Several allocation models have been developed, aimed at explicitly addressing these biases.

Cline and Sargen (1975) propose an aid allocation model that determines allocations of development assistance according to need and performance criteria. Their approach starts, as most donors would, with a specified amount of assistance and a list of potential recipients. They then seek a linear path such that *per capita assistance* declines as per capita income increases. Thus they incorporate an explicit bias in favor of low-income countries and remove any bias based on population size. By stipulating a ceiling level of per capita income, at which assistance falls to zero, they can determine a unique linear relationship between per capita income and per capita assistance that just exhausts the amount of assistance available.[32]

The next step is to incorporate performance criteria, which are used to adjust in either direction the allocations determined by need criteria alone (i.e., per capita income). The factors that are taken into account in performance include savings, export growth, inflation, tax revenues, and efficiency in resource use as measured by an incremental capital output ratio. Two of these indicators—savings and tax revenues—are measured in terms of deviations from expected performance as predicted by per capita income. Thus, a low-income country's savings performance would be evaluated relative to the savings rate expected of a low-income country, rather than in comparison to savings performance of middle-income countries.[33] Each indicator is normalized by dividing by the respective standard deviation. For each country the five indicators are aggregated into a single composite performance indicator, using an arbitrary weighting scheme. This indicator is then used to adjust per capita allocations upward or downward according to whether performance has been above or below average.

A broadly similar allocation model, following the work of Isenman, has been developed and implemented at AID (Crosswell 1979). Operationally, the model is used to arrive at indicative medium-term planning levels for development assistance, according to broad need and performance criteria. The model assigns a weight, $W_i$, to each recipient country according to population, per capita income, and performance, that is,

$$W_i = (\text{Pop}_i)^a (\text{PCI}_i)^b (\text{Perf}_i)^c$$

The weights are summed and each country's share of total assistance is determined by its weight relative to the total. The ratio of one country's allocation to another's will reflect the ratio of the two weights, which in turn will depend on relative population size, per capita income, and performance.[34] The exponents are determined according to policy judgments about the importance that each variable should have in determining the allocations. The exponent attached to the population variable allows more or less bias with respect to country size, depending on how close the value chosen is to 1.0—the value at which there is no bias. The value of the exponent associated with per capita income is typically negative, so that assistance tends to decline as per capita income increases. The exponent on performance, along with the scale chosen for the performance variable, determines the importance of performance considerations in affecting the indicative allocations. The allocations are determined subject to two general constraints that specify the minimum and maximum levels of assistance that may be allocated to countries.

There are policy issues surrounding each of the variables.[35] One question is whether the population variable ought to reflect total population or poor population, the number of people below a poverty line. The allocation model described above has been developed in a framework in which increased satisfaction of basic needs is taken as the primary objective of development assistance, and need for outside assistance is an explicit allocation criterion. This might suggest that need for assistance should be considered in terms of the extent of poverty (roughly measured by the number of poor people) compared with domestic resource availability (as indicated by per capita income). However, each country faces the task of achieving the satisfaction of basic needs of all its inhabitants. Therefore, both the scope of the problem and domestic resource availability depend on the number and income of the nonpoor. Considered in this light, it can be shown that *total* population is the more appropriate population variable. Domestic resource availability would be ideally measured not by per capita income alone, but rather by the ratio of per capita income to the poverty line, defined as the average per person cost of a standard of living that meets basic needs.[36] This ratio would indicate need in terms of the margin by which per capita income exceeds the income required to meet basic needs. In practice, the Kravis factors described in the first section provide an approximation to this adjustment to the extent that differences in poverty lines among countries reflect the differences in the purchasing power of a dollar.[37]

The performance variable pertains not simply to aggregate growth but to other factors that are also related to poverty alleviation and increased satisfaction of basic needs. For instance, performance with respect to literacy, infant mortality, life expectancy, and so on are important, as are other criteria having to do with distribution.[38] Cline and Sargen argue that this unduly penalizes poor people in countries with an unfavorable orientation toward equity and poverty alleviation. However, assistance is likely to be less effective in such countries in enhancing satisfaction of basic needs. Further, there may be some value to reinforcing good performance at the expense of poor performance in the distributional area.

A second major difference with the Cline/Sargen approach is that the measures of performance reflect not only quantitative factors but also judgmental evaluations.[39] On the basis of both kinds of analysis, numerical values are attached to the performance variables.

## FOREIGN ASSISTANCE AND GROWTH

### Empirical Evidence

The discussion so far has pointed to a concentration of the LDC poverty problem in low-income countries, and a concentration of concessional foreign assistance in middle-income countries. Given a concern with poverty alleviation, the argument for an increase in concessional assistance to low-income countries rests on two propositions: that growth will be effective in alleviating poverty in these countries, and that increased foreign assistance can make a significant contribution to growth. We now turn to this latter proposition.

The main evidence against the argument that increased assistance accelerates growth rests on the finding that foreign capital inflows and domestic savings rates are inversely correlated. Weisskopf estimated that "approximately twenty-three percent of net foreign capital inflow substitutes for domestic savings," and regards that figure as a lower bound.[40] Griffin and Enos estimated that an extra dollar of aid would increase investment by only $.25.[41] Other authors have found similar negative correlations.

Papanek (1972) provides a review and criticism of this literature that accepts the observed negative correlation between foreign inflows and domestic savings, but sets forth several arguments against a conclusion that foreign assistance causes savings effort to decline. One argument is that some foreign assistance is explicitly directed toward activities commonly classified as consumption—emergency food aid, military assistance, recurrent cost financing of some government services—such as health, education, and agricultural inputs—and so forth. Such assistance will lead to a decline in recorded domestic savings, the difference between gross investment and the current account deficit. Yet insofar as it is provided as a grant, it has no bearing on domestic savings effort.[42] A second argument rests on the tendency for assistance to rise in times of crisis caused by exogenous factors such as war, weather, or adverse movements in terms of trade. In these situations, savings are likely to fall more sharply than income. This would produce an observed negative relationship between foreign assistance and savings rates, again without reflecting causality from increased aid to diminished savings effort. Other more recent examples are provided by oil exporters such as Venezuela, Nigeria, and Indonesia, which are able to generate a large proportion of development expenditures from oil exports, and therefore are judged to have less need for foreign assistance. Papanek concludes that "As long as both savings and inflows are substantially affected by third factors, the negative correlation between the two found in many studies sheds little or no light on their causal relationship." [43]

Even if a dollar of foreign assistance increases investment by somewhat less than a dollar, the effects on growth can nonetheless be positive and substantial. In a subsequent paper, Papanek (1973) tests the effects of domestic savings, foreign assistance, private foreign investment, and other foreign flows—all measured as ratios to GDP—on growth of GDP. The samples tested include a group of thirty-one Asian countries and a larger group of thirty-five developing countries. His results are reproduced in Table 5–8.

The various sources of investment collectively explain a substantial portion of observed growth performance. What are particularly noteworthy are the relatively high coefficients for aid, which appears to have a more significant effect on growth than domestic savings or other forms of foreign resource flows. However, the validity of these coefficients depends on whether aid is correlated with other sources of growth not included in the equation, particularly variations in efficiency of resource use. If aid flows disproportionately to countries that make better use of resources, then the coefficient for aid in Papanek's results is overstated.[44]

The most prevalent analytical framework for relating flows of foreign assistance to growth in GNP is the two-gap model.[45] Chenery and Strout used this model to formulate projections of growth and foreign assistance requirements over the 1962–1975 period for fifty developing coun-

**Table 5–8. Results of Papanek's Tests**

|  | Savings | Aid | Foreign Investment | Other Flows | $R^2$ |
|---|---|---|---|---|---|
| Growth = (n = 85) | 1.5 + .20 (2.5)   (6.0) | + .39 + (5.8) | .17 (2.5) | + .19 (2.1) | .37 |
| Growth = (n = 31) | 1.5 + .21 (1.5)   (5.0) | + .46 + (4.4) | .35 (1.7) | + .13 (0.8) | .46 |

(*T* values in parentheses)

tries. Chenery and Carter (1973) provided an interim review of development performance relative to these projections for the period up to 1970. Lewis and Michalopoulos (1980) have recently looked at the Chenery/Strout and other projections of performance through 1975. These reviews provide some scattered insights into the contribution of foreign assistance to more rapid growth.

Chenery and Carter note that growth over the sixties was on the whole fairly close to projections. Of thirty-seven countries, twenty-five were within 1.2 percentage points of projected rates, five grew substantially more quickly, and seven grew much more slowly. Overall there was a considerable shortfall in foreign capital inflows as well as a hardening of terms that affected their distribution among countries. On the other hand, export performance was much better than projected. Of five countries for which growth was high absolutely and relative to projections, the foreign capital inflow was of major significance in explaining the surprisingly good performance in Kenya and Thailand, of less significance in Korea, and unimportant in Iran and Taiwan. For thirteen high-growth countries, the foreign capital inflow was about as projected. For eleven "normal-growth" countries and for thirteen low-growth countries, there were substantial shortfalls, on the order of 40 to 70 percent of projections. For the latter group of thirteen countries, only four received amounts of assistance even close to their projected needs. Naturally, the causality between poor performance and low aid levels can run both ways. Chenery and Carter single out India as an important case where shortfalls in foreign assistance severely constrained growth. They argue that, based on India's savings and export performance, aid allocated to India on a basis comparable to other countries would have raised the growth rate from 3.5 to 5.8 percent, or well over a doubling of per capita growth given a population growth rate of 2.1 percent.

The review by Lewis and Michalopoulos for the 1960–1975 period confirms the continuation of the trends highlighted by Chenery and Carter. They provide an analysis by region that compares the foreign capital inflow in 1975 with the level projected by Chenery and Strout. For South Asia, the projections called for $8.1 billion, whereas the actual foreign capital inflow was $2.6 billion. There was a corresponding shortfall in the growth rate of investment over the period (4.6 percent actual versus 7.9 percent projected) and of output (3.8 percent versus 6.1 percent projected). For sub-Saharan Africa the foreign capital inflow in 1975 exceeded the projections ($5.4 billion versus $3.7 billion), but investment growth fell well short (5.8 percent versus 7.3 percent projected). Nonetheless, the GNP growth rate was close to what was projected (4.4 percent versus 4.8 percent projected). Insofar as large amounts of aid were used in Africa for relief of drought and famine during the first half of the 1970s, this may explain the low savings and investment growth.

The evidence presented by Chenery and Carter and by Lewis and Michalopoulos on the importance of foreign assistance in achieving accelerated growth is ambiguous, in part because the experience of various countries and regions was mixed, and in part because there is not a clearly valid methodology for identifying the contribution of increased foreign assistance to accelerated growth, or the lack of foreign assistance to slow growth.[46] For our purposes, the experience of South Asia in general and India in particular is important, insofar as both papers suggest that inavailability of foreign capital severely constrained investment and growth.

## Projections

Some insights into the effects of increased ODA flows on growth prospects in low-income countries can be gleaned from a comparison of the base and high scenarios for 1980–1990 contained in the *World Development Report 1979*.[47] In the base scenario, ODA flows to low-income countries would amount to $5.7 billion (1977 prices) in 1980 and rise to $11.6 billion (1977 prices) by 1990. The growth rate in GDP for low-income countries in this scenario would be 4.9 percent. The "high" scenario assumes more rapid growth of exports, ODA and private capital flows, and also more expensive energy. More rapid annual growth of ODA (6.7 percent compared with 3.6 percent in the base) would raise ODA allocations to low-income countries to $15.6 billion by 1990, about $4 billion higher than in the base scenario. Flows of private capital in the high scenario would increase at a rate of 6.3 percent, compared with 3.9 percent in the base. However, the share of private loans in the financing of external resource requirements of low-income countries is expected to drop from 23 percent in 1976 to 4 percent in 1985 and 1990, so that the impact of the change in this assumption is apparently quite minor. Finally, merchandise exports of developing countries are to increase at 6.5 percent annually in the base scenario, and 7.5 percent in the high scenario, reflecting mainly more rapid growth of manufactured exports. Insofar as the low-income country share in this trade remains small, and the role of manufactured exports in low-income country exports is small, the effect of this assumption is probably also relatively minor. On the negative side, there are no offsetting factors to dampen the effects of the assumption of moderately higher energy prices. Overall, the main positive effect of the high scenario for low-income countries appears to be that of more rapid growth of ODA flows, an increase between 1980 and

1990 of about $6 billion in the base scenario and $10 billion in the high scenario. The effect on growth would be to raise the growth rate from 4.9 percent in the base scenario to 5.9 percent in the high scenario. With population growth estimated at 2.2 percent over the decade, the difference in per capita GDP growth would be 3.7 percent versus 2.7 percent. The estimates of the effects of more rapid growth on the incidence of poverty presented earlier suggest that this would make a substantial difference in the extent of poverty by the year 2000.

## An Illustrative Scenario

Most discussions of basic needs have stressed the need for sizable increases in the volume of ODA if substantial progress toward eradication of global poverty is to be achieved over the next several decades. For instance, Burki and Voorhoeve (1977) estimate that the *additional* investment costs required to meet basic needs in the low-income countries by the year 2000 would amount to about $12 billion annually in 1975 prices, or approximately $13.5 billion in 1977 prices. Resource requirements in terms of recurrent costs associated with this investment would be even higher. They conclude that "Development assistance would have to . . . grow at a very rapid real rate, if basic needs were to be met by the year 2000." [48]

The figures in Table 5–8 suggest that a reorientation of ODA toward low-income countries could result in major increases in the volume of assistance allocated to countries where the bulk of the world's poor are located. For instance, if 80 percent of ODA were allocated to countries that account for 80 percent of the world's poor, the volume of assistance committed to that group would increase from $11.3 billion to $20.3 billion.

This reallocation could be effected through various combinations of the following three measures: imposing an income ceiling on eligibility for ODA, or otherwise reducing the number of middle- and high-income countries that receive ODA; explicitly incorporating a bias in favor of low-income countries; and diminishing or removing the bias against large countries. For instance if the IDA-eligibility criterion (1977 per capita income of $580) were adopted for all allocations of ODA, then over 80 percent of recipient populations would be in countries with per capita incomes below $300. Allocating assistance on a per capita basis alone (without regard for per capita income) would be sufficient to effect the redistribution.

What would be the significance of that assistance in economic terms? The total population of the group of countries with per capita incomes at or below $300 is about 1.25 billion, and the (weighted) average per capita

GNP of the group is about $170.[49] Aggregate GNP of the group is, therefore, approximately $212 billion, so that $20 billion of assistance would come to almost 10 percent of aggregate GNP. In the same group of countries, gross domestic savings accounts for about 18 percent of per capita income, so that a reorientation of ODA could potentially raise the investment rate to around 28 percent, compared with a current rate of 21 percent.[50]

For middle-income countries—those with per capita incomes above $300—ODA accounted for roughly 22 percent of *net disbursements* of medium- and long-term loans and grants in 1976.[51] A reorientation of ODA along the lines described above would reduce the share of middle-income countries in total ODA from 56 percent to 20 percent. This reduction of ODA to middle-income countries would therefore amount to roughly 14 percent of medium- and long-term loans and grants. Much of this could be made up by expansion of non-ODA lending, at little real cost to donors.

The scenario described above is merely illustrative. The point of the discussion is that the current distribution of ODA does not reflect very well the distribution of global poverty; that there is considerable scope for increasing resource flows to the countries where most of the world's poor are located through a reorientation of ODA; that such a reorientation could be of major significance to this group of countries in macroeconomic terms; and that the negative macroeconomic effects on middle-income countries would be of a much smaller order of magnitude.

A combination of increases in the total volume of ODA and reorientation of ODA towards low-income countries would, of course, soften this negative impact. For instance, the Brandt Commission report (1980) recommends an increased level of assistance for countries in "the poverty belts of Africa and Asia" of at least $4 billion per year in real terms for the next two decades. In 1977 prices, this would amount to about $3.2 billion, or one-third of the assistance that might be redistributed.

## POSTSCRIPT

Since the bulk of this chapter was written, the *World Development Report 1980* has been issued. Prospects for the low-income oil-importing countries—essentially the low-income countries discussed in this chapter with the exclusion of Indonesia, Angola, and Zaire—are quite dim. Over the next decade, the average annual growth rate in per capita income for this group is projected to fall somewhere between 1.1 and 2.0 percent. Growth at these rates will result in only very slow progress in reducing the high incidence of poverty in the group of countries that account for most of the world's poor and quite possibly implies an increase in the absolute numbers of poor. The urgency of international measures to accelerate the flow of concessional assistance to low-income countries, as well as domestic policies to ensure that foreign assistance effectively contributes to their growth, has never been greater. In the absence of such measures, discussions of whether growth does or does not result in substantial reductions of poverty will be purely academic.

## NOTES

1. One can define the poor as those who cannot meet their basic needs, so that poverty alleviation and increased satisfaction of basic needs are equivalent. Empirically, estimates of poverty tend to focus on the capacity to meet needs for goods such as food, clothing, and shelter that are typically available through markets. They usually ignore the costs of needs such as health, education, and clean water, which might or might not be available through functioning markets.
2. Some characterize this latter endeavor as *the* basic needs approach and regard it as complementary to (but distinct from) efforts toward achieving equitable growth. Others consider that the basic needs approach is primarily an equitable growth strategy, modified to include supply-side considerations of the composition of output, including the provision of public services.
3. See the first chapter in this volume for discussion of these arguments.
4. See Ahluwalia, Carter, and Chenery (1979) and Kravis, Heston, and Summers (1978).
5. A more detailed account and critique of the KHS work is contained in Crosswell (1979a); Isenman (1979); and Marris (1979).
6. More specifically, estimates of income distribution were based on Ahluwalia's (1976) estimates of the "Kuznets Curve."
7. Of the countries listed as low-income or middle-income in the *World Development Report 1979,* this criterion excludes Bhutan, Kampuchea, Rhodesia (Zimbabwe), South Africa, Uruguay, Iraq, Yugoslavia, Trinidad and Tobago, Hong Kong, Venezuela, Singapore, and Spain.
8. $T$ values in parentheses; all coefficients significant at the .001 level.
9. $\text{PPK} = 90.54 - .101 \, (\text{PCIK}) + .000032 \, (\text{PCIK})^2 - .858 \, \text{YD}$
   $\qquad\quad (11.60) \qquad (-10.95) \qquad\qquad (8.04) \qquad\qquad (-2.19) \qquad R^2 = .87$
10. For Cape Verde, Vietnam, Djibouti, and French Guiana, the values for PCIK were "guesstimated" on the basis of information on nominal per capita income. For several small countries, trend growth rates were taken from the *1979 World Bank Atlas.*
11. Ahluwalia, Carter, and Chenery (1979). The data and estimates in this paper were revised substantially in later versions.
12. See International Labour Office (1977), p. 15, and Chenery and Associates (1974), p. iii.
13. *World Bank Annual Report 1978,* Statistical Annex, p. 118.
14. International Labour Office (1977), pp. 22–23.
15. See Chenery and Associates (1974), particularly the introduction and first chapter.
16. Obviously, data on variations in the incidence of poverty over time (rather than across countries) would be needed to nail this argument down. A review of some evidence in this respect is presented in the next pages.

17. Regression results for the LDC portion of the Kravis sample (Table 5–1) indicate that an increase of 1 percent in per capita income as conventionally measured corresponded to an increase of .82 percent in "real" per capita income. In other words, cross-section data suggest that as income measured in constant prices increases, income measured in ICP dollars increases somewhat more slowly. See Crosswell (1979a).
18. Ahluwalia (1976), pp. 301–313. The data on income shares in Table 5–2 confirm this trend; however, for the low-income group, nine of these observations are based on the Kuznets Curve.
19. Fields (1979), p. 15. This paper summarizes the analysis forthcoming in *Poverty, Inequality and Development* (New York: Cambridge University Press, 1980).
20. Ahluwalia, Carter, and Chenery (1979), p. 322.
21. Ahluwalia, Carter, and Chenery (1979), p. 307. The authors note that $600 in 1975 prices (equivalent to $670 in 1977 prices) is the turning point for the share of the lowest 60 percent, and that the shares of lower groups turn at successively higher levels of GNP.
22. Fields (1979), p. 15.
23. Despite negative growth and worsening income distribution, Fields reports that the evidence on Bangladesh is mixed and judges poverty to have fallen. In the Philippines, which grew at 2 percent, the conclusion that poverty rose is based on a decline in the average annual income among the poorest quintile.
24. Ahluwalia, Carter, and Chenery (1979), pp. 318 and 328.
25. Ibid.
26. Leipziger and Lewis (1980). For a further discussion, see pp. 116–123 of this volume.
27. Organisation for Economic Cooperation and Development (1979), p. 209. The "grant element" reflects the extent to which the financial terms of the loan—the interest rate, maturity, and grace period—are more concessional than the terms of a commercial loan.
28. *World Development Report 1979*, p. 9.
29. Organisation for Economic Cooperation and Development (1979), Table C.4. These data are on a commitment basis.
30. Ibid., Table D.4.
31. For instance, French Guiana, Guadalupe, Martinique, Reunion, and French Polynesia together receive $1.25 *billion* of ODA annually, but they have an aggregate population of less than 1.5 million.
32. Mathematically, they seek to determine per capita assistance, $a_i$, as a linear function of per capita income, $Y_i$, that is, $a_i = a_0 - by_i$. They can determine the values of the intercept and slope parameters by imposing two constraints. First, per capita assistance should fall to zero at a specified per capita income level, $Y_u$, that is, $a_0 - by_u = 0$. Second, total assistance $A$ should equal the sum of the allocations to each recipient, $A_i$, the product of per capita assistance times population, that is, $A = \Sigma A_i = \Sigma a_i n_i$.
33. One could argue that this procedure should also be applied to the efficiency variable since in low-income countries infrastructure may claim a larger share of investment, with a gestation lag significantly longer than the two-year lag assumed by Cline and Sargen. The capacity for sustained export growth may also vary with the level of development.
34. In particular, the ratio of assistance levels for any two countries will be expressed by

$$\frac{A_i}{A_j} \qquad \left(\frac{\text{Pop}_i}{\text{Pop}_j}\right)^a \left(\frac{\text{PCI}_i}{\text{PCI}_j}\right)^b \left(\frac{\text{Perf}_i}{\text{Perf}_j}\right)^c$$

35. This paragraph is based on the analysis contained in Crosswell (1980).

36. A formal derivation of this argument is presented in Crosswell (1980).
37. Recall note 34, which shows that the relative assistance levels of two countries depend on the ratio of their per capita incomes. Suppose these are expressed in dollars of equivalent purchasing power. If poverty lines expressed in ICP dollars are the same for each country, then the ratio will not change if each per capita income figure is divided by the same poverty line.
38. As with savings, actual performance is evaluated in terms of expected performance at various income levels.
39. Presumably, this reflects the fact that Cline and Sargen were concerned with formulating a testable model and did not have access to judgments of policymakers in multilateral institutions about performance of individual countries.
40. Weisskopf (1972), p. 37.
41. Griffin and Enos (1970), p. 321.
42. If provided as a loan, the country is financing current consumption through borrowing, i.e., dissaving. Another question, of course, is whether such "consumption" is more properly classified as investment.
43. Papanek (1972), p. 950.
44. Michalopoulos and Jay (1973) consider export growth a plausible indicator of increased efficiency in resource use and find a weak positive relationship between export growth and net foreign capital inflow, which they do not disaggregate. Inserting export growth into an equation similar to Papanek's results in a decline in the value of the coefficient for foreign capital.
45. Chenery and Strout (1966); McKinnon (1964).
46. Perhaps because of disillusion regarding the efficacy of growth in improving welfare, there appears to have been little work on the relation between foreign assistance and growth since the early 1970s.
47. *World Development Report 1979,* Chapter 2, particularly Tables 8, 9, and 16.
48. Other discussions of resource requirements for alleviating poverty and meeting basic needs are contained in Stern (1976) and Tinbergen (1976).
49. *World Development Report 1979,* Table 1. This average is calculated on the basis of a slightly different sample that includes Bhutan and excludes Cape Verde, Gambia, the Solomon Islands, and Guinea Bissau.
50. The fact that the investment rate is only three percentage points above the savings rate reflects several factors. First, net receipts of ODA were about two-thirds the level of commitments in 1977. Second, some of the foreign assistance consists of transfers directed toward consumption (e.g., some forms of food aid) and therefore does not directly contribute to investment.
51. *World Development Report 1979,* p. 9. These figures are not strictly comparable, but they do serve to indicate orders of magnitude.

## Appendix Table

| Country | Per Capita GNP-1977a ($) | Population 1977a (millions) | Average Annual ODA-1976-1978b ($ millions, commitments) | Per Capita ODA ($) | Per Capita Income-1975 (ICP $) | Percentage of Population in Absolute Poverty |
|---|---|---|---|---|---|---|
| Bangladesh | 90 | 81.22 | 1139.1 | 14.02 | 200c | 64c |
| Laos | 90 | 3.20 | 43.0 | 13.44 | 213 | 57 |
| Ethiopia | 110 | 30.24 | 140.7 | 4.65 | 237c | 68c |
| Mali | 110 | 6.13 | 189.7 | 30.95 | 152 | 62 |
| Nepal | 110 | 13.32 | 162.1 | 12.17 | 243 | 55 |
| Somalia | 110 | 3.66 | 251.7 | 68.77 | 216 | 57 |
| Burundi | 130 | 4.16 | 241.7 | 57.96 | 196 | 58 |
| Chad | 130 | 4.22 | 119.0 | 28.20 | 179 | 60 |
| Rwanda | 130 | 4.38 | 141.1 | 32.21 | 177 | 60 |
| Upper Volta | 130 | 5.47 | 151.9 | 29.60 | 181 | 60 |
| Zaire | 130 | 25.69 | 341.8 | 13.30 | 281c | 53c |
| Cape Verde | 130 | .31 | 38.7 | 124.84 | 195 | 59 |
| Burma | 140 | 31.51 | 254.3 | 8.07 | 237c | 65c |
| Malawi | 140 | 5.60 | 160.8 | 28.71 | 232 | 56 |
| India | 150 | 631.73 | 2100.5 | 3.32 | 300c | 46c |
| Mozambique | 150 | 9.69 | 112.2 | 11.58 | 421 | 41 |
| Niger | 160 | 4.86 | 168.6 | 34.69 | 230 | 56 |
| Vietnam | 160 | 50.65 | 270.1 | 5.33 | 298 | 50 |
| Afghanistan | 190 | 14.30 | 74.6 | 12.21 | 272 | 52 |
| Pakistan | 190 | 74.91 | 1365.2 | 18.22 | 299c | 43c |
| Sierra Leone | 190 | 3.21 | 39.3 | 12.24 | 421 | 42 |
| Tanzania | 190 | 16.36 | 596.9 | 36.49 | 297c | 51c |
| Benin | 200 | 3.23 | 90.4 | 27.99 | 207 | 58 |
| Sri Lanka | 200 | 14.10 | 322.7 | 22.88 | 471c | 14c |
| Gambia | 200 | .55 | 36.4 | 66.18 | 345 | 47 |

**Appendix Table** (*continued*)

| Country | Per Capita GNP-1977[a] ($) | Population 1977[a] (millions) | Average Annual ODA-1976-1978[b] ($ millions, commitments) | Per Capita ODA ($) | Per Capita Income-1975 (ICP $) | Percentage of Population in Absolute Poverty |
|---|---|---|---|---|---|---|
| Guinea | 220 | 4.99 | 64.0 | 12.83 | 232 | 56 |
| Haiti | 230 | 4.75 | 110.7 | 23.30 | 324 | 48 |
| Lesotho | 240 | 1.25 | 66.1 | 52.88 | 214 | 57 |
| Madagascar | 240 | 8.09 | 120.3 | 14.87 | 302 | 50 |
| Solomon Isles | 250 | .21 | 39.1 | 186.19 | 599 | 30 |
| Central African Empire | 250 | 1.87 | 52.2 | 27.91 | 309 | 50 |
| Kenya | 270 | 14.61 | 333.8 | 22.85 | 413[c] | 55[c] |
| Mauritania | 270 | 1.50 | 197.6 | 131.73 | 405 | 43 |
| Uganda | 270 | 12.05 | 27.8 | 2.31 | 280[c] | 55[c] |
| Guinea Bissau | 280 | .75 | 56.3 | 75.07 | 459 | 39 |
| Sudan | 290 | 16.92 | 521.4 | 30.81 | 281[c] | 54[c] |
| Angola | 300 | 6.58 | 44.0 | 6.69 | 389 | 44 |
| Indonesia | 300 | 133.51 | 889.0 | 6.66 | 280[c] | 59[c] |
| Togo | 300 | 2.35 | 94.2 | 40.09 | 358 | 46 |
| Egypt | 320 | 37.80 | 2797.3 | 74.00 | 561[c] | 20[c] |
| Cameroon | 340 | 7.88 | 232.9 | 29.56 | 490 | 37 |
| Yemen, PDR | 340 | 1.72 | 135.4 | 78.72 | 346 | 47 |
| Ghana | 380 | 10.63 | 163.2 | 15.35 | 628[c] | 25[c] |
| Honduras | 410 | 3.32 | 126.3 | 38.04 | 646 | 28 |
| Botswana | 410 | .73 | 87.5 | 119.86 | 749 | 22 |
| Liberia | 420 | 1.68 | 64.4 | 38.33 | 603 | 30 |
| Nigeria | 420 | 78.99 | 42.8 | .54 | 433[c] | 35[c] |
| Thailand | 420 | 43.33 | 260.2 | 6.01 | 584[c] | 32[c] |
| Senegal | 430 | 5.24 | 197.9 | 37.77 | 550[c] | 35[c] |
| Yemen Arab Republic | 430 | 4.98 | 388.9 | 78.09 | 308 | 50 |

| | | | | | | |
|---|---|---|---|---|---|---|
| Philippines | 450 | 44.47 | 294.4 | 6.62 | 469[c] | 33[c] |
| Zambia | 450 | 5.13 | 187.4 | 36.53 | 798[c] | 10[c] |
| Congo, P.R. | 490 | 1.42 | 68.3 | 48.10 | 656 | 27 |
| Papua New Guinea | 490 | 2.86 | 3⁻0.8 | 108.67 | 746 | 22 |
| El Salvador | 550 | 4.26 | 59.1 | 13.87 | 770 | 21 |
| Morocco | 550 | 18.31 | 3⁻0.8 | 16.97 | 643[c] | 26[c] |
| Guyana | 560 | .82 | 68.9 | 84.02 | 840 | 18 |
| Djibouti | 580 | .30 | 52.1 | 173.67 | 557 | 33 |
| Swaziland | 610 | .51 | 47.5 | 93.14 | 749 | 22 |
| Bolivia | 630 | 5.15 | 174.7 | 33.92 | 554 | 33 |
| Ivory Coast | 690 | 7.46 | 126.2 | 16.92 | 695[c] | 25[c] |
| Jordan | 710 | 2.89 | 959.8 | 335.57 | 716 | 24 |
| Colombia | 720 | 24.61 | 140.9 | 5.72 | 851[c] | 19[c] |
| Paraguay | 730 | 2.81 | 37.3 | 13.27 | 762 | 22 |
| Ecuador | 790 | 7.32 | 75.2 | 10.27 | 870 | 17 |
| Guatemala | 790 | 6.44 | 33.1 | 14.46 | 1128[c] | 10[c] |
| Korea, Republic of | 820 | 35.95 | 300.0 | 8.34 | 797[c] | 8[c] |
| Nicaragua | 830 | 2.41 | 58.8 | 24.40 | 1111 | 8 |
| Dominican Republic | 840 | 4.98 | 67.0 | 13.45 | 1135 | 8 |
| Peru | 840 | 16.36 | 170.1 | 10.40 | 1183[c] | 18[c] |
| Tunisia | 860 | 5.90 | 335.9 | 56.93 | 992[c] | 10[c] |
| Syria | 910 | 7.84 | 1298.3 | 165.60 | 764 | 21 |
| Malaysia | 930 | 12.96 | 94.8 | 7.31 | 1006[c] | 12[c] |
| Algeria | 1110 | 17.15 | 143.0 | 8.34 | 809 | 19 |
| Turkey | 1110 | 41.95 | 156.8 | 3.74 | 914[c] | 14[c] |
| Mexico | 1110 | 63.32 | 42.4 | .67 | 1429[c] | 14[c] |
| Jamaica | 1150 | 2.10 | 98.2 | 46.76 | 1211 | 6 |
| Lebanon | n.a. | 2.94 | ⁻29.2 | 43.95 | 1205 | 6 |
| Chile | 1160 | 10.55 | 71.4 | 6.77 | 798[c] | 11[c] |
| Taiwan | 1170 | 16.79 | 40.9 | 2.44 | 1075[c] | 5[c] |
| Fiji | 1210 | .59 | 35.9 | 60.85 | 1089 | 9 |
| Panama | 1220 | 1.77 | 28.6 | 16.16 | 1440 | 5[d] |
| Costa Rica | 1240 | 2.06 | 68.4 | 33.20 | 1346 | 5[d] |

**Appendix Table** (continued)

| Country | Per Capita GNP-1977[a] ($) | Population 1977[a] (millions) | Average Annual ODA—1976–1978[b] ($ millions, commitments) | Per Capita ODA ($) | Per Capita Income—1975 (ICP $) | Percentage of Population in Absolute Poverty |
|---|---|---|---|---|---|---|
| Brazil | 1360 | 116.10 | 157.0 | 1.35 | 1136[c] | 15[c] |
| Surinam | 1470 | .38 | 186.4 | 490.61 | 2175 | 5[d] |
| Argentina | 1730 | 26.04 | 60.8 | 2.33 | 2094[c] | 5[c] |
| Cyprus | 1830 | .64 | 56.8 | 88.75 | 1651 | 5[d] |
| Malta | 1870 | .33 | 38.8 | 117.60 | 2376 | 5[d] |
| Portugal | 1890 | 9.58 | 140.2 | 14.63 | 1676 | 5[d] |
| French Guyana | 1980 | .06 | 97.1 | 1618.33 | 1422 | 5[d] |
| Iran | 2160 | 34.78 | 59.2 | 1.70 | 1257[c] | 13[c] |
| Oman | 2540 | .81 | 104.2 | 128.60 | 1020 | 11 |
| Guadalupe | 2560 | .32 | 274.7 | 858.43 | 1728 | 5[d] |
| Netherlands Antilles | 2780 | .24 | 48.0 | 200.00 | 2400 | 5[d] |
| Greece | 2810 | 9.23 | 47.0 | 5.09 | 2370 | 5[d] |
| Israel | 2850 | 3.60 | 1085.3 | 301.47 | 3232 | 5[d] |
| Reunion | 2900 | .50 | 487.4 | 974.8 | 1491 | 5[d] |
| Martinique | 3470 | .32 | 321.7 | 1005.3 | 2238 | 5[d] |
| Bahrain | 3790 | .34 | 102.5 | 301.47 | 2079 | 5[d] |
| Gabon | 3860 | .50 | 49.3 | 98.00 | 1767 | 5[d] |
| New Caledonia | 4470 | .15 | 76.9 | 512.67 | 2939 | 5[d] |
| French Polynesia | 4770 | .15 | 78.7 | 524.67 | 3362 | 5[d] |

[a] Data are from Ahluwalia, Chenery, and Carter.
[b] Development Cooperation 1979, Table D.4.
[c] World Development Report 1979 and 1979 World Bank Atlas.
[d] Value of 5 percent imposed.

## BIBLIOGRAPHY

Ahluwalia, Montek. 1976. "Inequality, Poverty and Development." *Journal of Development Economics* 3, no. 3 (September).

Ahluwalia, Montek; Nicholas Carter; and Hollis Chenery. 1979. "Growth and Poverty in Developing Countries." *Journal of Development Economics* 6, no. 3 (September).

Ahluwalia, Montek, and J. H. Duloy. 1977. "Poverty Alleviation and Growth Pessimism: A Re-examination of Cross Country Evidence." Development Research Center, IBRD (draft). April.

Brandt Commission. 1980. *See* Independent Commission on International Development Issues.

Burki, S. J., and J. J. C. Voorhoeve. 1977. "Global Estimates for Meeting Basic Needs: Background Paper." *Basic Needs Papers: No. 1.* The World Bank, August.

Chenery, Hollis, and Associates. 1974. *Redistribution with Growth.* London: Oxford University Press.

Chenery, Hollis, and N. Carter. 1973. "Foreign Assistance and Development Performance 1960–70." *American Economic Review* 63, no. 2 (May).

Chenery, Hollis, and A. M. Strout. 1966. "Foreign Assistance and Economic Development." *American Economic Review* 56, no. 4 (September).

Cline, William R., and Nicholas P. Sargen. 1975. "Performance Criteria and Multilateral Aid Allocation." *World Development* 3, no. 6 (June).

Crosswell, Michael. 1979a. "Some Notes on the Kravis Estimates of Real GDP and Their Usefulness." AID Mimeo, January.

———. 1979b. "Basic Human Needs and the Distribution of Development Assistance Among Countries: The Indicative Planning Allocation Procedure." AID Mimeo, August.

———. 1980. "Need as a Criterion for Allocating Development Assistance." AID Mimeo, July.

Dudley, L., and Montmarquette. 1976. "A Model of the Supply of Bilateral Foreign Aid." *American Economic Review* 66, no. 1 (March).

Edelman, John, and Hollis Chenery. 1977. "Aid and Income Distribution." *The New International Economic Order: The North-South Debate,* edited by Jagdish N. Bhagwati. Cambridge, Mass.: MIT Press.

Fields, Gary. 1979. "Poverty, Inequality and Development: A Distributional Approach." Paper delivered at American Economic Association meetings, December. This paper summarizes the analysis forthcoming in *Poverty, Inequality and Development* (New York: Cambridge University Press, 1980).

Griffin, C. B., and J. L. Enos. 1970. "Foreign Assistance: Objectives and Consequences." *Economic Development and Cultural Change* 18, no. 3 (April).

Independent Commission on International Development Issues (Brandt Commission Report). 1980. *North-South: A Program for Survival.* Cambridge: MIT Press.

International Labour Office. 1977. *Employment, Growth and Basic Needs: A One-World Problem.* New York: Praeger.

Isenman, Paul. 1975. "The Middle-Income and Country-Size Biases in Aid Allocations." *IDS Communication 115.* Sussex: Institute of Development Studies, July.

———. 1976. "Biases in Aid Allocations Against Poorer and Larger Countries." *World Development* 4, no. 8 (August).

———. 1979. "Inter-Country Comparison of Real (PPP) Incomes: Revised Estimates and Unresolved Questions." World Bank Staff Working Paper No. 358. September.

Kravis, Irving; Alan Heston; and Robert Summers. 1978. "Real GDP per Capita for More Than One Hundred Countries." *The Economic Journal* 88, no. 350 (June).

Leipziger, D. M., and M. A. Lewis. 1980. "Social Indicators, Growth and Distribution." *World Development* 8, no. 4 (April).

Lewis, Theodore, and Constantine Michalopoulos. 1980. "Developing Countries' Growth: Projections, Performance and Implications for a New International Development Strategy." AID Mimeo, January.

McKinnon, Ronald. 1964. "Foreign Exchange Constraints in Economic Development." *Economic Journal* 24, no. 294 (June).

Marris, Robin. 1979. "A Survey and Critique of World Bank Supported Research on International Comparisons of Real Product." World Bank Staff Working Paper No. 365. December.

Michalopoulos, Constantine, and Keith E. Jay. 1973. "Growth of Exports and Income in the Developing World: A Neoclassical View." AID Discussion Paper No. 28. November.

Morawetz, D. 1977. *Twenty-five Years of Economic Development, 1950 to 1975.* Washington, D.C.: The World Bank.

Organisation for Economic Cooperation and Development. 1979. *Development Cooperation 1979.* Paris, November.

Papanek, G. F. 1979. "The Effect of Aid and Other Resource Transfers on Savings and Growth in Less Developed Countries." *The Economic Journal* 82, no. 327 (September).

———. 1973. "Aid, Foreign Private Investment, Savings and Growth in Less-Developed Countries." *Journal of Political Economy* 81, no. 1.

Tinbergen, Jan. 1976. *Reshaping the International Order: A Report to the Club of Rome.* New York: E. P. Dutton.

Weisskopf, T. 1972. "The Impact of Foreign Capital Inflow on Domestic Savings in Underdeveloped Countries." *Journal of International Economics* 2, no. 1 (February).

World Bank. 1978a. *World Bank Annual Report 1978.*

———. 1978b. *World Development Report 1978.*

———. 1979a. *1979 World Bank Atlas.*

———. 1979b. *World Development Report 1979.*

# Index

**Danny M. Leipziger** is a member of the Policy Planning Staff of the U.S. Department of State. He has published widely in the fields of development and international economic policy. Formerly with USAID, Dr. Leipziger is editor of *The International Monetary System and the Developing Nations* and coauthor of *Seabed Mineral Resources and the Economic Interests of Developing Countries.*

**Michael J. Crosswell,** a research economist with USAID, holds a Ph.D. from Northwestern University. He has been at the forefront of efforts to rationalize the allocation of foreign assistance and has written extensively about basic needs.

**Martha de Melo,** previously with USAID, is an economist with the World Bank. She holds graduate degrees from Columbia University and the University of Maryland. Dr. de Melo has researched and written about agricultural policy and economic planning in developing countries.

**Maureen A. Lewis,** who holds a graduate degree from Georgetown University, is an economist with USAID. She has developed health and fertility determinants research programs at AID and in the field.

**Paul P. Streeten** is Director of the Center for Asian Development Studies at Boston University. Formerly, he was an advisor to the World Bank and Warden of Queen Elizabeth House, Director of the Institute of Commonwealth Studies, and Fellow of Balliol College, Oxford. Professor Streeten is the author of numerous books about international development, including *Unfashionable Economics; Trade Strategies for Development;* and *Transnationals and Developing Countries.* He is Chairman of the Board of *World Development.*